THE WAR TO END WARS
END WARS
——1914-18——

FOREWORD

To celebrate the turn of the century and the new millennium, **THE EVENTFUL CENTURY** series presents the vast panorama of the last hundred years—a century which witnessed the transition from horse-drawn transport to space travel, and from the first telephones to the information superhighway.

THE EVENTFUL CENTURY chronicles epoch-making events like the outbreak of the two world wars, the Russian Revolution and the rise and fall of communism. But major events are only part of the glittering kaleidoscope. It also describes the everyday background—the way people lived, how they worked, what they ate and drank, how much they earned, the way they spent their leisure time, the books they read, and the crimes, scandals and unsolved mysteries that set them talking. Here are fads and crazes like the hula hoop and Rubik's cube . . . fashions like the New Look and the miniskirt . . . breakthroughs in entertainment, like the birth of the movies . . . medical milestones like the discovery of penicillin . . . and marvels of modern architecture and engineering.

THE WAR TO END WARS describes the most searing of conflicts, the first truly global war. An assassination triggered it—the shooting of an Austrian archduke by a Serbian nationalist in Sarajevo—and when it broke out in August 1914, many thought that it would be no more than a short, sharp battle . . . "all over by Christmas," they predicted. Almost alone the English author H.G. Wells predicted a long and bloody confrontation, the "war to end wars" in his words. He was right: by the time the bloodletting had run its course, some 8.5 million men lay dead, slain in places as far apart as East Africa and China. Caught in the stagnant nightmare of the trenches—a world, it seemed, that had lost all meaning—many succumbed to "shell shock"; a handful wrote poems that offer some of the most probing insights into life on the Western Front. When the Armistice was finally agreed to in November 1918, the world was exhausted—and transformed. Communism had established itself in Russia; new nations were sprouting from the ruins of the old Habsburg Empire. Ominously, many Germans, including an Austrian-born corporal named Adolf Hitler, felt cheated, robbed of victory by the duplicity of their leaders. In the unfinished business of the First World War lay the seeds of the Second.

THE 20th
EVENTFUL CENTURY

THE WAR TO END WARS

——1914-18——

Reader's
Digest

The Reader's Digest Association, Inc.
Pleasantville, New York/Montreal

THE WAR TO END WARS
Edited and designed by Toucan Books Limited
Written by John Man
Edited by Helen Douglas-Cooper and
Andrew Kerr-Jarrett
Designed by Bradbury and Williams
Picture research by Julie McMahon

FOR THE AMERICAN EDITION
Produced by The Reference Works
Director Harold Rabinowitz
Editor Geoffrey Upton
Production Antler DesignWorks
Director Bob Antler

FOR READER'S DIGEST
Group Editorial Director Fred DuBose
Senior Editor Susan Randol
Senior Designers Carol Nehring, Judith Carmel
Production Technology Manager Douglas A. Croll
Associate Designer Jennifer R. Tokarski
Editorial Manager Christine R. Guido

READER'S DIGEST ILLUSTRATED REFERENCE BOOKS
Editor-in-Chief Christopher Cavanaugh
Art Director Joan Mazzeo
Operations Manager William J. Cassidy

First English Edition Copyright © 1998
The Reader's Digest Association Limited,
11 Westferry Circus, Canary Wharf,
London E14 4HE

Copyright © 2000
Reader's Digest Association, Inc.
Reader's Digest Road
Pleasantville, NY 10570

Copyright © 2000
The Reader's Digest Association (Canada) Ltd.
Copyright © 2000
The Reader's Digest Association Far East Limited
Philippine copyright © 2000
Reader's Digest Association Far East Limited

Printed in the United States of America

Library of Congress
Cataloging in Publication Data:
The war to end wars, 1914–18.
      p. cm. — (The Eventful 20th century)
Includes index.
ISBN 0-7621-0288-8
    1. World War, 1914–1918. 2. World War,
1939–1945—Causes. I. Reader's Digest
Association. II. Series.

D521 .W335 2000
940.3—dc21
                                        00-028607

FRONT COVER
From top: U.S. Army recruiting poster; one of the
first tanks used in war; French infantrymen march to
the front.

BACK COVER
From top: Canadian soldiers resting in their trench;
the Lusitania; an American soldier leaving his family.

Page 3 (from left to right): British soldier, Mons,
1914; advertisement for the Voluntary Aid
Detachment; Australian Imperial Forces medal;
Armistice celebrations in Paris.

Background pictures:
Page 15: British troops going over the top, Battle of
the Somme, 1916
Page 101: German women taping cartridges in a
munitions factory
Page 127: Crowds outside Buckingham Palace on
Armistice Day, November 11, 1918

Address any comments about The War to End Wars
to:
Reader's Digest, Editor-in-Chief, U.S. Illustrated
Reference Books,
Reader's Digest Road, Pleasantville, NY 10570

To order additional copies of The War to End Wars,
call 1-800-846-2100

You can also visit us on the World Wide Web at:
www.readersdigest.com

CONTENTS

THE BUILD-UP TO WAR

IN THE BALKANS A SHOT WAS FIRED, AND WITH REMARKABLE SPEED THE WHOLE EDIFICE OF EUROPEAN PEACE AND STABILITY CRUMBLED

Sarajevo, Bosnia-Herzegovina, June 28, 1914: at 9:45 a.m. on this sunny Sunday, the Archduke Franz Ferdinand, heir to the Austro-Hungarian throne, arrived at the train station. With his wife Sophie, he had come for a state visit to this Balkan outpost of imperial rule to inspect military maneuvers that were to take place close to the city. Austria-Hungary, an empire that dominated central Europe, had annexed Bosnia-Herzegovina only six years earlier, a move that had caused nothing but trouble, stirred by local Serbs who wanted to re-unite with neighboring Serbia. The archduke hoped that a show of military and political power would subdue the unruly province.

In the crowds that morning were half a dozen Serbian terrorists, teenage members of a group known as the Black Hand, and all of them were out for Franz Ferdinand's blood. Their leader, Colonel Dragutin Dimitrijevic, had good reason to keep a low profile. Better known by his alias, "Apis," he not only ran the Black Hand, but was also head of Serbia's military intelligence. His hidden agenda brought him into conflict with his political superiors, who knew that Austria-Hungary did not need much excuse to move against Serbia, the natural sanctuary of pro-Serbian, anti-Austrian extremism.

The motorcade drove along the columns of Austrian troops drawn up on the parade ground outside the station, then turned toward the town hall. As it sped through the crowded streets, one of the terrorists tossed a bomb at the royal car. It landed on the folded canopy, bounced off backward and exploded under the following car. Flying fragments wounded 20 people, including two royal aides, who were taken to a military hospital. The culprit leaped into the river, but was dragged out and arrested. Strangely, the police assumed he was acting alone, and did not search the crowd or increase their security measures.

After this brief halt, the motorcade continued with its schedule, but the Archduke soon decided to change plans and visit his injured aides. On the way, the leading car took a wrong turn, and the military governor, General Oskar Potiorek, who was accompanying the royal couple, shouted

at the driver to stop. The car came to an abrupt halt on the corner of a bridge, and the driver started wrestling with the controls to reverse. By chance, several terrorists were loitering nearby, morosely contemplating

ASSASSINAT DE L'ARCHIDUC HÉRITIER D'AUTRICHE ET DE LA DUCHESSE SA FEMME A SARAJEVO

DEATH ON A SUNDAY MORNING Soldiers drag away the assassin, Gavrilo Princip (in civilian clothes, on the right). Left: A French newspaper gives a dramatic picture of the scene. Top: The archduke's blood-stained tunic.

EUROPEAN POWERS IN AUGUST 1914

- Allied Powers
- Central Powers
- Countries joining Allied Powers
- Countries joining Central Powers
- Neutral countries

Kristiania (Oslo)

Stockholm

St. Petersburg (Petrograd)

Moscow

RUSSIAN EMPIRE

GREAT BRITAIN

Danzig

London

Hamburg

NETHERLANDS

EASTERN FRONT

Berlin

POLAND

Warsaw

BELGIUM

Cologne

Kiev

Tsaritsyn

WESTERN FRONT

GERMAN EMPIRE

Paris

Prague

Vienna

FRANCE

SWITZERLAND

AUSTRO-HUNGARIAN EMPIRE

Budapest

Odessa

ITALIAN FRONT

ITALY

Belgrade

ROMANIA

Bucharest

ROMANIAN FRONT

PORTUGAL

SPAIN

Marseilles

Sarajevo

SERBIA

BLACK SEA

CAUCASUS CAMPAIGN

Madrid

MONTENEGRO

BULGARIA

Lisbon

Rome

BALKAN FRONT

Constantinople

ALBANIA

Salonica

DARDANELLES CAMPAIGN

OTTOMAN EMPIRE

Gallipoli

GREECE

Athens

Baghdad

Damascus

With France in the west allied to Russia in the east, Germany and its ally Austria-Hungary inevitably faced a war on two fronts. The Ottoman Empire joined the war on the side of the Central Powers in November 1914; Italy, on the Allied side, in May 1915.

THE ASSASSINATION OF ARCHDUKE FRANZ FERDINAND

Borijove Jevtic, one of the conspirators, recalled how the plot to assassinate Archduke Franz Ferdinand was hatched at a small table in a humble café in Belgrade in April 1914:

"June 28 is a date engraved deeply in the heart of every Serb, so that the day has a name of its own. It is called *vidovnan*. It is the day on which the old Serbian kingdom was conquered by the Turks at the Battle of Amselfelde in 1389. It is also the day on which in the Second Balkan War the Serbian arms took glorious revenge on the Turk for his old victory and for the years of enslavement.

"That was no day for Franz Ferdinand, the new oppressor, to venture to the very doors of Serbia for a display of the force of arms which kept us beneath his heel.

"Our decision was taken almost immediately. Death to the tyrant!

"Then came the matter of arranging it. To make his death certain twenty-two members of the organization were selected to carry out the sentence. At first we thought we would choose the men by lot. But here Gavrilo Princip intervened. Princip is destined to go down in Serbian history as one of her greatest heroes. From the moment Ferdinand's death was decided upon he took an active leadership in its planning. Upon his advice we left the deed to members of our band who were in and around Sarajevo under his direction and that of Gabrinovic, a linotype operator on a Serbian newspaper. Both were regarded as capable of anything in the cause."

the failure of their cause. Suddenly, fate presented them with the perfect target; 19-year-old Gavrilo Princip pulled out his pistol, ran to the stationary car, leaped on the running board and fired at close range.

The archduke was hit in the neck (the bloody uniform can still be seen in Vienna's Military History Museum), and Sophie in the stomach. She slumped into his lap, and before he lost consciousness he muttered: "Sophie, Sophie, don't die. Live for our children." The car sped them to Potiorek's house, where a doctor attended them. There was nothing he could do. Both died within the hour.

The European powers

In Vienna the assassination was, of course, a shock. But it was not exactly a tragedy, given that Sophie was *persona non grata* at court and the archduke not much loved. In the rest of Europe, it caused no panic. Assassinations of heads of state were not unknown—the Empress of Austria, the Tsar of Russia, the Kings of Italy and Portugal, and the Presidents of the United States and France had been killed over the previous 20 years. No one had reason to suspect that a shot in a Balkan province would echo around the world and destroy a system of such seeming stability.

In part, the descent into war occurred because war was thought impossible. Europe had largely been at peace for half a century, secured by an everlasting round of shifting alliances. Britain's last war in Europe had been against Russia in the 1850s, and France and Germany had been at peace since 1871. Though all nations had huge armed forces, it was universally assumed that these would be for local conflicts or colonial wars. For two generations, the political interests and military forces had been kept in check by diplomacy. In fact, no permanent solution was possible, for each new development—a local war, or the appointment of a new foreign

1908 Assassination of King Carlos I of Portugal

1912 Outbreak of First Balkan War

1913 Assassination of King George I of Greece

1914 Assassination of Franz Ferdinand; outbreak of war

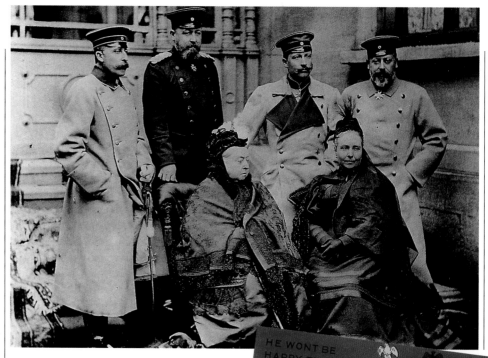

minister, or the revelation of a secret pact—affected all the others, and each attempt to resolve the strains created another problem.

The main players in the game of European power-politics were France, Germany, Italy, Russia, Austria-Hungary, Turkey and Britain. After the Franco-Prussian War of 1870-1, Germany had kept Alsace Lorraine, to the chagrin of many French patriots, some of whom felt eager for revenge in Europe, others for new imperial acquisitions in Africa. France saw Russia as a potential ally against Germany, whose Emperor Wilhelm II reinforced Germany's alliance with Austria. France's previous disputes with Britain had

been largely rendered obsolete by an entente in 1904.

Germany was the brash new power at the center of Europe. Unified in 1871, with formidable industrial might, the country's steadiest ally was neighboring Austria-Hungary. In the event of war, Germany would need to counter France and Russia, facing the possibility of fighting on two fronts at once. This inspired a massive investment in arms, coupled with a naval shipbuilding program which brought Germany up against British naval power.

Also newly unified, Italy sought to complete its territorial acquisitions by claiming "unredeemed" borderlands in Austro-Hungarian lands. In seeking territory in Africa, Italy also came up against French imperial ambitions and looked for alliances with Germany and Austria-Hungary—the very power it sought to rival.

Russia's main national interest was to maintain an exit route for its trade and its navy from the Black Sea through the Dardanelles and the Bosporus. The collapse of the Ottoman Empire would set Russia at odds with any other power seeking influence in the Balkans. France, with no involvement in the Dardanelles, was an obvious ally, as was the Slavic Serbia.

LEADING PLAYER Austria-Hungary's foreign minister, Count Berchtold, had an uncertain grasp of the events unfolding around him and was easily swayed by belligerently anti-Serbian army officers.

Austria-Hungary felt threatened by nationalist movements in the Balkans, which became ever more unstable as countries there became independent of Turkish rule. Turkey, known as "the sick man of Europe" because of its empire's steady decline over the previous century, straddled the Bosporus Strait and the geopolitics of access from the Black Sea to the Mediterranean.

And, finally, there was Britain, with an empire held together by trade and naval power. This had allowed the country to stand to one side in "splendid isolation" until the spread of Russian power into central Asia had seemed to threaten British imperial interests and until the rise of Germany threatened its traditional naval authority.

Within this context, there were three wild cards. One was the rise of Slav nationalism. Already the Balkans, once under Turkish rule, had split into six rival nations in two series of wars (in the 1870s and in 1912-3), with the Serbs of Bosnia-Herzegovina eager to join the rush to independence—from

Austria-Hungary, not Turkey. A second was the determination with which Austria-Hungary countered Serbian nationalism. The driving force behind this disastrous policy was the Austrian foreign minister, Count Leopold Berchtold. Berchtold was an extremely rich landowner, charming and urbane, but he was under the influence of the bellicose chief of staff, Conrad von Hötzendorf. Together, the two were set on war with Serbia.

The wildest card of all was the German emperor, Wilhelm II. As Queen Victoria's grandson, he loved and feared Britain almost to the point of schizophrenia. Two years after succeeding to the throne in 1888, Wilhelm had fired his chancellor, Otto von Bismarck, and set about creating unrivaled armed forces. When the British built a powerful new type of battleship, the dreadnought, Wilhelm ordered a German version, doubling the size of the German fleet and challenging Britain's naval supremacy. In an interview with the *Daily Telegraph* in 1908, he had tried to assuage the fears of the British by calling them "mad as March hares" not to see how friendly he was.

The complexity of European politics was reflected in the growing complexity of relations outside Europe. In Africa, newly divided between European powers scrambling for imperial possessions, Germany, France, Britain and Italy had rival interests. The United States, now a Pacific as well as an Atlantic power, had annexed Hawaii and had gained the Philippines from Spain. Japan, only recently emerged from medieval isolation, had acquired astonishing industrial, military and political clout, enough to form an alliance with Britain in 1902, and to defeat Russia in a war in 1904-5. Should Europe go to war, other regions of the world would inevitably become embroiled.

Indeed, there was a growing feeling in the corridors of power that a short war might be necessary

DREADNOUGHT—GIANT OF THE SEAS

The growing rivalry between Germany and Britain focused on a naval race. German naval construction began in earnest in 1898—a challenge taken up by Britain's First Sea Lord, Sir John "Jackie" Fisher, in 1904. Even without a race, Fisher's jingoism was a match for Kaiser Wilhelm's. He used to advocate destroying the German fleet in its home ports, without a declaration of war—"Copenhagened" was his phrase, a reference to Nelson's destruction of the Danish fleet in Copenhagen in 1801.

In 1906, the first of a new type of battleship, the HMS *Dreadnought,* was launched. Displacing 21,000 tons, and carrying ten 12-inch guns instead of four, it would make all existing battleships obsolete. At once, Germany responded by building her own "dreadnoughts." The British government proposed to build eight of these monster ships every year, then fell behind in construction. The popular press, spearheaded by the *Daily Mail,* ran scare stories about Germany's shipbuilding program, coining the slogan: "We want eight and we won't wait!" As a result the naval budget and production were increased. By the time war broke out, Britain had 20 dreadnoughts to Germany's 14.

NOTHING TO FEAR
HMS *Dreadnought* was fast as well as well-armed, capable of 21 knots (24 mph).

to sort out the problems that beset the major players. Some in Vienna argued that force would restore Austro-Hungarian power in the Balkans. Ministers in Russia wanted to secure the Dardanelles. Naval officers in Germany were anxious to use their version of the dreadnought in order to gain imperial possessions. Very soon, they would be able to deploy their new ships rapidly from their Baltic base through to the North Sea via the Kiel Canal, the widening of which was almost complete. The French eyed Alsace Lorraine. Britain would gain by curbing Germany's industrial and military expansion.

PULP PROPAGANDA
A German cartoon depicts Russia's Tsar Nicholas II as a bloodthirsty bully.

Even so, the events in Sarajevo did not in themselves inevitably lead to war. There was one final link to be forged—Austria-Hungary's move against Serbia. The assassination gave Berchtold the pretext he needed to act. Much was therefore made of the deaths in Sarajevo. The press reported the sorrow of the emperor and the wide-ranging aims of the youthful assassins. As Princip and his accomplices were interrogated, private reports "revealed" that Serbia was behind the plot, that the bomb and pistol had come from the Serbian arsenal, and that the assassination had been designed to precede the arrival of the Serbian army and the creation of a Greater Serbia.

Shock waves from Sarajevo

This fabrication, for which no hard evidence has ever emerged, was what Serbia's leaders had feared. Their country was still recovering from two years of war, against Turkey in 1912 and Bulgaria in 1913, and still busy absorbing its gains. The last thing they needed was another war, in which their new frontiers—indeed, their very status as an independent nation—would be threatened. They did have

full-time, followed by four to five years in the reserves, and 17 years more as a territorial reserve and a veteran reserve. In other nations, the manpower available was also staggering: France could field 1.3 million, Austria-Hungary 450,000, Russia 1.4 million.

Britain was the least prepared for land warfare. Despite the demands of policing its massive empire, the country had only 120,000 regular soldiers, all of them volunteers. This reflected a tradition in which the army was a missile to be launched by a vastly superior navy in some imperial campaign. Neither the men nor their officers had any experience in European warfare.

Each of these European soldiers required a uniform, a gun, ammunition and food. There were also millions of horses to be harnessed, moved and fed, for every nation assumed that, as always, the horse would play a key role in the action to come. No one, except one or two eccentrics, foresaw static

one advantage, however: they relied on Russia for support, and Russia had good reason to support them. If Austria-Hungary advanced through the Balkans, it would control the Dardanelles, and consequently Russia's southern exit through the Mediterranean. Russia also supported Serbia's Pan-Slavic aspirations in the region.

To move against Serbia, therefore, Austria-Hungary would have to ensure that Russia was restrained, and this could be done only with German help. Berchtold fired off a request to the kaiser. Wilhelm, eager to avenge the shedding of royal blood, was enthusiastic: "We must clear the Serbians out of the way," he scribbled in the margin of a report, adding in a message to Vienna that Austria-Hungary could depend on Germany's complete support.

Since Berchtold did not wish to be seen as the aggressor, he planned to send an ultimatum. This would be a tricky task, for in his words: "What demands could be put that would be wholly impossible for Serbia to accept?" On July 23, the terms were delivered. All anti-Austrian propaganda was to be crushed. Austria-Hungary had to have the right to fire any Serbian official. There would have to be an inquiry into the assassination, with Austria-Hungary making the rules. A reply would have to come within 48 hours. These demands, which would in effect end Serbian independence, were termed "very moderate and proper" by Germany.

Serbia, eager for peace, sent a plea to the tsar, but then agreed to almost all of Austria's demands, and offered to refer the dispute to the International Court at The Hague. All was in vain—the Serbian reply arrived two minutes before the expiry of the 48 hours, but Berchtold never read it. Austria declared war on July 28, pre-empting entreaties for peace from Britain and Russia.

Europe prepares for war

Austria-Hungary's declaration was the act that precipitated general war. But the very possibility of war forced action, for no nation could go to war instantly. Troops had to be mobilized, armaments and stores prepared, and supplies rushed across countries by train.

There were unprecedented numbers of troops under arms in Europe in 1914. In Germany, from 1870, every able-bodied man—over 9 million of them in a population of 65 million—was liable for active service, providing a standing army of almost 2 million in 1914. All served two to three years

PRUSSIAN PLAN Anticipating war on two fronts—against France and Russia—Germany's chief of staff Schlieffen proposed a rapid knockout blow to France, before turning in force on Russia.

warfare or the arrival of the tank. In addition, there were huge quantities of field guns, machine guns and vehicles to be moved along narrow, poorly surfaced roads.

The train was the key to large-scale, industrialized warfare. By 1900, Europe had 175,000 miles of railway, crossing every river and mountain chain, linking industrial centers and ports, reaching far into agricultural backwaters, and spanning the major powers. Journeys that had once taken a month or two for foot soldiers could be completed in less than 24 hours. Germany had learned this lesson early. In the Seven Weeks' War against Austria of 1866, it had taken a week for the Prussian Guard Corps, traveling in 12 trains a day, to move from Berlin to the Austrian front, where overwhelming force won the day. Four years later, France's lack of a suitable railway system had contributed to defeat in the Franco-Prussian War. Every major power took the lessons to heart. In 1876, the German general staff set up a railway department, building new tracks and providing outposts along the French and Belgian borders with platforms a mile long to fit in several troop trains at once.

Germany's preparations were reflected in its war plan, which the facts of geopolitics dictated had to be uniquely aggressive. For the previous 20 years, Germany had planned

LEAVING FOR THE FRONT The atmosphere is light-hearted as French Zouave troops board a train for the front in August 1914. Virtually no one anticipated how long and grueling the war would be.

"BRAVO, BELGIUM" A *Punch* cartoon from August 1914 applauds Belgium's defiance of its giant neighbor. Attacking France through the Low Countries was an essential part of the Schlieffen plan.

for a war on two fronts, against both France and Russia simultaneously.

The plan was the brain child of Count Alfred von Schlieffen, chief of the general staff from 1891 to 1905. The assumption of this meticulous man was that Russia would be slower to mobilize than France. A relatively small force would hold the Russians at bay initially, while France was taken out. This would demand a massive operation: 500 trains of 50 wagons each, shifting four corps—750,000 men—to the border. France had a narrow entrance, the 150 miles of frontier between Switzerland and Belgium. Most of it ran along the Vosges mountains, behind which was a line of defenses it would be foolhardy to assault. The solution was to go around the line to the north, through Belgium and Holland. A huge force of 53 divisions would sweep right through the Netherlands plain. Schlieffen hoped that this would not mean violating the borders of a neutral country: with luck, the massing of German forces would persuade the French to do that first. The Germans would then be free to sweep in. Meanwhile, a much smaller force would invite attack in the south. If the French advanced across their frontier, they would not be available for defense in the north.

In this "revolving door" strategy, the northern force would swing in a vast arc around Paris in 39 days, and on to victory—in just six weeks. The timing was crucial: any longer than six weeks, and the Russians would have a chance to build up their forces in the east. Once victory had been achieved in the west, the armies would be released to strike east. Everything hinged on the speed and overwhelming weight of the armies sweeping through the Low Countries. "The struggle is inevitable," Schlieffen is supposed to have said on his deathbed in 1913. "Keep the right flank strong!" It was not to be. His successor, Helmuth von Moltke, lacked Schlieffen's

EAGER FOR BATTLE French infantrymen step out briskly on their way to the front. Their overcoats, with buttoned-back skirts, had scarcely changed since the mid-19th century.

nerve. When more divisions became available, he allotted them to the left flank (the French frontier), not to the right (the Low Countries). Moreover, he did not trust Schlieffen's idea of forcing the French to be the ones to violate Belgian neutrality. There would be no diplomatic nicety—a change that later assumed particular significance when Britain used Germany's advance through Belgium as a reason to go to war.

The French, despite their line of frontier fortresses, had come to place their faith not in defense but in attack, in all-out assault delivered with a peculiarly French ingredient, *élan*. French Field Regulations, reflecting the influence of the chief of the general staff, General Joseph Joffre, insisted that "success comes not to him who has suffered the least but to him whose will is firmest and morale strongest."

In brief, the French, with only one-sixth of Germany's industrial might and two-thirds of Germany's population, placed their faith not in the weight of firepower but in Plan XVII. They had only one really effective piece of armament: the light, quick-loading 3-inch gun, though there were those who

discounted even this weapon, believing that heavy artillery would destroy the mercurial essence of French soldiering. Vastly underestimating the strength of the German forces, they assumed that the Germans would strike through the Ardennes in northeast France. Indeed, anyone with an inside knowledge of both nations' armies might well have gambled that Germany had a good chance of achieving Schlieffen's aim: victory in six weeks.

Given the urgency to gear up the machinery of war, and the belief that it would all be over by Christmas—the phrase was British, but the attitude universal—the overriding need was to give orders in time to get the trains moving. And once the trains were rolling, no one could stop them. It would take several days to engage, but the leaders who might have pulled back from the brink in that time released a beast over which they no longer had control. In the historian A.J.P. Taylor's phrase, this was war "by timetable."

Declarations of war

Once the balance was tipped, the descent into war happened at frightening speed, unleashing rumors and fears that swept governments and whole populations into a frenzy. Behind the frenzy, the peace in Europe unraveled with the precision and

inevitability of clockwork.

With Austria's declaration of war, Russia had no option but to act. If she did not, Austria-Hungary might be able to dominate the Dardanelles, effectively boxing Russia in. When the Russian foreign minister, Sergei Sazonov, learned of the Austro-Hungarian ultimatum, he saw at once what would happen. "This means a European war," Sazonov declared. Even before the tsar received the Serbian appeal, he had decided on a partial mobilization, intending to rattle sabers on the Austro-Hungarian frontiers to deter an attack on Serbia. His military leaders explained that this was not possible. The timetables did not allow for such a course. If the tsar wished to threaten Austria-Hungary, he would have to threaten Germany as well. It was total mobilization, or nothing. On July 30, two days after the Austrian declaration of war against Serbia, and a day after Austria-Hungary had committed the first act of war by bombarding

FOOT SOLDIER IN BRITAIN A "Tommy" holding his Lee-Enfield rifle and carrying webbing straps and bags filled with field equipment such as ammunition and food rations.

chancellor, telegraphed an ultimatum to Russia demanding that mobilization be reversed. It was, he knew, an impossible request. When, on August 1, the Russians refused, Germany declared war on Russia. Bethmann-Hollweg telegraphed France, demanding that in the event of war with Russia, France should remain neutral. This was equally impossible. In Germany's plans, there was no such thing as war against Russia alone. To mobilize against Russia, German armies would first have to invade France. But to get to France, the German armies had to go through Belgium. On August 2, the Germans demanded from Belgium the right to send troops through their country. Naturally enough, the Belgians refused.

Meanwhile, Britain might have remained aloof from events on the Continent, for it had little interest in Serbian independence; indeed, Wilhelm, drawing on the anglophile side of his schizophrenic personality, believed that the English and the Germans were natural partners in withstanding Slav

WAR FEVER IN VIENNA Like their counterparts all across Europe, Austrian troops clearly had few apprehensions about the coming conflict.

Belgrade, the tsar ordered total mobilization. The next day, Austria did the same. With the trains in motion, diplomacy took a back seat.

In Germany, the immediate need was to counter the Russian mobilization. Theobald von Bethmann-Hollweg, an experienced

THE COMING OF WAR IN A FRENCH VILLAGE

Mémé Santerre, a woman in a village on the Belgian border, recalled the scene among those working in the fields when the church bells started ringing on August 1:

"'The tocsin [alarm]!' cried someone in the field. 'There's a fire in the fields!' Then we saw men running and yelling on the road bordering the field. We couldn't hear what they were saying, but as they passed, the workers dropped their tools, running wildly, seized with some madness after a second of shock. Soon the field was swept with a wave of agitation. As the words reached them, people began running. My husband and I stared without understanding, before we heard, right in our faces, the news that a neighbor, in his turn, was yelling. 'War! It's war!'

"We were stunned. I remember that Auguste, turning toward me, said 'War, but what war?'

"Then we dropped our tools, the little hooks that we used to pile up the sheaves, and joined the crowd, running as fast as our legs could carry us, to the farmhouse. Everyone was going there, in the great need that men feel to gather together when faced with catastrophe . . . In this coming-and-going of wagons and animals, I could hear disjointed phrases: 'General mobilization . . .' 'What a misfortune, what an awful misfortune!' 'I have to leave right away!'"

. . . IN FRANCE At the start of the war, French infantrymen still wore conspicuous uniforms of blue and red, a severe disadvantage in the conditions of modern warfare.

. . . IN RUSSIA Russians carried a horseshoe roll—a tent cloth and overcoat rolled together. Their uniforms had been modernized after defeat in the Russo-Japanese War of 1904-5.

. . . IN GERMANY The Germans' spiked *Pickelhaube* helmet, dating from the 1840s, was abandoned during the war in favor of a more effective steel helmet.

PARIS-BOUND German guardsmen scrawl cheerful graffiti and a caricature of France's General Joffre over the train that will take them to the front in August 1914. Trains were the key to speedy mobilization.

ambitions. Also, Britain's wait-and-see attitude up to that point had given many the impression that the country would remain neutral. However, Britain was by treaty already part of the coming war, because it had signed up as a guarantor of Belgian neutrality under the Treaty of London in 1839. Furthermore, the mood in Britain favored war. Germany was perceived as a threat, and needed to be taught a sharp lesson. It was expected to be a brief unpleasantness. "If we are engaged in war," Sir Edward Grey, the foreign secretary, told the House of Commons on August 3, "we shall suffer but little more than we shall suffer if we stand aside."

That day, Germany declared war on France and the following morning invaded Belgium. On August 4, Britain, on its own behalf and its empire's, declared war on Germany and ordered the mobilization of its small professional army: six divisions of infantry and one of cavalry. This was to be the British Expeditionary Force (BEF). No one in the War Office had much of an idea where it should go, until General Henry Wilson, director of military operations, reminded his colleagues that the agreed purpose of the BEF was to help the French. They would have to join the French left wing in Belgium. Since the BEF could only travel by train, they could only go to Maubeuge, near the Belgian border, and link up with the French there.

In a flurry of telegrams, all of Europe joined the rush to arms. Over the next ten days, Austria-Hungary declared war against Russia; Montenegro, another of the Balkan states, siding with Serbia, declared war against Germany and Austria-Hungary; France declared war against Austria-Hungary; and Britain against Austria-Hungary. Turkey, with a toehold in Europe across the Bosporus, would join Germany and Austria-Hungary after three months.

By the end of August, the heart of Europe was divided into two great blocks—the so-called Central Powers of Germany and Austria-Hungary versus the Allies, principally France, Britain and Russia. Of the other European powers, Italy, Portugal, Romania and Bulgaria were indifferent temporarily; Spain, Holland, Switzerland and Scandinavia remained neutral throughout the war.

It was initially, in the phrase of some American historians, a great European civil war. But it would not remain so. Britain's declaration also involved its empire: the semi-independent dominions of Canada, Australia, New Zealand and South Africa; and India, the colonial territories in the West Indies, Africa and the Pacific. Germany invited Japan to consolidate its position in China, but Japan judged it better to stick by its treaty with Britain and came out against the Central Powers on August 23.

At the time, however, no one, except perhaps a few far-sighted diplomats, had any idea that this was truly a European war, let alone what came to be called a world war. Every nation was fighting in its own corner, with limited aims. The Balkan states were fighting a Balkan war. The French were defending themselves against an aggressive neighbor. The British were fighting German naval and industrial power, fearing a blockade would result from German domination on the Continent. Outside Europe, the British, Russians and, later, the Arabs were squabbling over the ruins of Turkey's Ottoman Empire. It would take four years of appalling death and destruction for peoples and nations to see that the pursuit of their narrow self-interests was suicidal.

WAR ON ALL FRONTS

ALMOST BY ACCIDENT, THE OPPOSING ARMIES ON THE WESTERN FRONT DISCOVERED A NEW FORM OF WARFARE—IN WHICH MEN IN TRENCHES FACED ONE ANOTHER ACROSS A FEW HUNDRED YARDS OF MUD AND SLIME, NEITHER SIDE ABLE TO MAKE A DECISIVE BREAKTHROUGH. ON THE EASTERN FRONT, THE GERMANS AND AUSTRO-HUNGARIANS FOUGHT A MORE MOBILE WAR AGAINST THE SOLDIERS OF THE TSAR, UNTIL REVOLUTION PULLED RUSSIA OUT OF THE WAR.

THE OPENING CAMPAIGN

BY NOVEMBER 1914, TWO LINES OF TRENCHES FACED ONE ANOTHER, FROM THE ENGLISH CHANNEL TO THE SWISS BORDER

It would be a short war: on that point almost all the experts agreed. No nation could long sustain the immense investment in manpower and armaments needed for modern warfare. A victor would soon emerge and peace would be made. In any event, it would all be over by Christmas.

EARLY SHOTS German artillerymen heave a field howitzer into place in November 1914. A French poster (right) salutes the bravery of the Belgian defenders of Liège.

Beginning on August 1, 550 trains a day steamed and clattered over the Rhine bridges, pouring forth some 1.5 million men on Germany's borders with Belgium and France. On the 4th, German troops began to cross the border into Belgium. The first task facing the Germans was to clear away any obstacles to their advance toward the French border, and the first obstacle that faced them was the Belgian town of Liège, defended by a line of 12 forts,

34,000 troops and a network of underground passageways. The Belgians were well ensconced there, and the German assault was virtually useless. "They made no attempt at deploying," wrote a Belgian officer, "but came on line after line, almost shoulder to shoulder, until, as we shot them down, the fallen were heaped on top of each other in an awful barricade of dead and wounded." On August 6 a German force entered the city, and on August 7 the central citadel surrendered. The

August 3, 1914
Germany declares
war on France

August 4, 1914
Germany invades Belgium
Britain declares war on Germany

August 7, 1914
Liège falls to
Germans

August 23, 1914
British retreat
from Mons

September 9-17, 1914
Battle of the
Marne

October 19-
November 11, 1914
First Battle of Ypres

THE GERMAN INVASION OF BELGIUM AND FRANCE IN AUGUST 1914

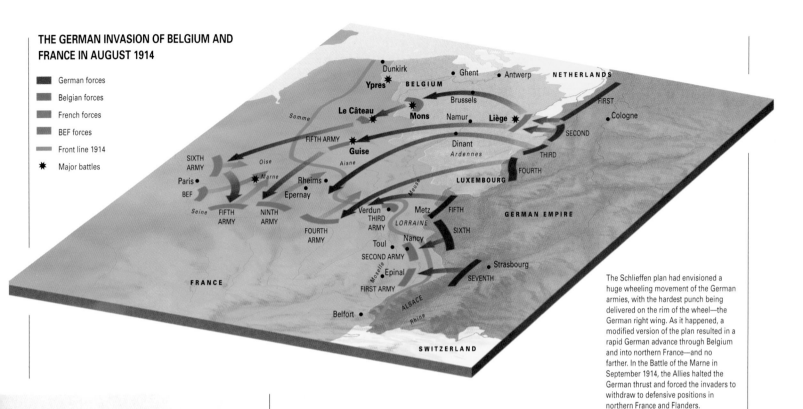

■ German forces
■ Belgian forces
■ French forces
■ BEF forces
— Front line 1914
✳ Major battles

The Schlieffen plan had envisioned a huge wheeling movement of the German armies, with the hardest punch being delivered on the rim of the wheel—the German right wing. As it happened, a modified version of the plan resulted in a rapid German advance through Belgium and into northern France—and no farther. In the Battle of the Marne in September 1914, the Allies halted the German thrust and forced the invaders to withdraw to defensive positions in northern France and Flanders.

forts remained in Belgian hands, however, and the Germans had to await the arrival of heavy howitzers—massive siege guns forged in the Skoda works in Austria-Hungary. It was assumed that these immense devices, which lobbed 1-ton shells measuring over 16 inches for a distance of 5½ miles, were made in the Krupp munitions works, so they were nicknamed "Big Berthas" after Frau Bertha Krupp von Bohlen und Halbach, daughter of the head of the Krupp family. By August 16, they had blasted all 12 forts into submission.

The battle of the frontiers

By then the German advance forces, pressing on through Belgium, found themselves up against a people as well as an army. When snipers picked off German soldiers, the invaders answered by burning homes and shooting groups of civilians—over 600 at Dinant on August 23. Louvain's ancient university library went up in flames. These atrocities—and many fabricated ones—were used as propaganda to whip up anti-German outrage among the Allies. But even at this early stage, the grim realities of war shocked

FIGHTING RETREAT Belgian troops man a barricade on a country road during the retreat to Antwerp. For all their bravery, the Belgians were hopelessly outnumbered and outmatched by the Germans.

Germans as well as their victims. One wrote: "When one sees the wasting, burning villages and towns, plundered cellars and attics . . . dead or half-starved animals, cattle bellowing in the sugar-beet fields, and then corpses, corpses, corpses . . . then everything becomes senseless, a lunacy."

The German advance forced the Belgians

to retreat to Antwerp, opening the capital, Brussels, to the Germans on August 20. Meanwhile, a second thrust to the south of Liège and Namur was advancing up the River Meuse. In two weeks, the Germans had taken 50 to 60 miles. It was another 150 miles to Paris. They were on schedule.

Farther to the south, in two determined offensives, the French advanced from their line of fortifications into Alsace Lorraine, where they discovered that *élan* alone made little impact against modern weapons. Nevertheless, the attacks had a beneficial effect, unwittingly undermining the battle plan laid down by Schlieffen. The German commander of the invasion, Moltke, was now 60 and in uncertain health—not the man to remain true to Schlieffen's vision. Seeing the French plight, he threw six new divisions into the battle, thus failing to strengthen his crucial right wing in its swing through Belgium.

What happened next revealed the inadequacies in Germany's high command. Moltke's order to his local commander, Crown Prince Rupprecht of Bavaria, was to detain as many French troops as possible. Rupprecht, through his chief of staff, Krafft von Delmensingen, said that he could only do this by attacking—which he would do unless specifically ordered not to.

"No," said General von Stein, Moltke's deputy. "You must take the responsibility. Make your own decision as your conscience tells you."

"It is already made. We attack."

"Not really! Then strike, and God be with you."

Rupprecht attacked—but failed to win a decisive victory, succeeding only in driving the French back to their well-prepared defenses. From there, they were free to send reinforcements north. In this sector, the outcome by August 23 was precisely the opposite of what Schlieffen had planned.

In Belgium, France received another setback. Learning of Liège's resistance, General Joffre had jumped to the conclusion that the main German thrust would come through the Ardennes, and planned a pincer movement to counter this move. It was wishful thinking: the Ardennes advance was not the main thrust, but even so he vastly underestimated it. His 20 divisions were up against 21 German divisions. When the two sides met, at Rossignol on August 22, it was the French, moving through fog with fixed bayonets in the face of withering machine-gun fire, who had to retreat.

To the northwest, the French 5th Army was on the point of coming up against the powerful German forces, 34 divisions, which had swung past Liège. At this moment, on August 20, the British Expeditionary Force (BEF) arrived to strengthen the French left wing at Mons.

Not since the Crimean War ended 58 years earlier had a British army set foot on the continent of Europe. They were well supplied for war in tropical Africa and India, with khaki uniforms, and they were skilled at handling rifles. Each division (some 18,000 men) had 5,600 horses, only 24 machine guns, and no telephones or radio—messages were carried by men on horseback. Their commander, Sir John French, was perhaps not the man for the job. He was 62, had a heart condition, was subject to rapid changes of mood, and was easily piqued by opposition from subordinates or colleagues.

Sir John's meeting with his French allies was not a happy one. The French general, Lanrezac, had just discovered how vulnerable his British counterpart was. "At last you're here,"

VICTOR OF THE MARNE

Joseph "Papa" Joffre (1852-1931), the French commander, was the son of a tradesman who had started his professional life as an engineer. His tubby shape and heavy jowls belied a ferocious fighting spirit, and it was this that underlay his war plan, the notorious Plan XVII. Yet when the attack came, and his plan, which underestimated German strategy, was in ruins, other traits emerged in Joffre's character: patience, composure, courage. It was his readiness to retreat and then fight back that saved France—and his reputation. Only later in the war, when he failed to devise a way out of trench warfare, was he forced to resign.

Lanrezac said irritably to French. "If we are beaten, we shall have you to thank!"

Two days later outside Mons, the BEF came up against the German 1st Army. Here, at least, British training was effective. Their rifle fire was so fast—the standard 15 rounds a minute—that the Germans mistook it for machine-gun fire and backed off. A 20-year-old in the Royal Irish Fusiliers, John Lucy, wrote that the German advance over open fields amazed him, but "after the first shock of seeing men slowly and helplessly falling down as they were hit, gave us a great sense of power and pleasure. It was all so easy." The 1,600 British casualties were low compared with battles in the Boer War, and perhaps for that reason the engagement saw the birth of a legend that angels had entered the battle on the British side.

Through a combination of circumstances—Lanrezac's caution, French's resentment, and a premature attack by the German 2nd Army—the French and British realized they were not up to attacking. Joffre saw that Plan XVII had failed. Between August 20 and 23, 40,000 French soldiers had been killed, 27,000 of them on the 22nd alone, the bloodiest day so far in French military history. "You may expect the German armies to be before the walls of Paris in 12 days," Joffre told the government, and ordered a retreat.

In Paris, there was near panic. The government fled to Bordeaux. Refugees blocked

the roads and turned the railroad stations into camps. As a British reporter wrote, the elderly knew well what a siege meant: they had endured one in 1870. They told the young "with shaking heads and trembling forefingers. 'Starvation! We ate rats if we

were lucky!'. . . Most of them had a haggard look and kept repeating the stale old word, *'Incroyable!'*"

In the countryside, the Allies crowded back 50 miles into France, where Joffre hoped to dam the German advance. The maneuver was completed just in time, for the German 1st Army was already trying to outflank them to the west. For the BEF, the retreat from Mons was a great achievement, marching 150 miles in 13 days in a heat wave. No one liked the scent of failure. "Scandalous," said a British sergeant. "In our hurry to get away guns, wagons, horses, wounded men were left to the victorious Germans and even our British infantrymen were throwing their rifles, ammunition, equipment and running like hell for their lives."

The British held together nevertheless. One action was fought at Le Câteau when an able general, Horace Smith-Dorrien, ignored French's orders to abandon ammunition and officers' kits, engaged the Germans, then retreated in good order. The retreat

GRIM REALITY Two British soldiers, followed by two Belgians, march determinedly in the retreat from Mons. Intense heat added to their discomfort during forced marches.

TAXI! Some troops were rushed to the battlefront on the Marne by Paris cabs (top). French artillerymen cheer the British cavalry in an illustration of the battle.

allowed the British to believe they would live to fight another day, on their own terms.

Fortunately for the Allies, Moltke failed to apply Schlieffen's *diktat*: "Only keep the right flank strong!" He had already used up seven divisions occupying Belgian fortresses. Now, on August 26, he robbed his right flank of four divisions to strengthen the Eastern Front. It was a decision born of overconfidence. Everything was going so well that army commanders were already talking of victory.

In fact, everything was going *too* well. The Germans, covering some 20 to 25 miles a day, had advanced so fast and so far they had outrun their communications and supplies. The German cavalry had made a point of destroying telegraph lines, with the result that the German high command, first in Koblenz, then in Luxembourg, was often out of touch with local commanders. One German officer wrote: "The men stagger forward, their faces coated with dust, their uniforms in rags, they look like living scarecrows. They march with their eyes closed, singing in chorus so that they will not fall asleep on the march. The certainty of early victory and the triumphal entry into Paris keeps them going." Then came another change of plan.

The German 1st Army was on its way

TAKE AIM ... German trenches in the Marne had built-in gunholes. Each soldier carried a leather knapsack on his back, with a rolled-up overcoat and tent cloth on top.

around Paris, but by now the first French troops were arriving by train in the region, east of Paris, after their removal from Alsace Lorraine six days earlier. To meet them, the 1st Army veered southward, heading *east* of Paris, not to the west as Schlieffen had directed. Moltke's scheme now was to envelop the French with a massive assault through Alsace Lorraine, sweeping around the French and British rear past Verdun.

General Joseph Gallieni, the military governor in Paris, saw an opportunity to strike at the flanks of the German 1st Army. Gallieni, who had been recalled from retirement after a career in the French colonies, knew a chance when he saw one. For two days, he struggled to convince both the British and General Joffre that the moment had come to attack. Slowly Joffre allowed himself to be persuaded. Every available French soldier was rushed to strengthen the line, including a fresh division that had just arrived in Paris from Tunis. But how were they to be moved to the front? Trains would only take half the division, and a march would get them into action too late. On September 7, with the help of the police, Gallieni rounded up 600 taxis, which then relayed the 6,000 men to the front line, 25 miles away.

Now, fatally, Germany's 1st Army—waving about "like the tentacles of an octopus," to use A.J.P. Taylor's phrase—turned to

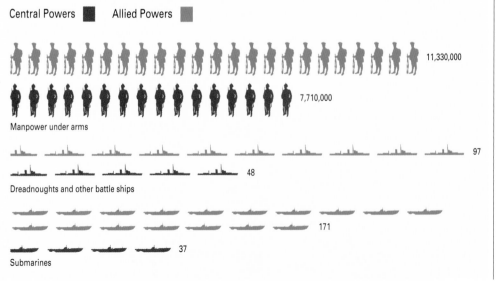

guard itself against attack from the Paris area. In doing so, it opened a 30-mile gap between itself and the German 2nd Army along the Marne, just as the British and French were mustering for attack along the whole line. Soon, the British advanced into the hole between the two German armies.

At the eastern end of the line, the Germans tried and failed to break through the French, first at Charmes, then at Nancy. The French held firm in the great fortress of Verdun, while not far away the kaiser waited in vain

HANDS UP   German soldiers take four French prisoners during their advance in early September. By September 9, the advance had turned into withdrawal.

for it to fall. The German failure to break through was hardly surprising, for it was the existence of those defenses that had driven Schlieffen to plan an attack through Belgium in the first place. The kaiser did not forgive Moltke for his failure to deliver the promised victory, and fired him a few days later.

Through all this, the German high command in Luxembourg had little idea what was happening at the front. The commanders on the spot were not much better informed. All of them, however, knew that the Schlieffen plan had been fatally compromised, and that victory on those terms was now impossible. The commander of the German 2nd Army, General von Bülow, was told that his aerial reconnaissance had spotted the British advancing into the 30-mile hole on his right. On the afternoon of September 9, the Germans started to pull back—and back, and back, across the ground they had seized only days before.

This retreat, known as the Battle of the Marne, saved the Germans from probable defeat, and it was the last great maneuver of open warfare on the Western Front. Some 25 miles back, the Germans crossed the River Aisne, blew up its bridges, regrouped and dug in. There, they made the discovery that shaped the war—that men in trenches, even when exhausted, can stop the most

RESOURCES AND ARMS, 1914

With nearly one-and-a-half times as many men under arms, the Allies outnumbered the Central Powers in manpower at the start of the war. The Allied naval strength was far superior to that of the Central Powers.

Central Powers ■   Allied Powers ▮

11,330,000
7,710,000
Manpower under arms

97
48
Dreadnoughts and other battle ships

171
37
Submarines

PARADING IN "WIPERS" British troops arrive in Ypres—which they pronounced "Wipers"—on October 13, 1914. The town would remain the center of a British salient until the end of the war. In the process, it was almost destroyed.

determined assaults. By September 17, the front line became static right along the French frontier. In the six weeks that should have led to victory, the Germans had done nothing but overwhelm Belgium. In France, they had gained a few miles, no more.

The race to the sea

With the opposing forces locked into the first primitive trenches in what would evolve into a new form of warfare, the only way to gain an advantage was by outflanking the enemies' trenches. Between the western end of the front lines and the sea was a gap of 200 miles. There now emerged two new objectives: the ports on the English Channel—Calais, Dunkirk, Boulogne, Ostend, Zeebrugge—and Antwerp, a base for Belgian offensives.

It was odd that the British had not already secured the ports to protect their supply lines. Only when the Germans began attacking Antwerp did they move, sending a small force to guard the ports and dispatching one infantry and one cavalry division to help the

Belgians. As it happened, they were not in time to save Antwerp—it fell on October 10—but they did manage to cover the retreat of the Belgians and secure the coast, and to provide a defendable base as the opposing forces leapfrogged each other from the entrenched front line toward the coast.

The Western Allies, using French railways to switch their forces ever farther northward, tried three times to outflank the Germans, on the Somme, at Arras and at Ypres. By the time the British began to advance from Ypres along the Yser River in mid-October, linking with the French and Belgians to form an impenetrable wall to the sea, the Germans had devised a countermove with forces released by the seizure of Antwerp; they aimed to force a way down the coast road, as the last possible chance to squeeze past their opponents. In addition, the Germans had had a stroke of luck: they had captured a British officer who had in his pocket the order for the next offensive. When it came, the Germans were well prepared. Both offensives opened almost simultaneously, on October 19 and 20. The First Battle of Ypres had begun.

While the Belgians secured their position to the north by flooding the area, the British at Ypres were brutally overstretched. The Germans, with six new divisions, outnumbered the Allies 2:1 in manpower and 5:1 in

artillery. But if the British could not break the German line, the Germans could not penetrate either. One attempt to do so, at Langemarck, led to an astonishing scene. The British saw long lines of gray uniformed men approaching, and heard them singing; the figures were arm in arm. They were student volunteers, comrades striding into battle as they had strode the streets of Heidelberg. With only six weeks of training, they had never been in action before. British shrapnel and machine guns tore the lines to pieces. In three weeks, 36,000 students died. The Germans still refer to this event as the "*Kindermord*," the Massacre of the Children.

The First Battle of Ypres was predominantly a British battle, in which the line held because British front-line soldiers kept up their "15 rounds rapid." Death and gallantry etched themselves into the memory, history and legend of every British unit. At Zaandvoorde, a hamlet southeast of Ypres, cavalrymen used to parading in burnished breastplates and plumed helmets were reduced to a week of hell in shallow, muddy trenches before being blasted and shot to bits. On November 11, 18,000 Germans streamed through the thin Allied line and advanced on a copse known as Polygon Wood, defended by 1,000 British. If the Germans broke through, the Channel ports lay ahead and quite possibly the war would be lost. The "Ox and Bucks," the 1st Kings and the Royal Engineers combined to deflect the attackers into a copse off to one side—Nonnebosschen, Nun's Wood. Then the British hunted the Germans out of the wood, and sealed the gap. That day, the fighting ended.

The three months of carnage and the ensuing stalemate changed the character of the war. There was no opportunity anymore for mobility, because there was nowhere left to move, at least in Western Europe. Defense had triumphed over attack. From the Swiss border to the Channel, the great machinery of war had ground to a standstill. Both sides were in for a long siege.

THE CHRISTMAS TRUCE

AS THE SEASON OF GOODWILL REACHED THE TRENCHES MEN SPONTANEOUSLY LAID ASIDE THEIR ARMS AND CLAMBERED OUT TO FRATERNIZE WITH THE ENEMY

On Christmas Eve 1914, it froze along the Western Front. The mud turned hard, shell-stunted trees were rimed with frost, and the terrible smell of rotting flesh in no-man's-land faded. The night was clear, crisp, clean and, for the most part, quiet. It was the Germans who celebrated first, exchanging schnapps and cigarettes, with a few candle-lit Christmas trees and Chinese lanterns showing above the trenches. Along the front south of Ypres, the lights attracted desultory fire from the British trenches, which died away as the British saw that no attack was pending. The night became silent. At one spot, the Germans began to sing: "*Stille Nacht, Heilige Nacht.*"

Rifleman Graham Williams of the London Rifle Brigade recalled: "They finished their carol and we thought that we ought to retaliate in some way, so we sang 'The First Noel,' and when we finished that they all began clapping; and then they struck up another favorite of theirs, 'O Tannenbaum.' And so it went on...when we started 'O Come All Ye Faithful' the Germans immediately joined in singing the same hymn to the Latin words '*Adeste Fideles*.' And I thought, well, this was really a most extraordinary thing—two nations both singing the same carol in the middle of a war."

At another spot, a Royal Field Artillery gunner remembered: "The Germans started shouting, 'Come over, I want to speak to you.' Our chaps hardly knew how to take this, but one of the 'nuts' belonging to the regiment got out of the trench and started to walk across towards the German lines. One of the Germans met him about halfway across, and they shook hands and became quite friendly. In due course, the 'nut' came back and told all the others about it. So more of them took it in turns to go and visit the Germans."

The next day, by tacit agreement, troops on both sides moved about within full view of each other. Services were held, without a shot being fired. A few individuals met in no-man's-land, and both sides waved at each other. Small groups formed, then larger ones, until in some places hundreds mixed, shaking hands and

CHRISTMAS BOUNTY   Gifts were distributed to British soldiers in the name of the king's daughter, Princess Mary.

offering each other drinks and cigarettes. In Belgium, the German Royal Saxon Regiment met up with the Scottish Seaforth Highlanders. A Scottish soldier produced a football and used hats as goalposts; the Germans did the same with their helmets. The game lasted an hour before the German commanding officer ordered the men back.

Perhaps two-thirds of the whole front observed the truce, which in some places lasted a week. "One of the Dublin Fusiliers was killed by a bullet," wrote Royal Field Artillery 2nd Lieutenant Cyril Drummond. "And the Saxons immediately sent over and apologized, saying it hadn't been anything to do with them, but from those so-and-so Prussians on their left... But of course the war was becoming a farce and the high-ups decided that this truce must stop."

No one believed the peace would last. Rain came again, the mud softened, the mood changed, the commanders ordered their men back into the trenches, and the guns opened up again. But the men at the front remembered that they and their enemies had, in a time of inhuman horror, reasserted their basic humanity.

PEACE TO ALL MEN   British and German soldiers mingle in no-man's-land at Ploegsteert in Belgium during the Christmas truce.

THE WESTERN FRONT

THE ALLIED GENERALS SEEMED TO HAVE NO ANSWERS TO TRENCH WARFARE—EXCEPT TO HURL MORE MEN AT THE ENEMY LINES

The deadlock in Belgium and northeast France left all three major combatants wondering what to do next. Moltke's replacement as commander, Erich von Falkenhayn, still believed that the war would be decided in France. Lacking new ideas to break the stalemate, he saw that a long conflict was inevitable and committed himself to a war of attrition. At home, this meant more railroads behind the lines, more munitions and an economy geared to war. Abroad, it meant undermining Britain's imperial subjects and winning new allies, specifically Turkey.

The British, who saw the German lines as (in Churchill's words) "a fortress that cannot be carried by assault," also accepted the burden of extended warfare. In this, the driving force was the Secretary of State for War, Lord Kitchener, who believed that Britain's small professional army would no longer suffice. Half of those who had crossed the Channel three months earlier were casualties. Some 10,000 had been killed at Ypres alone, and another 6,000 in previous engagements. What was needed now was a mass army of volunteers. In an upsurge of nationalism, volunteers flooded in. By the end of 1914, 1 million men had enlisted. With troops from the empire, Britain could now call on an army of 2 million.

To break the deadlock, Britain pursued two strategies. One was to cut through the

POINTING THE FINGER A hero of colonial battles, Kitchener became the chief feature of his recruiting posters in Britain.

Gordian knot of trench warfare with a machine that could cross trenches and was invulnerable to machine guns. Such a machine, soon to be known as the tank, was already on the drawing board, backed by the First Lord of the Admiralty, Winston Churchill. The other solution was to use the navy to attack a vulnerable part of the Central Powers' flanks—a policy that would lead to the Dardanelles, and Gallipoli.

GAS ATTACK German troops advance through a cloud of gas. Left: Moltke's successor, Erich von Falkenhayn, lasted as chief of the general staff until August 1916.

April-May 1915
Second Battle
of Ypres

September 1915
Allied offensive in Champagne
and around Loos

February 1916
Start of German
assault on Verdun

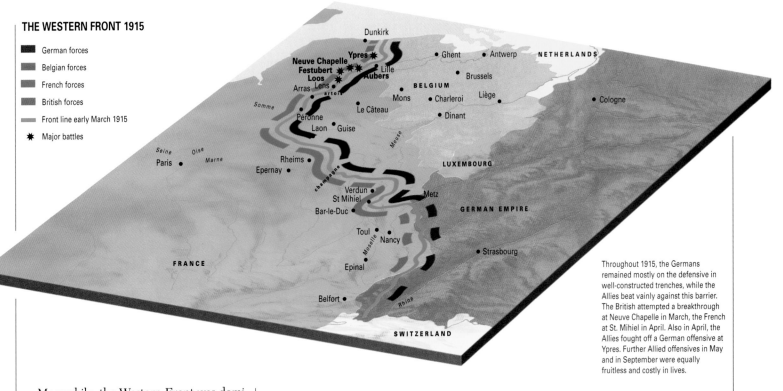

THE WESTERN FRONT 1915

- ▨ German forces
- ▬ Belgian forces
- ▬ French forces
- ▨ British forces
- ▬ Front line early March 1915
- ✳ Major battles

Throughout 1915, the Germans remained mostly on the defensive in well-constructed trenches, while the Allies beat vainly against this barrier. The British attempted a breakthrough at Neuve Chapelle in March, the French at St. Mihiel in April. Also in April, the Allies fought off a German offensive at Ypres. Further Allied offensives in May and in September were equally fruitless and costly in lives.

Meanwhile, the Western Front was dominated by the French, who were loath to accept the consequences of Ypres. Joffre's solution consisted of two converging blows from Artois and Champagne, followed by a large-scale attack in Lorraine. In February and March 1915, the French lost 50,000 men attacking the German trenches, gaining just 500 yards of ground. In April, they lost 64,000 attacking the St. Mihiel salient.

The British, too, tried to break through, spurred on by the arrival of several divisions of Indians and Canadians. Sir John French

SOUNDS FAMILIAR

The best-known Anglicized version of a Western Front name was "Wipers" for Ypres. Others in common use were:

Doingt: Doing It
Etaples: Eatables, Eat-apples
Achonvillers: Ocean Villas
Foncquevilliers: Funky Villas
Biefvilliers: Beef Villas
Poperinghe: Pop
Albert: Bert

needed a victory, and chose Neuve Chapelle as his target. On March 10, after an intense half-hour bombardment, the artillery lengthened their range, creating a defensive curtain—a barrage—behind which the British seized the battered German trenches. The key to these tactics was accuracy, strict scheduling and speed. But in repeating the maneuver, the artillery fire wavered, as did the command structure. A five-hour delay allowed the Germans to recover.

The British were short of weapons and ammunition, partly due to the fact that their military leaders had ignored the growing significance of the machine gun. Two per battalion had been considered enough in 1908, and it was with reluctance that Kitchener allowed four. When the consequences of this decision were made public, the outcry led to the establishment in 1915 of a new Ministry of Munitions under David Lloyd George. Shell production rose, and each battalion had 16 machine guns.

Stalemate in the trenches

If head-on assault could not achieve a lasting breakthrough, something new had to be tried. While the British experimented in secret with the tank, the Germans turned to a secret weapon of their own—gas. These weapons made their first public appearance on the afternoon of April 22, 1915, at the opening of the Second Battle of Ypres. The first victims of gas on the Western Front, Algerians fighting with the French and Canadians, staggered back from the line coughing and pointing to their throats. This

COMMITMENT FROM THE COLONIES Outside the British Isles, the largest imperial contribution in the war effort came from India, where about 1.3 million volunteers joined up. Of these, 49,000 would die in battle.

left a gap 4 miles wide, but the Germans had not been told what to do if they broke through, other than dig in. This they did, choosing safety over offense.

From this salient—a narrow projection of

1919

July-November 1916
Start of Battle of the
Somme

December 1916
Germans pull back
from Verdun

March 1917
Germans withdraw
to Siegfried Line

July 1917
Beginning of Third
Battle of Ypres

November 1917
British take Passchendaele;
end of Third Battle of Ypres

always succeed in the end. This attitude took no account of the Germans' defenses: trench-lines with walls of sand-bags and wire 30 feet deep, backed by mounds and dugouts for 219 yards, covered by machine-gun nests, communication trenches, concrete bunkers and reserve posts stretching back at least 1 mile.

In May, the French mounted an assault between Lens and Arras; the British did the same at Aubers Ridge. Here, the opening bombardment achieved little, and when the British troops, including many Indians, went over the top, "there could never before in war have been a more perfect target," according to the history of one German regiment. Both assaults shuddered to a halt, were renewed in mid-May and again in mid-June, and again faltered. Each of these immense attacks gained nothing but a few yards of mud, and led to losses of more than 200,000 Frenchmen.

Attempts to break through

In autumn 1915, France and Britain planned more massive attacks: the French in Champagne near Rheims, the French and British together on either side of Lens, and the British at Loos. The attacks were designed to spark a general offensive along the Western Front, compel a German retreat, and, in Joffre's words, "possibly end the war."

British support for the plan was not unanimous. Kitchener allowed himself to be bludgeoned into backing it by Joffre, justifying it as a means of taking the pressure off Russia. Sir John French vacillated. And General Haig was set against it—with good reason. The ground was bare and open, and the Germans well ensconced. The British, with only half the weight of artillery possessed by the French, were producing only 22,000 shells a day, compared with France's 100,000 and Germany's 250,000.

land beyond the Front—the very presence of the Germans threatened the Allies with future attacks. Sir John French, confident of imminent French reinforcements, ordered a counterattack, during which the Canadians suffered appalling losses. The British commander in the area, General Horace Smith-Dorrien, advised withdrawal. French, who had been annoyed with Smith-Dorrien ever since he had ignored his orders (yet saved the day) at Le Câteau, accused Smith-Dorrien of defeatism and forced his resignation. He then authorized the very withdrawal Smith-Dorrien had advocated. And so by May 27, the Second Battle of Ypres ended, with the loss of 2 miles of ground and 60,000 British and Commonwealth lives.

The Allies were still gripped by the ambition to seize territory, mainly because Joffre remained confident that the offensive must

MOVING TARGETS Members of an assault battalion of the Tyneside Irish are strung out in silhouette as they go over the top.

> ## GOING OVER THE TOP
>
> Private Fellowes of the Northumberland Fusiliers described what it was like to go over the top at the Battle of Loos:
>
> "We had five nights marching down to Loos. Our Company commander, Captain Powell, called together the companies and addressed us and told us there was a battle raging, several divisions had been in action… We were going up to relieve them. I can still remember the cheers.
>
> "On the way to the line, the Adjutant stopped me. He said, 'The CO's got a message for you to take up.' I can remember the words of this message even to this day. It was written on an old signal pad. It wasn't dated or signed, it just said, 'The CO wishes the attack to be carried out with the bayonets in the true Northumbrian fashion.' It was the first I heard that we were going into action.
>
> "When I got to the trenches all the lads were standing with fixed bayonets and as I walked through the back they started to climb out of the trench running as fast as the equipment would ever allow. They were just a mob! I was looking for Captain Powell to give him the message, and then I realized he was up there with the lads, so I followed on.
>
> "The leading men would be about 100 yards from the German wire and till then not a shot had been fired. Suddenly all hell was let loose. Some men began to stumble and fall, machine guns were firing from the front of us… A lad in front of me went down, and I tripped and fell over him. To this day I don't feel any shame—I stayed where I was.
>
> "I'll remember the sight until my dying day, the whole slope was full of prone figures. The Germans had suddenly stopped firing, just like they'd begun. Men started to rise to their feet, some stumbled and crawled any way to try to get back. Still the Germans never fired… They were so filled with bitter remorse and guilt at the corpses of Loos that they refused to fire another shot… When I got back in the trench I landed in the same place where I'd left. One of the lads handed me a water-bottle. We lay there and it was awful listening to the cries of the men on that field, some were screaming. Terrible! I'm afraid a lot were dead before the night.
>
> "All this time I still had the message for Captain Powell. I didn't find him until afterwards… I gave him the message. He read it. He said, 'It doesn't matter, Sonny, now.' I could see tears running down his cheeks."

Haig said he needed 36 divisions for a chance of success; he had only nine. And no one knew of a way to resolve the tactical paradox of this new form of warfare: an assault needed two elements, surprise and a huge artillery bombardment; but the bombardment undermined the surprise. Attack would, it seemed, be suicidal, and many senior officers knew it. But attack was ordered nevertheless.

The attack was launched on September 25 around Loos, with hopes of a breakthrough pinned on a bombardment and on gas, of which the British now had their own supplies. But the gas moved sluggishly and randomly in unhelpful breezes. The troops followed at 6:30 a.m., displaying great heroism. Men of the London Regiment dribbled a soccer ball across no-man's-land. Piper Peter Laidlaw of the King's Own Scottish Borderers rallied his

LINE OF COMMUNICATION Soldiers in a British communications trench are protected with barbed wire above. A telephone cable is strung along the left wall of the trench.

comrades by marching up and down in full view of the enemy playing "Scotland the Brave."

There was no breakthrough. Six British divisions made little impact on the two defending German divisions. On the second day of the battle, 10,000 British reserves advancing belatedly and slowly presented the Germans with a perfect target. Around 8,000 of them were killed or wounded in three and a half hours, all volunteers. So sickened were the German defenders by the slaughter that, when lone survivors rose and staggered back from no-man's-land, no shots were fired. The Germans sustained no casualties at all.

The only positive result of this slaughter was the departure of Sir John French, mainly because of the opposition of his junior, Haig. After a high-level dispute over the disaster at Loos, French was fired and Haig replaced him.

LOOKING OUT Periscopes provided the safest way of peering out of a trench. Barbed wire covers a front-line trench near Arras (below).

The defense of Verdun

During 1915, the war became truly global. But in 1916 attention again returned to the Western Front, for the increase in manpower and munitions there raised hopes of breaking the deadlock in trench warfare. Thirty-eight new British divisions increased the total number for the Allies on the Western Front to 139, against the Germans' 117. For the first time, too, the Allies—Britain, France, Italy, Belgium and Russia—planned to coordinate their attacks with a general assault in the summer of 1916. On the Western Front, the attack would fall on the Somme.

They were too slow. Germany moved first. Falkenhayn believed that Britain was the real problem because the country could blockade Germany into starvation while remaining safe beyond the Channel. The way to attack Britain was to knock out France. Bleed France dry, he had argued to the kaiser at the end of 1915, and victory would follow. The strategy should not be mass assault, but an attack at a single point so critical that France would have to respond with everything it had. That point, he said, was Verdun.

bombardment and a battle of unprecedented length. A million shells were fired on the first day alone. For three days, French lines crumbled into a mass of mud, wire and concrete, and German troops advanced with a new weapon, the flame-thrower. Douaumont, one of the two huge fortresses guarding Verdun, was taken with hardly a struggle. The

IN THE MUD An aerial photograph shows the land around Verdun reduced to a pockmarked wasteland. Below: French soldiers in a captured German trench near Douaumont.

"Cannon conquers, infantry occupies," he said, and even Joffre saw that this was now the only strategy likely to work in Verdun.

Under Pétain, the French fought the Germans to a standstill, following Pétain's edict: *"Ils ne passeront pas!"* ("They shall

Verdun was not well prepared to repel such an assault. The French had plenty of warning: it is hard to amass six infantry divisions and 1,300 pieces of artillery—including a number of Big Berthas—without anyone noticing. But Joffre wanted to focus on the build-up in the Somme, and failed to authorize new defenses.

At 7:15 a.m. on February 21, a 14-inch shell exploded in the archbishop's palace in Verdun and opened an unprecedented

French, told of the loss by propaganda leaflets scattered from German planes, despaired. Frozen roads became clogged with refugees and wounded soldiers.

In response, Joffre handed Verdun to General Henri-Philippe Pétain, who had won fame at Arras in May 1915. Already 60, he would become the aged leader of the Vichy government after Germany's victory in 1940. In 1915, he was an outspoken adversary of Joffre's obsession with offense.

not pass!") Though the Germans manufactured a zone of death with their artillery, whenever their infantry moved forward to secure the ground, they were pounded in turn by French artillery. Despite terrible conditions, French supplies managed to match those of the Germans. Where the Germans had good roads leading to the front, the French had poor rail links and one road, from Bar-le-Duc, along which up to 6,000 trucks passed every day, always under

SHOOTING DESERTERS

In October 1916, No. 12772 Private A. Botfield, 9th Battalion (Pioneers) South Staffordshire Regiment, while on a work party in the trenches, ran away "owing to the bursting of a shell and did not afterwards rejoin the party." He was accused of "misbehaving before the enemy in such a manner as to show cowardice." He was found guilty, and shot by firing squad at 5:50 a.m. on October 18.

One of the most heinous crimes in the trenches was variously called loss of nerve, cold feet, cowardice and shell shock. Most men were more frightened by fear itself than by death, and this held them together. Some, however, became nervous wrecks or faked illness, and were given medical leave; others simply ran, technically making themselves deserters: both reactions attracted accusations of cowardice. Desertion was seen as a disease stemming from a lack of self-control, which could spread like a plague and thus help the enemy. This form of cowardice was considered treachery, and was subject to military discipline.

Botfield was among the first to be shot for "cowardice," but he was not the last. "There was one poor little man came to me," wrote Captain C.S. Slack of the East Yorkshires. "He was a half-wit . . . he ran away, and he was caught and ran away again, deserted, and he was court-martialed to be shot, and I had to pick, together with my sergeant-major, ten men to shoot him, which we did . . . I wrote to his mother, 'Killed in action,' and I think that's what they were told in every case."

In the French army, cases of desertion rose from 509 in 1914 to 21,174 in 1917. Mostly these were individual acts, but there was one notable exception. In the spring of 1917, during the April assaults on the Chemin-des-Dames ridge between Verdun and Paris, some 25,000 men were killed or wounded for a gain of some 500 yards. The men had had enough and mutinied. On June 1, at Missy-aux-Bois, French infantry troops established their own anti-war government. Pétain, the new commander-in-chief, ordered mass arrests: 23,385 were judged guilty, of whom 50 were shot. However, conditions for the troops were improved and the threat of mutiny ended.

FORM OF DEATH The British authorities issued special forms for those sentenced to death by courts-martial.

horrors counted it a victory, and it made Pétain's reputation. In fact, the heart went out of the battle long before its final end, for beginning in mid-June 1916 the Germans, pressed on the Eastern Front, received no fresh divisions, and the French were able to regain some of the ground lost the previous autumn. In June, the Western Front acquired a new focus: the Somme.

The Battle of the Somme

If Verdun was France's great self-sacrifice, Britain's was the Somme. The inspiration came from Joffre, who had spoken of a massive break-through in an operation between the two allies; this had to be at the point where their armies joined, on the River Somme. But since France was being bled into immobility at Verdun in the south, and drawing in forces from the north—the French front shrank from 25 miles to 8 miles, and their troops from 40 divisions to five—most of the action would have to

fire. Both sides became locked into a conviction that the town had to be taken, or had to be saved, at whatever cost.

The cost was frightful, the sights atrocious. At any one time, up to 115 divisions—over 1 million men—were crammed against each other along a mere 8 miles. For ten months, these men lived a nightmare of shattered bodies, whistling shells and explosions that racked the mind. Some 40 million artillery shells contributed to the deaths of at least 160,000 Frenchmen and 130,000 Germans. Another 600,000 men were wounded.

This was the war's longest battle, lasting from February 21 to December 18, 1916—a grisly monument to the power of industrialized warfare, and for France an epic tragedy that bled the country dry of men and materials. But those who did not experience the

"FRENCH TROOPS RESTING" The British war artist C.R.W. Nevinson uses an almost Cubist technique to depict a group of weary French soldiers taking a break at the side of a road.

come from Britain. By the summer of 1916, the British army, its 17 divisions fed by the stream of volunteers during 1915, held almost 80 miles between Paris and the sea.

Haig's plan relied on a massive artillery barrage to break the enemy's spirit and to destroy the barbed wire, the trenches and the machine-gun posts. For this he had some 1,500 guns, of which 467 were heavy ones, a gun for every 60 feet of front. The second vital element—surprise—was never a possibility, for the preparations were obvious to the Germans from February. The British plan was further compromised by a divergence of opinion in the high command: Haig wanted a breakthrough, while others believed that only a limited advance would be possible. Both tactics were trapped in the paradox of trench warfare. Only a long bombardment would cut through the enemy lines; but the longer the bombardment, the greater the resources required, and the longer the Germans would have to prepare their rear defenses.

In the last week of June, as 2 million men faced each other, the British on their 18-mile front opened a massive artillery barrage, firing off more than a million rounds, dumping 20,000 tons of metal and explosive on the German lines, and creating a roar that could be heard beyond the Channel more than 100 miles away. Much of this turned out to be completely useless. The guns were distributed evenly along the front, with no effort to focus on weak points. Many guns were obsolete, and could not penetrate the German dugouts or gun emplacements. Thus the prime, indeed the only, aim of the barrage—to allow an infantry advance by pulverizing the enemy lines—was not achieved. Yet the infantry were sent forward just the same.

The only hope for the infantry was to race across no-man's-land before the barrage lifted, but racing was impossible. For one thing, every man was burdened down with more than 60 pounds of gear, over ground

BLOOD AND SLAUGHTER

The Battle of the Somme still ranks as the bloodiest battle in the history of warfare. In 142 days between July and November 1916, 1.2 million men were killed or wounded.

ploughed into a morass of mud and craters. For another, the men were to advance at "a steady pace," in lines as neat as ninepins, and just as vulnerable. The result was a catastrophe, the most intense bloodletting in British military history.

July 1 dawned hot and full of hope. The

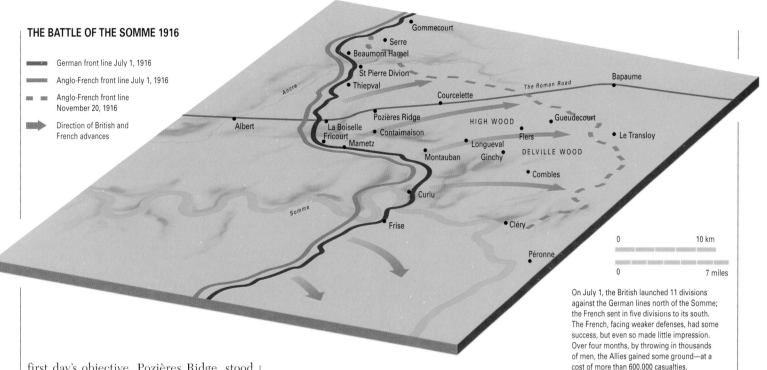

THE BATTLE OF THE SOMME 1916

▬▬▬ German front line July 1, 1916

▬▬▬ Anglo-French front line July 1, 1916

▬ ▬ Anglo-French front line
November 20, 1916

➡ Direction of British and
French advances

Gommecourt
Serre
Beaumont Hamel
St Pierre Divion
Thiepval
Ancre
Courcelette
The Roman Road
Bapaume
Albert
Poziéres Ridge
HIGH WOOD
Gueudecourt
La Boiselle
Contaimaison
Le Transloy
Fricourt
Flers
Mametz
Longueval
Ginchy
DELVILLE WOOD
Montauban
Combles
Curlu
Cléry
Frise
Péronne
Somme

0   10 km

0   7 miles

On July 1, the British launched 11 divisions
against the German lines north of the Somme;
the French sent in five divisions to its south.
The French, facing weaker defenses, had some
success, but even so made little impression.
Over four months, by throwing in thousands
of men, the Allies gained some ground—at a
cost of more than 600,000 casualties.

first day's objective, Poziéres Ridge, stood out clearly 4 miles ahead. "The sun was just topping the mist and catching the dewdrops on the grass and thistles around us," wrote Major H. Bidder, of the Royal Sussex Regiment. "The stakes of the barbed wire threw long shadows towards us. The guns were blazing away; and great black mushrooms were shooting out of the surface of the white sea in front . . . There was a wonderful cheery air of expectancy over the troops . . . I have never known quite the same universal feeling of cheerful eagerness."

When 120,000 men, riding the final wave of the barrage, went over the top at 7:30 a.m., they advanced shoulder to shoulder, in waves 300 feet apart. Ahead, the barrage of falling shells lifted, supposedly to flatten more distant trenches. The front-line Germans, sheltering in their dugouts, dragged out their machine guns and raked the British infantry as if they were in a carnival's shooting gallery. At the same time, undamaged German guns rained down artillery shells. "We never got anywhere near the Germans," recalled Corporal W. Shaw of the Royal Welch Fusiliers. "Our lads was mown down . . . You couldn't do anything . . . The machine guns were levelled and they were mowing the top of the trenches . . . The officers were urging us on, saying, 'Come on lads, follow the flash!' [on the back of the officers' collars]. But you just couldn't. It was hopeless. And those young offi-

FIELD HOSPITAL British wounded lie on stretchers waiting to be tended by medics. Below: Men of the Wiltshire Regiment advance to attack Thiepval in August 1916.

THE WESTERN FRONT 1916-17

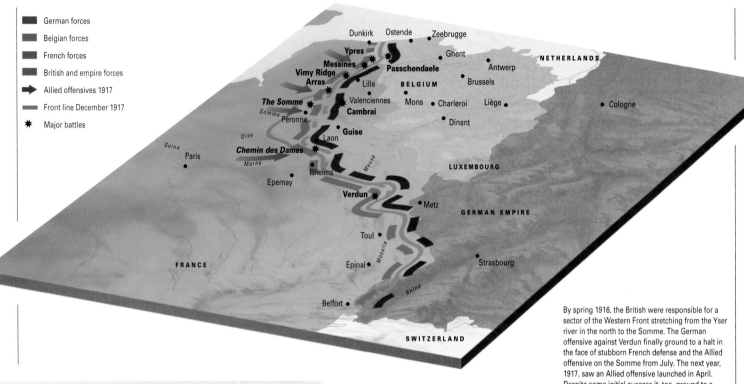

German forces

Belgian forces

French forces

British and empire forces

Allied offensives 1917

Front line December 1917

Major battles

By spring 1916, the British were responsible for a sector of the Western Front stretching from the Yser river in the north to the Somme. The German offensive against Verdun finally ground to a halt in the face of stubborn French defense and the Allied offensive on the Somme from July. The next year, 1917, saw an Allied offensive launched in April. Despite some initial success it, too, ground to a halt—as did British offensives in June and July.

LANDSCAPE OF WAR   With splintered tree trunks and ground raked again and again by shellfire and mining, the Messines Ridge in 1917 presents a picture of almost unsurpassed desolation.

the French, along their much smaller front, took 4,000.

After two weeks, General Sir Henry Rawlinson suggested renewing the attack on a 4-mile front, aiming at spots on the ridge marked by Delville Wood and High Wood. Over five days, the 3,000 men of the South African Brigade attacked, often fighting hand-to-hand. When relief came, only 758 survived.

With the idea of a breakthrough gone forever, Haig might have called a halt; but he had promised a great victory, and could not—would not—stop. Failing to break through, Haig opted instead for "methodical progress." This course of action entailed steady battering on Pozières Ridge against an immovable force. In one sector, held by the Anzacs—the Australian and New Zealand Army Corps—23,000 men were killed or wounded to gain a mile of mud.

Many Anzacs became appalled at what they saw as murder by an incompetent, callous, vain and self-deluded leadership.

The last attack on the Somme was in mid-November. The British had advanced at most 5 miles, but so slowly that the German lines had been rebuilt as strong as ever. The British and their Dominions had suffered 420,000 casualties, the French 200,000, the Germans about 450,000. In the words of A.J.P. Taylor: "The Somme set the picture by which future generations saw the First World War: brave helpless soldiers; obstinate generals; nothing achieved."

The Allies on the offensive

If Britain and France had fought themselves to a standstill, the Germans had suffered as well, with nothing to show, and they needed a new commander. Falkenhayn was put in charge of fighting Romania, which had just entered the war on the Allied side, while the new face on the Western Front turned out to be an old one: the aged titan, Paul von Hindenburg, a legendary figure after his victory over the Russians at Tannenberg in the first month of the war.

Hindenburg came with his quartermaster-general, Erich Ludendorff, the two forming a military equivalent of president and prime

cers, going ahead, that flash flying in the breeze, they were picked off like flies." All that was left of the advancing British were pockets of men cowering in shell-holes.

There was progress of a sort in the south. The French, straddling the Somme itself, moved forward with only small losses, partly because their advance was less rigid, and partly because the Germans had focused on the British sectors. But the British advanced, in one spot only, just over a mile to seize a village, Montauban. Every assault led to a bloodbath. Along their whole front, the British took less than 2,000 prisoners, while

UNDERMINING THE ENEMY

minister in which Ludendorff exercised power, while Hindenburg conferred gravitas. Ludendorff chose good sense over high risk, and had his troops on the Western Front prepare an even more impregnable wall, known to the Allies as the Hindenburg Line and to the Germans as the Siegfried Line. It lay well behind the front and was protected by a dead zone of razed houses and poisoned wells. With this defense, Germany would never be taken in the west and was free to fight elsewhere. Ludendorff opted for unrestricted submarine warfare to raise the British blockade of German coasts. And he had promised Poland independence to secure Polish help against the Russians.

In France, Joffre had delivered too little for too many deaths and, although promoted to marshal, he was effectively replaced by General Robert Nivelle, a hero of Verdun. Nivelle's plans for an attack won the backing of Britain's new prime minister, David Lloyd George, who, disillusioned with Haig, arranged for the British general to be placed under Nivelle's control.

ON THE MOVE German artillery (below) is dragged through a war-damaged town en route to Verdun.

DIGGING DEEP German sappers work on a tunnel (above); a French sapper in full uniform (right).

A major element in the war of the trenches was the impact of sappers—tunnellers with the job of digging under no-man's-land to lay mines beneath the enemy lines. The greatest mine explosion of the war was on Messines Ridge, south of Ypres, in June 1917. It took British, Canadian and Australian sappers six months to dig the 4^1/$_2$ miles of tunnels under the German trenches. By early June, 19 mines had been laid with a total of some 500 tons of explosive.

At 3:10 a.m. on June 7, 17 of the mines erupted simultaneously. "It seemed as if the Messines Ridge got up and shook itself," wrote a Royal Engineers captain. "All along its flank belched rows of mushroom-shaped masses of debris, flung high in the air. Gradually the masses commenced to disintegrate, as the released gases forced their way through the centers in pillars of flames. Then along the enemy line rolled dense columns of smoke, tumbling into weird formations as they mounted into the sky, at length opening like a row of giant umbrellas, spreading a dark pall over the yawning cavernous craters below."

To the Germans on Messines Ridge, the effect was cataclysmic. Some 10,000 were killed, either in the blasts or buried alive, and another 7,000 were taken prisoner in the advance that took the ridge. One explosion blew a crater 430 feet across. The next morning, a major-general, Charles Harrington, entered a dugout near the crater. He found "four German officers sitting round a table—all dead—killed by shock. They might have been playing bridge."

Of the two mines that failed to explode, one was blown up in 1955; the last remains below ground, undiscovered.

GERMAN SUPREMO General Hindenburg had served in the Austro-Prussian War of 1866 and the Franco-Prussian War of 1870-1. An imposing figurehead, he would later become German president, from 1925 until his death in 1934.

The attack, in April, coincided with two events that would change the course of the war: America's intervention and the arrival in Russia of Lenin, who was intent on pulling his country out of the war. Thereafter, the Allies in the west, unable to count on Russia, would increasingly look across the Atlantic for salvation.

On April 9, the British attacked at Arras as a distraction from a later, greater offensive. It began with a barrage by almost 3,000

THE MENIN ROAD By 1918 the landscape around Ypres was so pitted with craters that only packhorses could get through carrying supplies of shells and other ammunition.

guns, lasting five days. The Germans had all the warning they needed, and the Allies undermined their own plan by allowing all the supplies to come through a bottleneck at Arras. Fighting in unexpected snow flurries, the Canadians quickly took a much-disputed strong point, Vimy Ridge, which dominated

the northern French plain. But after five days, the arrival of German reserves stopped the advance. After a month, the British called a halt. Another 250,000 British, French, Imperial and German casualties had fallen, with nothing much to show for the sacrifice.

Meanwhile the French, following Nivelle's plan, attacked the Germans on the Aisne and were stopped in their tracks. The French advanced 600 yards, taking only a single ridge, the Chemin-des-Dames, instead of the promised 6 miles, and lost heavily. Nivelle's battered troops mutinied and deserted en masse. He was cast aside for Pétain, under whose rule more than 20,000 men were found guilty of desertion. At last Pétain had his way: defense, not offense, would govern France's military strategy. The French would await the Americans—and the tanks.

By June 1917, Haig believed that everything was up to him. Just another six months,

he argued, and Germany would fall. He now claimed that the Somme had been the wrong battle in the wrong place, and that the right place was, once again, Ypres—the mud notwithstanding, nor the massive German fortifications. Ypres was no more than 30 miles from the coast, and a breakthrough at this little salient would put the British within reach of the German submarine bases on the Belgian coast.

The attack at Ypres opened on June 7 with a successful limited advance on Messines Ridge. The keys to seizing this strongpoint were some 4$^1/_2$ miles of tunnels—in which were placed 19 mines containing 500 tons of explosive. When these blew, in conjunction with a barrage, the shock to the German soldiers was so intense that the ridge was taken in three hours, yielding 7,000 prisoners for the loss of "only" 16,000 British killed and wounded.

The main attack followed three weeks later. Again, there was a massive bombardment; again, all hope of surprise vanished; and again, the area to be taken was reduced to mud—much worse in this case, because the British shells destroyed the drainage and the weather was rainy. The Germans were well prepared. In this swampy Belgian landscape, trenches were unsuitable; instead, machine-gun posts dominated the marshes. On July 31, in this, the Third Battle of Ypres, the British cast themselves into the marshes that guarded the approach to the village of Passchendaele (today's Passendale), the name by which the battle became known.

In ten days, over 3,000 guns fired 4.25 million shells—more than 4 tons of metal and explosive for every yard of front. Then the infantry went in. They advanced 2 miles and farther, as several blows in the next two months pushed the front line back over ground marked by familiar names such as Gheluvelt and Polygon Wood. The weather was frightful, the battleground a morass. Despite the mud, there was progress, until Passchendaele Ridge loomed ahead, offering an objective that seemed to be worth any risk. But when the attack came, on October 9, mud jammed the guns, damped the shell-bursts, bogged down tanks, and swamped the men.

The Germans held back, conserving their strength and using mustard gas. On November 4, a sudden advance by British and Canadian troops seized Passchendaele village, and on the 10th the battle was brought to an exhausted close, the Allies having advanced 4$^1/_2$ miles, far short of their target on the Belgian coast.

New tactics

Yet there was light in the darkness, lit by the new Tank Corps. In August, the Tank Corps commanders had suggested a raid near Cambrai, 50 miles south of the mud of Passchendaele, into land well drained by two canals. The aim would have been to surprise the enemy with silence and speed, without a preliminary bombardment; then destroy, demoralize and get out quickly, without capturing ground. Haig, who dismissed tanks as "a minor factor," delayed. With time, the plan grew in scale, though it retained the two crucial elements: tanks and the lack of an opening bombardment. Almost 400 tanks

"WE ARE MAKING A NEW WORLD" A lowering sun shines on a hell of devastation, in a painting by British war artist Paul Nash. With its ironic title, the work sums up the nightmarish world created by the war.

would spearhead a breakthrough between the two canals across the Hindenburg Line. They would then press on toward Valenciennes, 25 miles to the northeast.

After meticulous preparations, the tanks went in on a 6-mile front at 6:20 a.m. on November 20. In many places, by midday, the tanks and infantry had sliced through the German lines and advanced for up to 5 miles. This phenomenal success was greeted by the ringing of church bells in London.

But then came hours of delay. While the Germans rushed reinforcements to block the gap, there were no British reserves to follow the exhausted attackers. Over the next nine days, front-line pockets were won and lost several times. Then, on November 30, the Germans counterattacked, in places forcing the British back behind their original start-line. In three days everything gained had been lost again, leaving only the inspiration of that first tank-driven advance—a seed that would take another year to bear fruit.

LIFE IN THE TRENCHES

MUD, RATS, AN ALL-PERVASIVE STENCH AND BOREDOM—ALL THESE WERE STAPLE INGREDIENTS OF EVERYDAY LIFE IN THE TRENCHES

They thought they would be home by Christmas; but the soldiers who dug in along the first 90 miles of the Western Front at the end of 1914 were breaking the ground for a way of life that would remain much the same for four years. This was a new type of war: a siege fought not around the enemy's prize fortresses, but in a straggling city of mud. "When all is done and said," wrote the poet Siegfried Sassoon, "the war was mainly a matter of holes and ditches."

As daily maps in the newspapers showed, the Western Front extended some 400 miles, running from the Belgian coast across Belgium, bulging around Ypres as it entered the 90-mile British sector, then south into France. After the River Ancre, where the French took over, the front veered eastward, bulging again past Verdun, before cutting down to the Swiss border. But those 400 miles—that heavy line on the maps—concealed another world, intricate as a nervous system. In all, with both sides of the front included, there were an estimated 25,000 miles of trenches—enough, if stretched out, to circle the Earth.

A stinking world of sticky earth

Between major offensives, the British front line was manned by some 80,000 soldiers, concentrating on two main areas—the Ypres salient and the Somme. At Ypres, the front was like the bow of a battleship jutting into German territory, always a focus for German artillery firing from three sides, with the blackened ruins of Ypres itself surrounding the gutted remains of the medieval Cloth Hall. In the Somme sector, at least, the fire came from only one direction.

Typically, there were three lines of trenches—the "firing" trench at the very front, which was anything from 150 feet to 1 mile from the German lines. From the firing trench, smaller ditches known as "saps" probed no-man's-land, leading to observation posts, grenade-throwing positions and machine-gun posts. Out in front, beyond grenade range, was barbed wire. In the early days, this was nothing more than a few strands, but it eventually grew into a wild thicket.

Between 20 and 100 yards back from the firing trench was a "support" or "cover" trench, with a "reserve" trench in the rear. All were linked with communication trenches, which might reach back a mile or so to a nearby village or town. Each trench, over 6 feet deep and protected by a bank of earth tossed out when it was dug, would be 2 to 3 feet wide at the base, with sloping walls, making it 4 to 5 feet wide at the top. Along the enemy side of main trenches were fire-steps, about 2 feet high, on which soldiers stood to shoot when repelling an attack. Trench floors had drains cut into them, which were covered with

BATTLING WITH THE MUD   French troops scoop up waterlogged soil in their trench—a familiar routine on the Western Front.

April 1915
Germans use gas
in battle at Ypres

September 1915
British use chlorine
gas at Loos

January 1916
Britain introduces
conscription

front meant making new trenches, or, often, the reclamation of old ones. Many systems changed hands several times. "In these mazes," a young officer wrote, "where we have fought each other so often and each side has held the ground in turn, you can never be quite sure whether a trench won't lead you straight to the German lines."

One reason the British trenches were so miserable was that they were not intended to be permanent. What point was there in expending energy on digging in when the troops would soon be going over the top and advancing? In the words of one participant, George Coppard: "The whole conduct of our trench warfare seemed to be based on the concept that we, the British, were not stop-
(continued on page 40)

NOT EXACTLY HOME With decorative touches, these British troops (left) attempted to make a home of their dugout hovel. German troops (below) had shuttered windows and even a doormat to wipe their feet.

boards. It was, one soldier wrote, a "stinking world of sticky, trickling earth ceilinged by a strip of threatening sky."

One British lieutenant described it as a "world of moles, burrowing always deeper and deeper to get away from the high explosives: an underground city with avenues, lanes, streets, crescents, alleys and crossroads, all named and labeled and connected by telegraph and telephone. 'No. 3 Posen Alley' was my last address, and you reach it via 'Piccadilly,' 'Victoria Station,' and 'Sackville Street.'" Dugouts with walls and ceilings made with sandbags were given familiar or comical names, such as Savoy Grill or Trembling Terrace.

An Irish Guards 2nd Lieutenant explained what it was like to his family: "There are all sorts of odd turn-offs, to officers' dugouts, or other lines of trenches. At other places, there are steps down and other unknown steps up where a piece of parapet has been blown in, or some walls or a traverse have collapsed." An advance or retreat would force the abandonment of old trenches, but a new

August 1916
Falkenhayn sacked as
German chief of general staff

December 1916
Lloyd George becomes
British Prime Minister

June 1917
First American troops
reach France

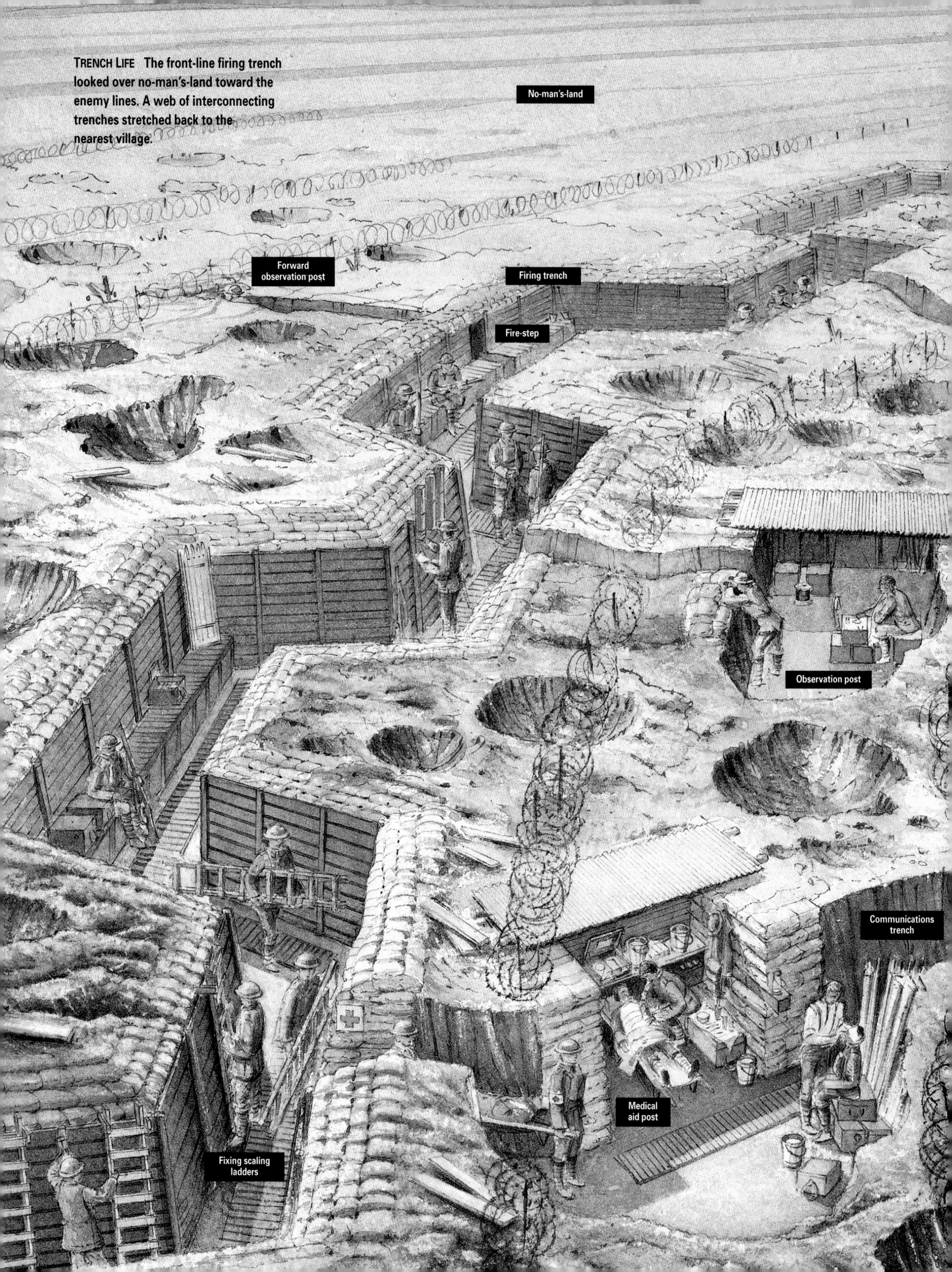

TRENCH LIFE The front-line firing trench looked over no-man's-land toward the enemy lines. A web of interconnecting trenches stretched back to the nearest village.

No-man's-land

Forward observation post

Firing trench

Fire-step

Observation post

Communications trench

Medical aid post

Fixing scaling ladders

Latrine sap

Mortar emplacement

Support trench

B COY HQ

Repairing trenches

Company HQ

Cooking shelter

PICCADILLY

Trench name

houetted against the morning sky; in the evening, the Germans had the advantage. What the men actually saw and noted, mostly, was sunrise and sunset. For those with artistic sensibility, these were moments both of anxiety and beauty, amidst the misery and tedium and the horror of battle.

After the morning stand-to, everyone "stood down" for breakfast. If they were lucky, there would be a ration of rum, two tablespoons each, served out with ritual care. Though there was generally enough to eat, the food was seldom fresh, and often a tedious repetition of

TRENCH CUISINE French officers (above) maintain standards with a tablecloth and a bottle of wine. British Tommies (right) dine where they can, clutching their cooking pots.

ping in the trenches for long, but were tarrying awhile on the way to Berlin."

In contrast, the German trenches were built to last. Coppard described what he saw when the British advanced on the Somme: "Some of the dugouts were 30 foot deep, with as many as 16 bunk-beds, as well as door-bells, water tanks with taps, and cupboards and mirrors." The walls, floor and ceilings of the dugouts were boarded and there were even wood-

en staircases, electric lights and furniture.

Limbo land

Though historians focus on the battles, those in the trenches spent much of their time in limbo between war and peace.

Typically, officers and men would have to rise before dawn, the favored time for launching an attack, and check the enemy trenches. This was the "stand-to," short for "stand to arms," the order to repel an attack. Repeated at dusk, the stand-to was a moment of solemnity when men on both sides, along the whole length of the front, stared across at each other, watching for any movement, checking on any change from the day before. In the morning, the British and French looked for Germans sil-

tinned corned beef— Bully beef—and a tinned meat-and-vegetable stew named Maconochie after its makers. The day would be spent cleaning weapons, repairing trenches, writing home. Officers would inspect and encourage, and answer requests from headquarters brought by runners.

A private, Kenneth Garry of the Honourable Artillery Company—destined to die after living in the trenches for two years— described a typical drizzly day in December 1915. His first task, at 7 a.m., was to thread his way back through the communication trenches to collect water in 2-gallon gas tins, perhaps from a surviving pump on a derelict farm, more often from a water-wagon. On his return, a soldier in his dugout had a Primus stove going to boil water for tea, while in the regimental canteen, the

RATIONS IN TINS Fresh food was a rarity in the British trenches— usually sent in parcels by relatives at home. Most of the time, rations were tinned meat and vegetables and hard, dry biscuits.

ANGELS AND OTHER MYTHS OF WAR

Men in the trenches were so miserable, so helpless, and so close to death that their imaginations constantly sought comfort in another reality. The result was the creation of rumor, myth and superstition. In this upside-down world, wrote the French historian Marc Bloch, "anything might be true, except what was printed." Almost every soldier had his little piece of magic, his amulet—a coin, button, dried flower, Bible, medal or doll. Others believed in little rituals that would act as life-preservers.

The number "three," regarded as a mystic number from ancient times, was given added significance by the realities of trench life. Land forces were divided into infantry, artillery and cavalry. There were three lines of trenches. Each unit was divided into three: one alert, two resting. No one would light three cigarettes with the same match, in deference to the imagined tripartite orders from the enemy trench: Ready, Aim, Fire.

The most famous myth was that of the Angel of Mons, reputed to have appeared in the sky, blocking the German advance during the Battle of Mons in August 1914. The object that caused the most myth-making, however, was a statue of the Virgin Mary on the cathedral tower in Albert, which was left hanging at an angle from the top of the tower after a German bombardment in January 1915. The legend grew that whichever side brought down the statue would lose the war. Meanwhile, various interpretations were placed on the statue's continuing survival in its precarious position. Some said that the Virgin was holding out the infant Jesus as a peace offering, others that she was reaching out to save the child, who was about to fall, others again that she was diving to her destruction. In April 1918, the British finally brought down the tower, and the statue with it, to prevent the Germans from using the tower as an observation post.

One of the most potent myths was that, somewhere between the lines, a battalion of deserters from all combatant nations had joined together and taken over the abandoned front-line trenches. The wild band of deserters, it was said, holed up during the day and crept out at night to pillage corpses and gather food. Like all good myths, this one distilled a number of emotive issues: the misery of working in the open only at night; the guilt of being forced to abandon the wounded; the desire to disobey; the urge to be at peace with the enemy; and the fear that trench warfare turned men mad.

THE VIRGIN FALLS The hanging statue of the Virgin Mary in Albert was brought down by the British in April 1918.

barbed wire and spare boards, before being handed a spade and set to work shoring up the collapsed wall of a communication trench. He left the exposed top, for that could only be repaired at night. Then he had a turn on guard. He got out his rifle, worked his way to a firing-bay, and fixed a mirror on his bayonet at a 45° angle. With this improvised periscope—everyone had his own—he could look over the parapet at the enemy trenches. Every now and then, a well-aimed bullet would shower the trench with shards of glass.

"There was nothing to be seen," Garry wrote. "Only a line of earth and sandbags with occasional pieces of timber lying about, the whole looking like a mound of earth thrown up by workmen excavating a drain. When you get tired of sitting you can get up and have a peep between the sandbags, and if extra bored you can fire a shot. But a man can be in the trenches a year and need never have a shot, for he would probably not have seen a Hun." Relief came after three hours, then coffee, another brief spell on guard, and finally "stand-to" and a return to his dugout.

The real work happened after dark. Soldiers would be out digging saps farther into no-man's-land, creeping out to repair or extend the wire, or bringing up a constant flow of timber, sandbags, boards,

cook managed to get the damp fuel in the brazier to catch in order to cook bacon for breakfast. Garry was then collected by a cor- poral and made part of a fatigue on trench-repair. He donned gumshoes and a cape, was led to a dump of sandbags, spades, picks,

SIMPLE COMFORTS An Australian "digger" enjoys a cup of tea, courtesy of the Australian Comforts Fund. Right: Open-air ovens bake bread for the front.

IMPROVISED PHOTO FRAMES One sergeant found an ingenious use for the famously tough biscuits issued to British troops: he made them into frames for photos of him, his wife and their twin children.

corrugated iron, tarpaulins and pumps. It was for this reason that men tried to get as much sleep as they could during the day.

At home on the Western Front

Boredom was sometimes the hardest thing to bear. "Heat, flies, and monotony," moaned a young lieutenant in the summer of 1916. To pass the tedious hours, to come to terms with the mud and the suffering, men wrote as never before—letters home (which were vetted and censored by officers), letters to

NEWS FROM THE FRONT While his comrades rest, a Canadian soldier writes a letter home. Most men treasured any sense of contact with wives and sweethearts—celebrated in a French postcard (below).

L'INSTANT DIVIN

newspapers, diaries, songs that were by turn bawdy, mawkish and patriotic, and doggerel that captured the truth of their lives.

The most notorious of the miseries were the wet conditions. Drains were never good enough, trenches were always collapsing under the pressure of the sodden earth, and they were often feet deep in water. Waterproof boots and trousers were standard issue. The

HANGING TROPHIES   Rat hunts helped to keep down vermin and relieve the tedium on the French front (right). British troops take a dip behind the lines (below).

poet Wilfred Owen wrote to his mother in early 1917: "In two and a half miles of trench which I waded yesterday there was not one inch of dry ground. There is a mean depth of two feet of water."

Then there were the lice and rats. Behind the lines, cleaners with steam vats and hot baths did their best to delouse clothes and men, without lasting success. Rats fed on the corpses of men and horses, and then invaded the trenches, consuming anything they could find—including, in at least one instance, the cat imported to hunt them. The smell was horrific. From no-man's-land spread the stench of rotting flesh. Corpses of men, horses and other domestic animals often remained in the open for months. Occasionally, work parties would creep out at night and scatter lime over the most offensive sites; this smell added to the appalling cocktail of stenches.

In this surreal and horrifying world, where there were no old people, no children and

THE ENTERTAINERS   A traveling theater company puts on a performance for troops behind the French lines.

no women except for a few nurses, the men did their best to create a semblance of normality, creating newspapers like the "Wipers Times," named after the popular English pronunciation of Ypres. They held sports events—horse races for the cavalry, soccer matches, boxing tournaments. They formed drama groups and put on shows in village halls, in barns and in tents, with young men acting the women's parts.

The Zulus of the South African Native Labor Corps devised an entertainment of dancing with drums and grass skirts.

Inevitably, in the towns and villages behind the lines, there were brothels, with those favored by officers distinguished by blue lights from the men's red-lit ones. At the front itself, sex found expression in close male friendships. Officers and men alike formed friendships of agonizing intensity, but in the context of stern hierarchies, these remained predominantly platonic.

THE EASTERN FRONT

RUSSIA SCORED SOME SUCCESSES, BUT IN THE END ITS ARMIES WERE NO MATCH FOR THE BETTER-LED, BETTER-EQUIPPED GERMAN FORCES

As the German invasion in the west ground to a halt, the Russian army moved into action, urged on by her western ally, France. Russia's mobilization brought the size of its army up to 4.5 million, with another 2 million in reserve—a massive force that the Russians were sure would soon crush neighboring Germany into submission. In early autumn 1914, a force of 370,000 gathered in western Russia (present-day Poland) on the borders of East Prussia, Germany's most easterly region.

The plan in this low-lying region of forests and lakes consisted of a two-pronged attack: the first from the east to draw the German defenses, then a second from Warsaw in the south to cut the German forces from their roots. But the Russians faced several problems. First, the

THE TSAR'S MEN
Russian troops, wearing the distinctive sheepskin *papakha* hats, fire from their trench during a gas attack.

Russian agreement with France called for Russia to have 800,000 men under arms by the 15th day after mobilization—a feat far too fast for efficiency, but the Allies needed the German troops pinned down in the east while they launched the Marne offensive. The Russian commander-in-chief, Grand Duke Nicholas, a cousin of the tsar, therefore forced his troops into action before they were ready. The second problem was that the Masurian Lakes and the fortress of Königsberg would force the eastern thrust, under General Paul Rennenkampf, through a gap only 40 miles wide. Third, the southern thrust, under General Alexander Samsonov, would have to cross an area that the Russians themselves had left almost devoid of communications as a defense against German invasion.

Schlieffen had planned how to counter such a move. The Germans were to wait and then throw almost everything they had at whichever force came within reach first. Meanwhile, the other thrust would be delayed until troops could be freed to deal with it. The German commander, General Max von Prittwitz, however, lacked the nerve to rely on Schlieffen's plan. When the attack came on August 20, Prittwitz split his forces, was driven back on both fronts, panicked and telephoned General Moltke, chief of the German general staff, to say he would have to retreat if he did not get reinforcements.

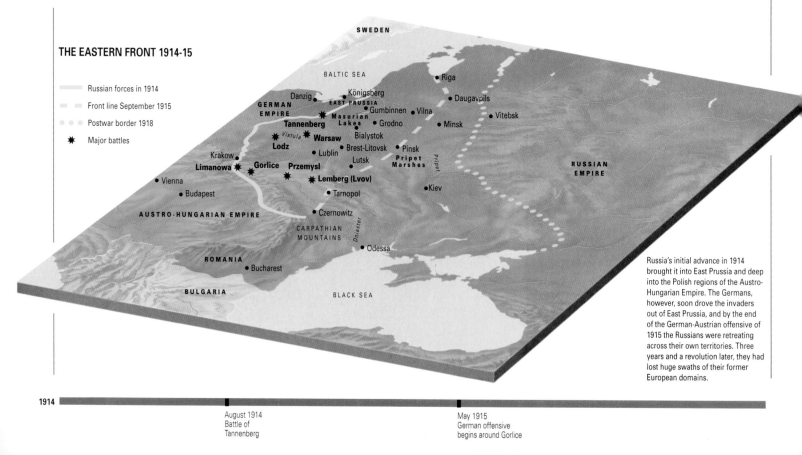

THE EASTERN FRONT 1914-15

— Russian forces in 1914

- - - Front line September 1915

••• Postwar border 1918

✳ Major battles

SWEDEN

BALTIC SEA

Riga

Danzig
Königsberg
Daugavpils

GERMAN EMPIRE

EAST PRUSSIA
Gumbinnen • Vilna
Masurian Lakes • Grodno
Tannenberg
Vistula • Warsaw
Bialystok
Lodz
Lublin • Brest-Litovsk • Pinsk
Minsk
Vitebsk

Krakow
Lutsk
Pripet Marshes
Pripet

RUSSIAN EMPIRE

Limanowa
Gorlice • Przemysl
• Vienna
Lemberg (Lvov)
• Budapest
• Tarnopol
• Kiev

AUSTRO-HUNGARIAN EMPIRE

• Czernowitz
Dniester

CARPATHIAN MOUNTAINS

ROMANIA
• Odessa
• Bucharest

BULGARIA

BLACK SEA

Russia's initial advance in 1914 brought it into East Prussia and deep into the Polish regions of the Austro-Hungarian Empire. The Germans, however, soon drove the invaders out of East Prussia, and by the end of the German-Austrian offensive of 1915 the Russians were retreating across their own territories. Three years and a revolution later, they had lost huge swaths of their former European domains.

August 1914
Battle of
Tannenberg

May 1915
German offensive
begins around Gorlice

As he was telephoning from his own quarters, one of his officers, Lieutenant-Colonel Max Hoffmann, was proposing a counterattack based on Schlieffen's original premise. Hoffmann knew that the two Russian generals were notorious rivals who

A PHILOSOPHER'S WAR

In 1914, the 25-year-old Viennese Jewish philosopher Ludwig Wittgenstein, newly returned from studying logic and philosophy in Cambridge, England, volunteered as a gunner in the Austrian army. Eager for danger, he soon found himself fighting Russians in the front line.

On a river gunboat in October, he mused gloomily about "the terribly sad position of our race—the German race. Because it seems to me as good as certain that we cannot get the upper hand against England. The English—the best race in the world—cannot lose. We, however, can lose and shall lose, if not this year then next year."

The thought did not deter him. In 1916 and 1917, he was twice decorated with the Silver Medal for Valor for the accuracy of his gunnery and his fortitude under fire. In June 1918, on the Italian front, when a hit buried his senior officer and three crew members, he took charge of the gun they were manning, for which he won Austria's highest award, the Gold Medal for Valor. In November he was among the 300,000 Austrians taken prisoner.

Wittgenstein arrived safely back in Vienna in August 1919. Two years later, working as a teacher, he published his *Tractatus Logico-philosophicus*, which laid the foundations for Logical Positivism, the philosophical doctrine focusing on language and its limitations. In 1929, he returned to Cambridge, and stayed.

had once come to blows. He also knew that the Russians were careless in their communications: they transmitted wireless orders "in clear," or uncoded. It was easy to intercept the orders and discover the Russians' plans. The Germans would be able to pick off one force, then the other.

Prittwitz approved Hoffmann's plan. But he did not tell his staff of his call, nor did he tell Moltke of the revised plan. Moltke, meanwhile, had been horrified by Prittwitz's call. He sent for the up-and-coming Erich Ludendorff, who had led the successful assault on Liège just the day before. Ludendorff dictated his initial orders directly to the

corps commanders—bypassing Prittwitz's headquarters—then took a train east.

Ludendorff was not well enough established to exercise the authority needed. In order to provide him with extra clout, Moltke summoned from retirement a grand old man of the German military world, Paul von Hindenburg, a survivor of the Franco-Prussian War. Now 67, he was to be Ludendorff's mentor; the two met up in Hanover and headed east together. Ludendorff found that Rennenkampf's forces were resting after the great initial success of their advance against East Prussia. Samsonov, on the other hand, was driving forward in an attempt (as

MASTERS OF WAR
Hindenburg (left) and Ludendorff (right) made a formidable partnership. A German officer (top) directs fire during fighting around the Masurian Lakes.

March 1917
Tsar Nicholas II
abdicates

July 1917
Successful German
counteroffensive on Eastern Front

December 1917
Russian-German
armistice

he thought) to cut off the retreating Germans. This move spread his army thinly across 60 miles of bad roads and scattered lakes and woods. Taking a risk, Ludendorff withdrew troops from the east and threw them against Samsonov—in effect putting Schlieffen's plan, and Hoffmann's, into action.

It worked. In one incident, a Russian division was backed against a lake, and many were drowned. Then a German bombardment broke the exhausted Russians, who scattered even before the German infantry attacked. A cross-country march trapped Samsonov's men in the forests. Almost 30,000 died there and 100,000 were rounded up. Samsonov himself got lost in the forest, and shot himself before he could be captured. With no possibility of support, Rennenkampf retreated.

The battle and the German victory had vast ramifications—military, political and social. Two German corps dispatched from the Western Front to help Ludendorff allowed France to survive on the River Marne. Altogether,

ROUNDED UP Huge columns of Russian prisoners are a measure of the scale of the German victory in the fighting around the Masurian Lakes.

Russia lost 250,000 men and vast amounts of weaponry and supplies.

Hoffmann suggested that the success be reported from the village of Tannenberg, where in 1410 the Teutonic Knights, the spearhead of German medieval imperialism, had been defeated by a Polish-Lithuanian army. This was a masterstroke of propaganda, for the Battle of Tannenberg, as it became known, reassured Germany that

after 500 years the Germans had avenged themselves against the forces of eastern barbarism. To the German public, Hindenburg and Ludendorff were saviors.

The forging of the Eastern Front

Victory in the north was offset by disaster in the south for Germany's ally, Austria-Hungary. It was in large measure the fault of Austria, and in particular the Austrian chief

ON THE MARCH With their officers on horseback, the men of a German rifle company tramp through the vast open plains of the west Russian countryside.

ON THE MARCH With their officers on horseback, the men of a German rifle company tramp through the vast open plains of the west Russian countryside.

of staff, Conrad von Hötzendorf, that Europe was at war at all. He had convinced himself of a great strategic opportunity in the wedge of western Russia (part of today's Poland) that pushed in between Germany and Austria-Hungary. A quick dart over the Carpathian mountains and into the Polish plains, he believed, would swallow this chunk of enemy territory.

His empire was not up to the task. Of all the Great Powers, Austria-Hungary was the least equipped for war. The country had few field guns, old rifles, and transportation that still relied on farm wagons. If Hötzendorf had waited, the Russian advance might have run out of steam. As it was, he was hungry for victory and sure that Moltke would help. After sending cavalry on a 100-mile reconnaissance mission—Austria did not have enough planes for the task—he thought he had identified the main Russian army, and on August 20 groped northward. Actually, the Russians had decided to abandon the salient he was invading, and the bulk of the Russian army was already off to one side, intending to invade Austria from the east.

This region, now southern Poland, was far from any industrial centers. The few roads were terrible, and there were virtually no railroads. Warfare was cast back into the 19th century, when cavalry was king. Neither side knew where the other was. At first,

Austria had the advantage, defeating a small force under General Plehve. For a week, there followed a confused series of minor actions as elements of the two sides advanced, retreated and wheeled in attempted encirclements. Finally, the two met head on at Lemberg (today's Lvov), and fought themselves to a standstill. But Russia still held a trump card—Plehve's defeated army returning to the fray unnoticed from the north. The Austrians learned of his presence by overhearing uncoded Russian wireless messages. On September 11, Hötzendorf ordered a retreat and got out just in time. For days, men and horses, hauling guns and wagons up to their axles in mud, staggered back over the border. The Austrians were saved from outright defeat, but they had lost 350,000 men and retreated 150 miles.

After their success at Tannenberg, Hindenburg, Ludendorff and Hoffmann brought German help to the shattered Austrians. Tuning in to the Russian wireless messages, they knew what their enemy was planning, and used the German railroads to secure a front line against which the Russians beat in vain. In one massive confrontation, 250,000 Germans and 150,000 Russians fought over the city of Lodz. First, the Russians threatened to encircle the Germans, who escaped with 16,000 Russian prisoners. Then, reinforced from the west, the Germans stood on the verge of another great victory, balked only by swamps and approaching winter. Lodz fell to the Germans on December 6, but they could manage nothing more.

By mid-December the Eastern Front was in position, with East Prussia divided, a small

THE HEAT OF BATTLE Through rolling clouds of smoke, Russian artillerymen take aim and fire during action on the Eastern Front.

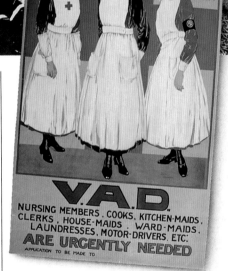

BLESSING THE WOUNDED
A priest stands among the casualties in a Russian field hospital, lodged in a church building. British women in the Voluntary Aid Detachment (below left) might serve anywhere from Russia to Egypt, France to Greece.

of them lying down in the dust . . . We had to wrench our skirts from their clinging hands . . . To the accompaniment of the thunder of exploding shells, and of the curses and prayers of the wounded men around and behind us, we hurried into the night."

This was what a breakthrough should be. Within two weeks, the Central Powers' front had ballooned outward for 80 miles, taking 400,000 prisoners. On June 3, they retook Przemysl; on June 22, Lemberg; then, resupplied from France, they turned north.

By this stage, it had become apparent to the German commanders that an advance from East Prussia could seal victory. Ludendorff, backed by Hindenburg, believed that a vast, two-pronged maneuver would achieve this, and in September he got his way. But the Germans were a long way from home, and with no railroads to help them, their advanc-

gain for Germany in Russia, and a large loss for Austria in the northeast of its empire. The Eastern Front was not as firm as the Western Front, however. These backwaters of peasant Europe did not have the roads and rails to deploy troops, materials and weapons on such a scale, and any attempted advance would simply run out of steam.

Russia in retreat

With a deadlock in the west, Germany contemplated the possibility of restoring some momentum in the east. But how? The Austrians, who could not resist Russia on their own, would need constant German aid; as a result, the Germans were not sure how best to proceed. Falkenhayn, who succeeded Moltke as chief of the German general staff,

suggested a compromise peace that would remove Russia from the war. The tsar, tied by his commitments to the Allies, and not wanting to appear weak, did not respond.

The next initiative came in spring 1915 when Germany, secure in the trenches of the Western Front, could afford to look eastward, attempt to rescue Austria from further threats and knock Russia out of the war, thereby releasing troops that would sway the balance in the west. The best place to cut through the Russian front was in the center, in Galicia, between the upper Vistula and the Carpathians. Through March and April, troop trains rolled across Germany, carrying 14 divisions and 1,000 guns to cement two Austrian armies along a 28-mile front north of the Carpathians between Gorlice and Tarnow.

On May 1, German troops ran across no-man's-land and dug in. The next day, the largest bombardment so far on the Eastern Front flattened the Russian trenches and scattered the soldiers, who were so poorly armed that the living had to seize rifles from the dead. Florence Farmborough, a British nurse serving with the Russians, described the retreat: "Those who could walk got up and followed us; running, hopping, limping by our sides. The badly crippled crawled after us; all begging, beseeching us not to abandon them in their need. And, on the road, there were others, many others; some

NURSING THE WOUNDED

Florence Farmborough, a British nurse with the Russian troops on the Eastern Front, described the horrors encountered by those working in a field hospital on the upper Dniester:

"As the fighting became more intense, the wounded lay massed outside our temporary dressing station, waiting for attention—countless stretcher cases among them. A few would crawl inside, beseeching the care they so urgently needed. We were working day and night, snatching a brief hour here and there for sleep. In the evening the dead would be collected and placed side by side in the pit-like graves dug for them on the battlefield. German, Austrian, Russian, they lay there at peace in a 'brothers' grave.' Swarms of flies added to the horror of the battlefield and covered the dead brothers, waiting in their open ditches for burial, as with a thick black pall. I remember the feeling of horror when I first saw that black pall of flies *moving*."

SOLDIERS OF HOLY RUSSIA The tsar holds up an icon to kneeling troops. In September 1915, Nicholas II took personal command of the Russian armies.

ing jaws moved too slowly to snap shut on the retreating Russians. Time and again, the Russians slipped out of salients before they could be surrounded. By mid-October, they had pulled back to a line stretching straight from the Baltic to Czernowitz, today's Chernovitsy, almost on the Romanian border. They were just 300 miles from their starting point; they had conceded some 750,000 prisoners (making total losses to date of over 1.7 million), and they had lost territory the size of France; but they were still able to fight.

The Germans had now accomplished precisely the opposite of what they had intended. If there had ever been the possibility of a compromise peace, it had vanished. Germany needed vast numbers of troops to occupy the conquered territory, and Russia had a real war aim—the liberation of the motherland.

The Brusilov Offensive

In Germany, Falkenhayn was now sure that Russia was paralyzed, and focused on the Western Front at Verdun. This allowed Russia a period of recovery. Suffering was immense, with food shortages everywhere and peasants being dragged off as cannon-fodder. Discontent mounted. But there was no shortage of men; the factories were producing more for the war; enough supplies flowed along the meager railways to keep the 2 million horses fed with grain; and the police knew exactly how to deal with strikers

and would-be revolutionaries. By spring 1917, Russia had 130 divisions facing 46 German and 40 Austrian divisions.

Nevertheless, a chance to take advantage of the crisis at Verdun forced premature action. In the northern sector, Russian troops were wasted on a fruitless assault, then drew back in order to plan a greater attack to coincide with the Battle of the Somme in the early summer. Those plans,

RUSSIAN MASTERMIND General Brusilov studies a map. At the height of his success in June 1916, the Russian general was depicted by a French illustrator (above) as a heroic figure, taking the surrender of fleeing Austrians.

too, were pre-empted in the south when Italy, on the Allied side, asked for help in their battle against the Austrians. For this, they requested that Austrian troops be pinned down by a Russian attack so that they could not be moved westward.

Russia's southern flank was under the command of Aleksei Brusilov, a 55-year-old veteran of the Russo-Turkish War almost 30 years before. With four armies numbering 38 divisions and 150,000 troops, Brusilov controlled 200 miles between the Dniester river in the south and the marshes formed by the Pripet river in the north. While the northern flank prepared for action he, supposedly, was on the defensive. Yet he knew that the Austrians would not be expecting an offensive. Carefully scattering concentrations of troops in order not to give the game away, he gambled on surprise—and won.

On June 4, 1916, what seemed nothing more than a reconnaissance mission toward the town of Lutsk met with little resistance. Then a 2,000-gun barrage blasted 50 breaches in the Austrian lines, through which the Russian troops poured. Lutsk fell and the Russians rolled on toward the mountain barrier of the Carpathians, 200 miles ahead. Prisoners were rounded up: 26,000 in the first 24 hours, 200,000 in two weeks, 375,000 in two months.

POPULAR PATRIOT A cartoon from a French magazine of June 1917 shows Kerensky being carried along by a soldier and a sailor amid scenes of revolutionary fervor.

Brusilov's offensive echoed across the European war zone. In the short term, it gave Russia command again of the western Ukraine and the northeastern corner of Austria-Hungary. It forced Falkenhayn to send help from the west, ruining his plans to hit back on the Somme. It encouraged Falkenhayn to have Hötzendorf fired, but it also fatally undermined Falkenhayn himself in his simmering dispute with Hindenburg and Ludendorff. Finally, it persuaded Romania to enter the war on the Allied side.

Germany fights back

Throughout 1916, Germany's leaders were embroiled in the continuing controversy over whether or not to negotiate peace with Russia. The Socialists, in Germany as elsewhere, were for it; Ludendorff was against, and carried the day. Falkenhayn, who was for peace, was sidelined to wage war against Romania, while Ludendorff assumed command of the Austro-Hungarian forces in the east as well as those of Germany. Refusing to contemplate giving up any of the territory he had conquered, Ludendorff promised independence for Poland on the assumption that Poles would flock to his banner. They did not, but his attitude guaranteed that the war

in the east would continue. Russia, however, was in no shape to fight on. Food shortages had sapped any remaining support for the war. In March 1917, the tsar was forced to abdicate and was replaced by a provisional socialist government, which at first remained committed to war. The new leader, Alexander Kerensky, dreamed of achieving national security by winning control of the Turkish straits. A victorious offensive would, he hoped, cause a burst of patriotic fervor and secure his position.

Brusilov was summoned as Supreme Commander, and launched Russian troops against the Austrians on June 18. Following a bombardment with 1,300 guns, 31 Russian divisions drove to recapture the much-disputed town of Lemberg, lying 50 miles to the west. That first day, during a rapid advance, they took around 10,000 prisoners. But the next day, Czech soldiers in the Russian army contacted Czechs in the opposing Austrian forces and refused to fight, standing with their arms folded in the face of their officers. Farther south, in a

BACK TO THE FRONT Would-be Russian deserters are beaten back to the front (right). The kaiser greets German troops at Tarnopol on the Eastern Front in July 1917 (below).

second prong of the campaign, the Russian General Lavr Kornilov took 7,000 prisoners and headed west to the Hungarian border. Kornilov, already a hero who had escaped from a year's captivity in Austria earlier in the war, was about to wield significant influence on the course of events.

On July 19, the Germans under General Hoffmann, now in effect the commander of the Eastern Front, counterattacked, precipitating a rout. Tens of thousands of Russians threw down their arms and fled, murdering officers who tried to stop them. "I should like to take a few more prisoners," wrote Hoffmann. "The fellows ran away so frantically that we couldn't catch any of them. Only 6,000 to date, and only 70 guns."

Steadily, the Germans regained lost ground, doing so with such confidence that the kaiser arrived to witness the taking of Tarnopol (Ternopol) in the

Polish Ukraine. At the end of the month, as they reached the Russian border, the German-Austrian army did not have to take prisoners—they were met by some 40,000 Russian deserters. By August, Russia had lost all of Brusilov's gains. Kerensky fired Brusilov, replacing him with Kornilov.

German-Russian peace

On September 15, Kerensky declared a republic, with every intention of continuing to fight. In early November, Russian troops on the Baltic front threw down their arms and began to fraternize with the Germans. Petrograd sank into turmoil, the Bolsheviks seized power with

ENOUGH IS ENOUGH Defiant Russian troops demonstrate against the war. Disaffection among the armed forces also led to mutiny in the Baltic Fleet in October 1917.

virtually no bloodshed, and on November 8, Lenin read out his first decree, the Decree of Peace—confident that peace would break out everywhere in the wake of his action.

To his surprise, the Western Allies rejected the idea of an armistice, for the United States had now entered the war, and salvation seemed to be on the way. Undeterred,

LEGENDARY HORSEMEN The Cossacks provided some of the most ferocious troops in the tsarist armies. They refused to acknowledge the Bolshevik government.

the new Bolshevik regime went ahead on its own. An armistice was agreed to, with one Bolshevik stipulation—that Germany should not move troops to the west until the armistice was signed. But Hoffmann moved them anyway, and there was nothing the Bolsheviks could do about it. The armistice was signed on December 15.

The former enemies met to work out terms at Brest-Litovsk. A team of Bolshevik intellectuals was strengthened by the arrival of Leon Trotsky, the revolution's theoretician. The Germans wanted to keep Russian territory, while the Bolsheviks refused to sanction these imperialist-capitalist gains. Moreover, Trotsky believed that he could curtail German demands through the threat of a world revolution, as workers in the

west rose up and overthrew their governments.

Trotsky's hopes were short-lived, however, and he returned to consult with Lenin, urging the continuation of the war—until Lenin pointed out that the soldiers had had their say. They "had voted with their feet by running away." Trotsky returned to Brest-Litovsk and said that there would be no treaty. The war was simply over, that was all: "No war, no peace," he declared. Hoffmann, furious, ordered his troops forward, toward Petrograd. The Bolsheviks suddenly saw their revolution vanishing before the German forces.

The Bolsheviks returned to the negotiations and, on March 3, signed away all the conquests made not only during the war but all those made by Russian tsars over the past two centuries. They lost 90 percent of their coal mines, all of their Baltic ports except Kronstadt, the granary lands of the Ukraine, and their Black Sea fleet. Meanwhile, Germany was freed to fight the war on one front only, and transferred forces as fast as possible in time for the offensive of 1918.

WHERE WERE THEY THEN?

GEORGE PATTON, DOUGLAS MACARTHUR, GEORGI ZHUKOV— MANY FAMOUS NAMES OF THE SECOND WORLD WAR HAD THEIR BAPTISMS BY FIRE IN THE FIRST

The war's mix of horrors and opportunities was a crucible that formed the character and attitudes of many future leaders. Some were already well established, such as Winston Churchill, Britain's First Lord of the Admiralty and future prime minister, and Philippe Pétain, French wartime general and head of the Vichy government during the Second World War. But under Pétain, during the Battle of Verdun, was Charles de Gaulle, then a 26-year-old infantryman; he was wounded by a bayonet through the thigh and taken prisoner for the rest of the war. In the Second World War, while Pétain deferred to Nazism at home, de Gaulle headed French resistance from abroad.

the defense of Moscow in 1941 and then the postwar Soviet Minister of Defense. In 1916, as a young cavalryman, he was awarded the St. George's Cross for capturing a German officer, and was later blown from his horse by a mine.

Several American officers established their careers in the war. George Patton served with the newly formed U.S. tank corps. Horrified by the futility of trench-fighting, he was to become a leading proponent of mobile tank warfare, leading the Allied campaign across

MEN WITH A FUTURE   Pétain (above) went from being a hero in the First World War to being condemned as a collaborator after the Second. More glorious fates awaited de Gaulle (right) and Churchill (far right).

He became head of government from 1944 to 1946, and head of state from 1958 to 1969.

Others played little part in the war. Russia's future Communist leaders were ideologically against war and stayed, or were kept, apart. One of Lenin's henchmen, Josef Dzugashvili, was in exile in a remote part of northern Russia. He would later become better known under his pseudonym "Man of Steel"—Stalin. One future leader who did serve was Georgi Zhukov, later the hero of

Europe in 1944-5. In March 1918, Colonel Douglas MacArthur captured a German machine-gun post, for which he was awarded the Distinguished Service Cross. He became one of the Second World War's most flamboyant leaders, commanding the American campaign in the Pacific.

The war had its greatest impact on those at its very heart, in Germany. Germany's defeat brought unprecedented political and economic collapse, and this was exploited by the architect of the next world war, Adolf Hitler. In 1913, Hitler had left Vienna—he hated Austria-Hungary's mixture of nationalities—for Munich and what he saw as the Bavarian capital's Germanic purity. At the outbreak of war, he joined a Bavarian regiment. On the Western Front, at the First Battle of Ypres, he won the Iron Cross, Second Class. In October 1916, at the Battle of the Somme, he was hit in the leg. Once he had recovered, he was promoted to corporal and in 1918 was awarded the Iron Cross, First Class, a rare distinction for a common soldier. In Italy, the Socialist journalist and firebrand Benito Mussolini advocated war as a stimulus

to revolution. When war came, he was called up and wounded by a hand grenade. In 1919, he played on fears of "Bolshevism" and the dissatisfaction of ex-servicemen to found the Fascist party. His own bombast and ambition led him to admire Hitler. Emerging from the ruins of one world war, the two would start a second.

FUTURE FÜHRER The First World War was formative, in different ways, for Hitler (below left, on the right), Stalin (left), and Douglas MacArthur (below).

WEAPONS OF WAR

WARFARE HAD CHANGED, AND COMMANDERS SLOWLY REALIZED THAT NEW TIMES CALLED FOR NEW WEAPONS—SUCH AS THE TANK

By 1914, science had transformed the reality of war: new technology meant that people could kill each other faster and in greater numbers than ever before. During the three years of the Boer War (1899-1902), the British had lost 22,000 men—16,000 of them to disease. Fourteen years later, on July 1, the first day of the Battle of the Somme, some 20,000 British soldiers died on just one day.

The most effective of the new weapons were the machine gun and the artillery shell. Infantry and the destructive force of flying metal were the

AUTOMATIC FIRE
Commanders were slow to appreciate the importance of the machine gun.

two prime elements that defined the nature of the war and made slaughter possible on an unimagined scale. No one in authority had foreseen a static war, or a war that involved a whole nation; no one had foreseen such wholesale destruction. The generals, raised in the days of cavalry, were slow to adapt.

The most easily available of the

BRINGING OUT THE BIG GUNS British 8-inch howitzers pound the enemy lines during the Battle of the Somme in August 1916.

new inventions was the machine gun. In fact, the lessons of rapid-firing weapons should have been learned long before. Richard Gatling's multi-barreled invention of 1862 could fire 300 rounds a minute. Its fully automatic successor, developed by Sir Hiram Maxim in 1884, could fire 600. The machine gun was, in effect, the "concentrated essence of infantry," placing in the hands of one man the firepower of 20 riflemen and delivering streams of lead that could scythe down a line of men like corn.

Yet in France and Britain, generals wanted to believe, as Haig originally did, that two machine guns per battalion were sufficient, when many times that number often proved inadequate. In December 1915, Lloyd George told the House of Commons that 80 percent of all casualties had been inflicted by machine-gun fire. By then, it was clear that no

THE WAR'S LARGEST GUN

Two types of giant German artillery were named Big Bertha. The first was the 16-inch howitzer used to bombard Liège and Namur with half-ton shells during the invasion of Belgium. Though the guns were made by Skoda in Austria-Hungary, they were nicknamed after the daughter of the head of the Essen-based Krupp munitions family, Bertha von Bohlen.

The name was later transferred to another type of gun, three of which were used to bombard Paris from Crépy-en-Laonnaise, a distance of some 75 miles. The guns weighed 142 tons. From their barrels, 110 feet 8¼ inches long, they fired high-velocity shells weighing 264 pounds. In the 140-day bombardment they killed 256 people, 156 of them all at once when a shell landed on the church of St. Gervais.

country could sustain such slaughter indefinitely. An answer had to be found, and the generals did not have one.

The war became a testing ground for a number of new weapons. Hand grenades, first used in the Russo-Japanese war of 1904-5, found ready use in trench warfare. So did the flamethrower, first used by the Germans at Verdun in late February 1915. But in the trenches, with their zigzag structures, these weapons were of limited use.

August 1914
Zeppelin raid on
Antwerp

January 1915
Zeppelin raid on Great Yarmouth
and King's Lynn, England

April 1915
Germans use gas
for first time

A GAS ATTACK

British Sergeant Bill Hay described one of the first gas attacks at Ypres on April 26, 1915:

"Word came down that the Germans had got through and they needed every man up the line, and we were sent up to St. Julien to stand by the Canadians ... A Canadian came down and he shouted to our Captain, 'The bastards have broken through; they've gassed us and they've broken through, so give them the bloody bayonet, Jock.' So then the order came, 'Fix bayonets,' right along the line. Of course, our hands were shaking, fixing the bayonets...[but] your main concentration was to get there, and not get killed yourself, so you lost these twitterings.

"Of course the chaps were all gasping and couldn't breathe, and it was ghastly, especially for the chaps that were wounded—terrible for a wounded man to lie there! The gasping, the gasping! And it caused a lot of mucus, phlegm, your eyes were stinging as well."

Artillery was a crucial adjunct to trench warfare. For most of the war, no advance would be ordered without a massive artillery barrage that rained down thousands of tons of metal and explosives on enemy trenches, sometimes for days at a time. Then, as the men went "over the top," the range would be lifted in a "rolling barrage" so that the shells would land farther beyond the advancing troops. It proved a self-limiting strategy, for a barrage destroyed any hope of a surprise attack. Defenders could dig deeper; and

the explosions churned up the approaches, slowing the attack and aiding the defenders. Only in the last months of the war did generals experiment with shorter, more intense bombardments.

Gas attacks

One way to attack the enemy was by releasing poison gas over their trenches. Smoke and tear gas were used by the Germans on the Western Front in October 1914, with another experiment against the Russians on January 31, 1915, but both times the gas, which was not lethal, proved ineffec-

GAS MASKS Both sides devised protective respirator helmets—here (from left to right) German, British and French.

GASSED Well-known for his high-society portraits, American artist John Singer Sargent painted *Gassed*, a scene of victims being shepherded to a dressing station.

tive. Gas made its first real impact as a weapon of war on April 22, 1915, when the Germans released chlorine during the Second Battle of Ypres. The Allied troops were quickly supplied with protective pads of cotton impregnated with a chemical that neutralized the chlorine. Respirator helmets soon followed. In response, the Germans switched first to phosgene, then to mustard gas, which was first used at Ypres in July 1917. The British quickly responded with gas attacks in September 1915 at the Battle of Loos. At first the gas was discharged from cylinders, but this method relied on a following wind to blow it over enemy lines. Beginning in 1916,

1919

September 1916
Tanks first used, in
Battle of the Somme

April 1917
French tanks
first see action

November 1917
British tanks see
action at Cambrai

March 1918
"Big Bertha"
bombards Paris

April 1918
German air ace,
Richthofen, shot down

THE HORROR OF GAS
An American soldier clutches his throat during a German gas attack in May 1918.

both sides used artillery and mortar shells to deliver gas.

From the first appearance of the strange green cloud of chlorine, gas was perhaps the most feared new weapon. Chlorine induces coughing fits and choking so severe that death results from asphyxiation. Phosgene, normally a colorless gas with the odor of freshly mowed hay, damages the capillaries, flooding the lungs with mucus until the victim dies of oxygen deficiency. Mustard gas—so called because of its smell—does not act immediately, but sets off a sequence of slow-acting effects, irritating the eyes, causing blisters, inflaming the whole respiratory system, and inducing bronchitis or pneumonia. Mustard gas was particularly feared because it attacks the skin, even through normal clothing, and the only defense—not available in the First World War—is to wear protective clothing over the whole body.

Though the gas masks issued to troops were clumsy and restrictive, they did provide a defense if used promptly and properly. Of the Americans who were killed and wounded during their nine months of fighting, a quar-

A TANK FOR THE KAISER The British and French led the way in designing and building tanks. The Germans had built just 20 tanks, like this one, by the war's end.

ter of all non-gas casualties died compared with only two percent of gas casualties—just a half of one percent of the total number of troops. Gas was not the tactic that would break the stalemate of trench warfare.

The first tanks

Even while both sides were experimenting with gas in 1915, the British were working on another potential answer to the stalemate. In 1912, an Australian civilian inventor, L.E. de Mole, presented the War Office in England with a design for a tracked and armored vehicle that could transport soldiers across barbed wire and enemy trenches without being riddled with machine-gun bullets. The War Office ignored it. In 1919, a Royal Commission would conclude that de Mole had been "in advance of his time" because "the occasion for its use had not then arisen."

Later historians came to a different conclusion. De Mole's design was an idea whose

time had come. Armored tractors had been used in the Boer War, and crawler tractors were at work on American farms. H.G. Wells's book *The Land Ironclads* had explored the idea of combining such concepts. De Mole's problem was that his design was mechanical and the War Office was wedded to cavalry.

In October 1914 a similar solution was proposed by Colonel Ernest Swinton, a military tactician who wrote under the pen name of "Ole-Luke-Oie." A visit to the front had convinced him that the combination of trench warfare and the machine gun demanded an armored and armed caterpillar-tractor. The Secretary of the Committee of Imperial Defense, Colonel Maurice Hankey, backed him, but Kitchener rejected the idea. It did, however, pass across the desk of Winston Churchill, then First Lord of the Admiralty. Churchill saw the potential and set up a committee to research what were called "land ships." Later, Swinton called the devices "tanks"—*réservoirs* in French—to mislead anyone intercepting the plans into thinking that Britain was producing water-storage tanks to ship to France. Independently, meanwhile, France was developing its own version of the tank, the Schneider, which was first tested in February 1916.

Once the tank's potential capabilities had been grasped by Allied commanders, it went into production. The idea was that they would be used en masse in a military *coup de théatre*. In any event, Haig was so desperate to gain ground on the Somme that he authorized their use when only 60 were available. The appearance of the machines astonished everyone who saw them. Built to

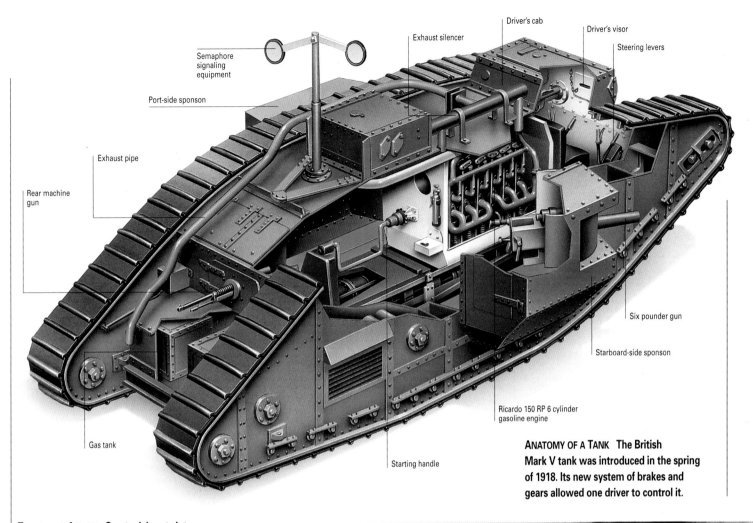

Semaphore signaling equipment

Port-side sponson

Exhaust pipe

Rear machine gun

Gas tank

Exhaust silencer

Driver's cab

Driver's visor

Steering levers

Six pounder gun

Starboard-side sponson

Ricardo 150 RP 6 cylinder gasoline engine

Starting handle

ANATOMY OF A TANK The British Mark V tank was introduced in the spring of 1918. Its new system of brakes and gears allowed one driver to control it.

TANKS INTO ACTION One tank bursts into flames, while another lumbers on, protecting a group of infantrymen on the attack.

span an 11-foot trench and climb over an obstacle 4¹/₂ feet high, they were 26 feet long and 14 feet wide. Weighing some 30 tons, their top speed was hardly more than walking pace. Inside was a crew of eight, two of whom operated a track each. The fuel tanks had a range of no more than 24 miles. They could go only about 50 miles before a track broke.

On the Somme, the tanks made very little difference to the outcome of the battle. Moreover, their disappointing performance allowed conservative officers to dismiss them altogether. "My poor 'land battleships' have been let off prematurely and on a petty scale. In that idea resided one real victory," Churchill lamented. Swinton was ousted from his position as commander of the tank unit in England.

After the Somme, the War Office tried to cancel an order for 1,000 new tanks and, when a few became bogged down in the swamps of Passchendaele, succeeded in cutting production down from 4,000 to around 1,300. "Instead of losing faith in their own judgment," wrote the military historian Sir Basil Liddell Hart, "the General Staff again lost faith in the tank."

The Battle of Cambrai in November 1917 revealed the tank's power to some, and its inadequacies to those who resisted the new machine. It took another year for the generals to realize that tanks could make many of the old weapons and tactics obsolete. They could flatten barbed wire, cross trenches, survive machine guns, take out machine-gun nests, and act as shields for infantry.

WAR IN THE AIR

SINCE THE DAWN OF HISTORY, MEN HAD FOUGHT ON LAND AND SEA, BUT NOW, FOR THE FIRST TIME, THEY WERE FIGHTING IN THE AIR AS WELL

One way to overcome the deadlock in two dimensions was to use the third. The air had been exploited by balloonists since the late 18th century, but although the Austrians had used unmanned balloons to drop bombs on Venice in 1849, balloons were used mainly for observation. By the late 19th century, most armies had regular balloon sections, with observers sitting in a basket moored to the ground or to a ship. Design changes allowed balloonists, reporting by radio, to watch for enemy movements or submarines from heights of up to 6,000 feet in winds of up to 50 mph.

Aerial war involved two other, far more significant developments—airships and airplanes. A German cavalry officer, Count Ferdinand von Zeppelin, who had seen how useful balloons were in the United States during the Civil War, had the idea of placing balloons in a line inside a rigid frame and driving them along using engine-driven propellers. The first one flew in 1900. With this head start, the German army acquired more than 100 airships, some of which were used to carry the war into the enemy's home territory. Designs improved. By 1918, Zeppelins could carry 50 tons of bombs and fly at 80 mph. But they were rendered useless by the development of the explosive bullet in 1916, which turned their hydrogen-rich interiors into burning infernos.

The role of the balloon was taken over by the airplane. Planes were first used for observation. With the development of radio, their role was extended to target-spotting for artillery, photography, and finally bombing. Air forces grew steadily. In

OBSERVATION AND ATTACK A German scout peers out from the basket of his observation balloon in 1915 (top). Men shelter as best they can beneath a Fokker biplane (bottom) during a raid on a German airfield.

1914, Germany had 200 planes, while Britain and France had about 100 each. By 1918, Britain's new Royal Air Force had 22,000.

In 1915, the German-based Fokker company invented a device that coordinated propeller revolutions with machine-gun fire, allowing a pilot to fire through his propellers, aiming with his whole plane. Soon, both sides had specialist fighter squadrons using fast, maneuverable biplanes. Their tasks were to hunt out targets and to protect spotter planes gathering information. Since both sides developed the same skills, it was inevitable that each should wish to knock the other out of the skies. Thus was born that most romantic of war figures, the fighter pilot.

Every nation had its ace flyers, but the most famous of all was Baron Manfred von Richthofen, known as the Red Baron. Richthofen, 23 years old, developed his flying skills as an observer on the Eastern Front and was brought west by Oswald Boelcke, who had formed 15 fighter squadrons, each comprising 12 men, in the summer of 1916. On September 17 Boelcke made his 27th kill, Richthofen his first. After Boelcke's death in an air collision in October, Richthofen shot down the British hero Major Lanoe Hawker and became a household name on both sides. Soon he was commanding his own squadron, then a whole "flying circus" of four squadrons.

In ten months of flying in 17 red-painted fighters, the Red Baron made 80 "kills." Cool in combat, he avoided unnecessary risks, but on April 21, 1918, he pursued an intended victim over Allied lines on the Somme, giving a Canadian, Captain Roy Brown, a chance to dive in from the rear. Though wounded, Richthofen managed to land his Fokker triplane on a roadside. He was dead when he was found, and was buried by his enemies in the Royal Air Force with full military honors.

FOUR ACES The air aces included (clockwise from top) Britain's Edward Mannock, France's René Fonck, America's Eddie Rickenbacker and, the most famous, Germany's Manfred von Richthofen, "the Red Baron."

WAR AGAINST TURKEY

**TURKISH TROOPS FOUGHT BACK EFFECTIVELY AT GALLIPOLI, BUT FARED
LESS WELL WHERE ARAB NATIONALISTS JOINED FORCES WITH THE ALLIES**

As the war sucked in other nations, Turkey joined the Central Powers, Germany and Austria-Hungary. Turkey's move stemmed partly from its failure to suppress revolution in the Balkans, and partly from its century-old fear of Russian designs upon the Dardanelles, the gateway out of the Black Sea. In early 1914, the war minister, Enver Pasha, had invited General Liman von Sanders, head of the German military mission to Constantinople (Istanbul), to reorganize the Turkish army. Pasha went on to conclude a secret pact with Germany just before the outbreak of war.

TURKEY'S GERMAN LEADER The courtly, Prussian-born Otto Liman von Sanders saved Turkey from military humiliation.

Turkey waited for two months, then declared war and sent a force to its frontier with Russia in the Caucasus. In brutal weather, 100,000 Turks pushed back Russian troops. Russia appealed to France and Britain for help and, as the new year dawned, counterattacked, defeating the Turks decisively at Sarikamis. The tsar's appeal struck a chord in England. Lord Kitchener was nervous that the Suez Canal might be vulnerable to a Turkish assault, and was also looking for a way out of the deadlock on the Western Front. He and Winston Churchill were convinced that the solution was to strike at Germany's ally, Turkey, and to get a supply route to Russia. Both were sure that the navy could do this job, without drawing any troops away from the Western Front.

In March 1915 a Franco-British naval squadron tried to force its way through the Dardanelles and into the Sea of Marmara, from where the Allied warships could bring their guns to bear on Constantinople. They failed to make it through. Three ships—one French and two British—were sunk and another three damaged by unsuspected mines. In London, the British War Council came to the conclusion that land forces were needed after all. There were troops already in the area, in Egypt—raw Australian and New Zealand soldiers, soon to be known as Anzacs. Plans were hurriedly drawn up for a Mediterranean

JOIN US An Australian recruiting poster invokes Gallipoli to encourage volunteers. Conscription was never compulsory in Australia.

Expeditionary Force (MEF), to be assembled on the Aegean island of Lemnos. It included British, Australian, French and New Zealand troops and was put under the command of General Sir Ian Hamilton, who was also a poet and novelist.

Meanwhile, the chance of an easy victory had been lost. The Turks guessed that a land attack was imminent and set up an army under Liman von Sanders, who took command on March 26. Viewing the cliffs and hills along the Gallipoli peninsula, von Sanders

November 1914
Turkey enters
the war

April 1915
Allied landings
at Gallipoli

December 1915
Allied evacuation
of Gallipoli

ANZACS: NATIONHOOD IN THE MAKING

Both Australia and New Zealand entered the war in support of Britain with scarcely a second thought. Both were fledgling nations eager to make a mark on the international stage. In September 1914, a joint New Zealand and Australian force set out for Britain. Before they arrived, the British government ordered them to disembark in Cairo to continue their training there. The order also stated they would be known as the Australian and New Zealand Army Corps, a name soon reduced to Anzac.

The troops were therefore on hand for the opening of the Gallipoli campaign, and it was this experience that forged the Anzacs. The first day of the Gallipoli landing, April 25, is still commemorated in New Zealand and Australia as Anzac Day. The troops went on to distinguish themselves in numerous actions. In the capture of Beersheba, which opened the way to Jerusalem in 1917, Australian cavalrymen swept through a numerically superior Turkish force, using their sharpened bayonets as swords. They also fought on the Western Front at the Somme, at Ypres and at Messines, where their tunnellers laid the war's biggest mines.

The suffering the troops endured, particularly at Gallipoli, contributed to a new self-image—that of the tough, independent, irreverent "Digger." Increasingly after 1918, "home" was "down under," not the "Old Country."

ARRIVING WITH HOPE Troops land at Anzac Cove (left). The medal (inset) was presented to those who fought with the Australian Imperial Force.

GALLIPOLI 1915-16

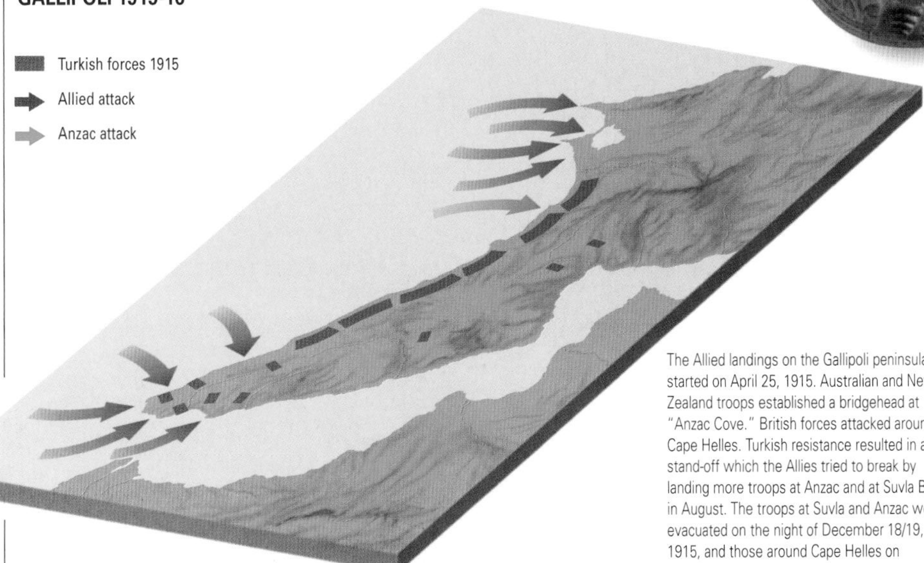

The Allied landings on the Gallipoli peninsula started on April 25, 1915. Australian and New Zealand troops established a bridgehead at "Anzac Cove." British forces attacked around Cape Helles. Turkish resistance resulted in a stand-off which the Allies tried to break by landing more troops at Anzac and at Suvla Bay in August. The troops at Suvla and Anzac were evacuated on the night of December 18/19, 1915, and those around Cape Helles on January 8/9, 1916.

prayed for a week's grace; he got a month. In that time he brought up six divisions, 84,000 men. It was the Allies' misfortune that the Turks had one particularly brilliant commander: Mustafa Kemal, later founder of the Turkish Republic.

The MEF was 75,000 strong. The plan was to attempt a difficult amphibious operation on beaches backed in many places by cliffs. Battleships and cruisers would bring the troops from Lemnos to positions offshore, from where flotillas of "tows"—towing boats, each pulling three barges—would take them to their beaches. The Anzacs would take the northern sector, a beach adjoining the headland called Gaba Tepe. The British would concentrate on Cape Helles, overlooking the entrance to the Dardanelles. French troops, sent from North Africa, would land on

1919

June 1916 Start of Arab Revolt | March 1917 British take Baghdad | July 1917 Lawrence takes Aqaba | December 1917 Capture of Jerusalem | September 1918 Battle of Megiddo | October 1918 Allies enter Damascus

the Asiatic side of the Straits at Kum Kale, chiefly to divert attention from the landings on the European shore. No one acknowledged the threat posed by the Turks, who were dismissed as inferior in every way.

It was still dark when the transports arrived off the coast in the early hours of April 25. In the northern sector, the Anzacs began their landing. At once, they were in trouble. In the darkness, the leading tow veered off course and all the others followed. By the time they had reached land, in what came to be called Anzac Cove, they were in the wrong place, bunched and in confusion, hemmed in by scrub-covered escarpments. In the grey light of dawn, the 500 defending Turks opened fire. As the first Australians struggled off the shore toward high ground, Kemal rushed up reinforcements. By early afternoon, the beach was a chaos of 8,000 men with no command and no objective.

Farther south, the British landing met with mixed fortunes. At either end of their section, there were only a few Turkish defenders, but

GERMAN INFLUENCE This Turkish belt and its cartridge pouches were made in Germany, as was most Turkish equipment.

the center was a deathtrap. Slowed by the current, the men landed after dawn and were met by withering fire while they were still in the water. At Kum Kale the French, after some initial delays, came ashore successfully.

On the Gallipoli beaches, the Anzacs and British dug in. On the 26th, the French were

withdrawn from Kum Kale, and redeployed on Cape Helles with the British. On the heights above, the Turks also dug in. Both sides expected further onslaughts. Neither was in any shape to attack. The conditions that developed at Gallipoli rivaled anything in the trenches of the Western Front.

In appalling heat, without shade and on hard ground, the troops were destroyed by disease, inaction and hopeless assaults. Only after almost three months did the British government attempt to break the deadlock by sending another five divisions. By then, the Turks had 15 divisions. Hamilton decided on a double blow: a fresh advance from Anzac Cove and a new landing by some 15,000 men at an inlet immediately to the north, Suvla Bay. Both attacks failed.

As the autumn rains set in and winter approached, and as frosts claimed their first victims, the Allies decided to cut their losses and ordered an evacuation. Trenches were booby-trapped and rigged so that they appeared to be fully manned. Guns were

SPLASHING THROUGH German artillerymen serving with Turkish forces heave a howitzer across a river in Mesopotamia.

fixed to fire automatically. On the nights of December 18 and 19, the last remaining 20,000 men slipped away undetected from Suvla and Anzac. By January 9, Helles was also cleared. The smooth evacuation was the only success for the Allies in a dismal, ill-planned campaign. In nine months, 46,000 Allied troops had died, with nothing gained.

The campaign in Mesopotamia

Meanwhile, Britain had become embroiled elsewhere in the Middle East, around the Persian Gulf. In November 1914, 4,500 British and Indian troops from Bombay landed at Fao (Al Faw) at the head of the Gulf, on the coast of what is now Iraq. Their

DIGGERS AT THE END Despite the aggressive postures of the men, this photo was taken at the end of the Gallipoli campaign, on December 17, 1915, just before the final evacuations.

THE ARMENIAN MASSACRES

LEAVING MORE THAN A MILLION PEOPLE BRUTALLY SLAUGHTERED, THE ARMENIAN MASSACRES CAN JUSTIFIABLY BE CALLED THE 20TH CENTURY'S FIRST GENOCIDE

After the Russians defeated Turkey in early 1915, the Turks vented their frustration on the 1.75 million Armenians living mainly in eastern Turkey, whom they accused of collaboration. This brought to a head a long and bitter struggle between Turkey and its Armenian subjects—a struggle marked by oppression and massacres that had already been the subject of international debate in the late 19th century.

In April, hundreds of thousands of Armenians were rounded up and some 50,000 men shot. The city of Van was besieged, with appalling Armenian losses. On April 24, later declared the Day of Mourning by Armenians, the head of the Armenian Church appealed to President Woodrow Wilson. Wilson could do nothing, but the killings received immense publicity.

On May 24, Russia, France and Britain denounced the massacres in Armenia as acts "against humanity and civilization." The Turks rejected the charge, saying that the killings were the fault of the Allies, who had fomented the Armenian revolt in the first place. Three days later, the Turkish government decided to eradicate the whole Armenian population, unleashing the century's first act of genocide (though the term was not coined until 1944).

In eastern Turkey, Baibourt had a population of 17,000 Armenians, of whom the bishop and seven leaders were hanged; 70 others were taken away and shot, and the rest deported. On the journey, all males

BRUTAL EVIDENCE Turkish atrocities against the Armenians continued after 1915. These bodies were photographed in Aleppo, Syria, in early 1919.

over 15 were bludgeoned to death. In Bitlis on June 17, 15,000 died, and hundreds more perished in Sirt. Between July 7 and 23, all but 100 of the 17,000 Armenians in the Black Sea port of Trabzon were killed. In seven months, some 600,000 Armenians were massacred and 500,000 were force-marched southward through the Taurus Mountains into Turkish Mesopotamia; of them 400,000 died. One eyewitness saw the dying crawling and begging by the roadside, while vultures flapped down to peck at corpses. The final death toll is estimated at over a million, with another 200,000 forcibly converted to Islam.

THE SLAUGHTER An illustration from a French newspaper offers a graphic depiction of the massacres.

For the Armenians, the massacres became what the Holocaust is to Jews. In 1939, Hitler urged his generals to act ruthlessly in Poland by asking: "Who today remembers the Armenians?" As the Armenian poet Avetik Isahakian wrote: "There are no words in the dictionaries for the hideousness of the terrors."

objective was to protect the pipeline that carried oil from British-dominated Persia into what was nominally still part of the Turkish Empire. To secure their position, they advanced up the Shatt al Arab waterway, taking Basra and Kurna (Al Qurnah).

In the spring of 1915, the Turks attempted a counterattack on Basra. In response the British and Indians, now reinforced, advanced up the Tigris and Euphrates rivers, which in this roadless plain were the only practical transport routes. The key to the area was the town of Kut (Al Kut), halfway between the coast and Baghdad, where the British general, Charles Townshend, scattered the Turks with his cavalry. Delighted by good news that did something to redress the disastrous deadlock in Gallipoli, army commanders urged Townshend on to attempt an even greater victory: the taking of Baghdad. Townshend, egocentric and ambitious for glory, accepted the challenge.

By now, however, he was far from his base, and came up against a Turkish force twice the strength of his own only a day's march from their headquarters. Just 20 miles southeast of Baghdad, at the ruined city of Ctesiphon, the ancient winter capital of the Parthian Empire, Townshend's advance ended in failure. Some 4,000 of his troops

GENERAL AND NATIONALIST Allenby, one of the last great cavalry commanders, had distinguished himself on the Western Front before arriving in the Middle East. Feisal, a son of Hussein, Sherif of Mecca, was a key Arab leader who would later be King of Iraq.

were wounded, and 600 were left struggling downriver to Basra on a vessel which, when it arrived, was said to be "festooned with stalactites of excreta" in which men lay, "their wounds crawling with maggots." Townshend retreated to Kut in November 1915, where his 11,500 men were surrounded by a far superior Turkish force.

Reinforcements set out from Basra, but got bogged down in the muddy banks of the Tigris. Three times in four months they tried to get through, to no avail. The British public had just endured the retreat from Gallipoli. Now another disaster loomed—and both at the hands of a nation disparaged by the British for its military weakness.

On April 29, 1916, after five months, Kut fell. While Townshend was whisked in comfort to Constantinople, the Turks' 13,000 British and Indian prisoners were

THE MIDDLE EASTERN CAMPAIGNS

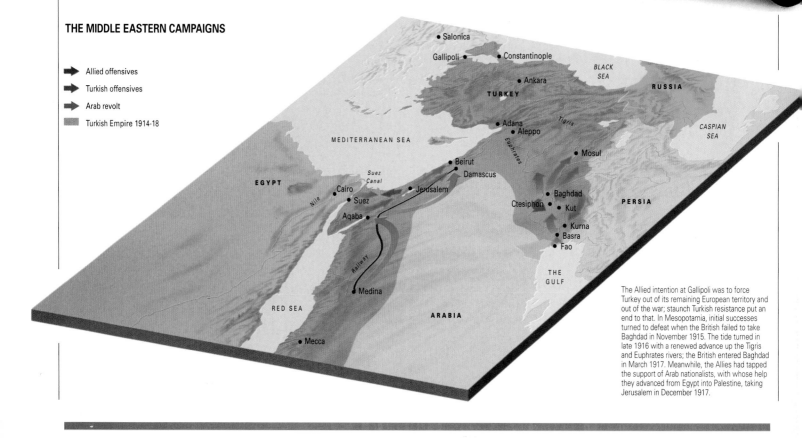

- ➡ Allied offensives
- ➡ Turkish offensives
- ➡ Arab revolt
- ▬ Turkish Empire 1914-18

The Allied intention at Gallipoli was to force Turkey out of its remaining European territory and out of the war; staunch Turkish resistance put an end to that. In Mesopotamia, initial successes turned to defeat when the British failed to take Baghdad in November 1915. The tide turned in late 1916 with a renewed advance up the Tigris and Euphrates rivers; the British entered Baghdad in March 1917. Meanwhile, the Allies had tapped the support of Arab nationalists, with whose help they advanced from Egypt into Palestine, taking Jerusalem in December 1917.

forced northward on a two-week, 1,200-mile death march to concentration camps in Anatolia. On the march or in the camps, 2,500 Indian soldiers and 1,750 British died—a humiliation avenged only when Kut was retaken ten months later. It was to take a force almost four times the size of Townshend's to achieve this victory.

Maneuvers in the Middle East

Still set on achieving a success of some sort against Turkey—and on re-establishing some prestige—the British decided to use the army defending the Suez Canal to seize the Turkish province of Palestine. For some time strategists had recognized that the key to success in this region lay in the support of the local Arabs. To this end, the British and French had negotiated with the Arab leader, Hussein, the Sherif of Mecca, about the future of Arab independence.

Talks stalled until July 1915, when an Arab agent told the British: support us now, on our terms, or we will turn against you. The British agreed. The Arabs would revolt and in return the British would back the formation of new Arab nations under British and French influence. Several issues remained unresolved, however, one being the future status of Palestine.

The Arab revolt broke out, disastrously, on June 5, 1916, with 50,000 Arabs routed by the Turks outside Medina. Nevertheless, the tables were soon turned. Hussein declared the independence of his state, the

LAWRENCE, THE SCHOLAR WARRIOR

The man who became a legend as Lawrence of Arabia was a living mirage, whose last name was not even Lawrence. That was what his father, Sir Thomas Chapman, had called himself when he ran away with the governess of his daughter.

The "Lawrences" raised "T.E." in Oxford. While at the university, he became fascinated by Middle Eastern history and archaeology. At the outbreak of war, when he was 27, he joined military intelligence and was sent to Cairo, where he became a political liaison officer with the Arabs fighting for independence from the Turks. His expertise, linguistic ability and readiness to adopt local ways endeared him to the Arabs. "Is this man God, to know everything?" asked a contact, Abdullah, one of the sons of the Sherif of Mecca. Lawrence proved a genius at guerrilla war. His raids on the Hejaz railway, his capture of Aqaba with a band of 2,500 men and his wraith-like ability to merge with the desert made him a living legend.

After victory, Lawrence became disillusioned by the political compromises made as Britain juggled its imperial ambitions with the claims of the Arabs, the French and the Jews seeking a homeland in Palestine. Returning home, Lawrence escaped from adulation by using pseudonyms, like his father. First as "Ross" he joined the air force and then as "Shaw" joined the tank corps, never seeking higher office. He died in a motorcycle accident in 1935.

Lawrence's death raised him to the status of a star—a unique blend of soldier and scholar (he translated the *Odyssey*, and his *Seven Pillars of Wisdom* became a fashionable best-seller). Intriguingly, he could have had wealth and power, yet he rejected it all, ending his life as he had begun it, an enigma.

Hejaz. The British shelled Jeddah and within weeks of the initial setback at Medina, the Arabs had seized both Mecca and Jeddah.

The British built on this success by advancing laboriously across the desert, laying a railway and water pipeline as they went. It was not until March 1917 that they could attack the coastal town of Gaza to seal their advance. Twice they attacked, and twice they were forced back again.

The British were saved from complete catastrophe by the behind-the-lines operations of T.E. Lawrence, "Lawrence of Arabia." In two legendary adventures, he led the Arabs to cut Turkey's key communications link, the Hejaz railway running south from Damascus, and on July 6 he seized the port of Aqaba. These two moves ensured that Turkey diverted valuable troops to defend the railway and was prevented from landing reinforcements on the British flank.

A new British commander, General Edmund Allenby, was in Cairo with orders to reach Jerusalem by Christmas and was building up his forces accordingly. Lawrence crossed the Sinai Desert and talked Allenby into paying the Arabs about $700,000 a month (some $9 million in today's terms), rising to $1.8 million. Allenby then tricked the Turks into thinking he was about to attack Gaza, and seized ill-defended Beersheba instead. British and French ships bombarded Gaza, and Allenby's infantry and cavalry—a mixed force including some Jewish soldiers—swept over its fortifications, killing 3,000. Pursuing the fleeing Turks, the cavalry overran the meager Turkish artillery, and the path to Jerusalem was open.

KEEPER OF THE KEYS The Mayor of Jerusalem (in the center, with a walking stick) surrenders the city's keys to two British sergeants on December 9, 1917. He and his party had been obliged to wander out of the city to find someone to surrender to.

WAR IN THE BALKANS

ALTHOUGH A SIDESHOW COMPARED WITH THE WESTERN FRONT, THE BALKANS SAW SOME CRUEL FIGHTING, NOTABLY IN SERBIA AND ROMANIA

Serbia had been the tinderbox that blew Europe and the world into war. Yet, for a year after that, the Serbs remained remarkably unscathed by the conflict, successfully beating off three Austrian attempts at invasion in late 1914. However, as they controlled a section of the rail link across the Balkans, the Serbs also dammed Germany's ambition to deliver supplies to Turkey. They would have to be dealt with.

Complicating the issue was the intricate Balkan power game. In their war of 1912-3, Serbia had seized territory from Bulgaria. It was likely, therefore, that Bulgaria would be an anti-Serbian player. King Ferdinand of Bulgaria—"Foxy" Ferdinand, the British called him—received bids from both sides, but in September 1915 he opted for Austria-Hungary and Germany. Serbia appealed to the Greeks for help, thus intensifying a rift within Greece, where the prime minister, Eleutherios Venizelos, was eager to support

"FOXY" FERDINAND The son of a German princeling, Ferdinand was elected ruler of Bulgaria in 1887. In 1908 he proclaimed his country's full independence from Turkey.

the Allies while the king, Constantine, was a supporter of the Central Powers. Their rivalry kept Greece on the fence. In the end, it was the Allies who took up the Serbian cause. Britain had troops nearby—in Gallipoli—and, ignoring Greece's neutrality, it landed 13,000 men at Salonica, intent on rushing forward to the Serbian border, 30 miles to the north. A few days later, 18,000 French troops arrived.

There would be no speedy advance, however, for the country was mountainous with few roads or bridges. In any case, the Allies were too late. On October 6, 1915, when the British were landing at Salonica, combined Austrian and German armies opened a bombardment across the Danube and then invaded Serbia. Bulgaria joined in two days later. The first contact between the major powers was when the French fought off the Bulgarians for control of a small railroad station, Strumica, just inside the Serbian border.

By then, the Serbs were already making a hard-fought retreat, one of the war's grimmest. Attacked from the north and east, and cut off to the south, their 250,000 troops had no option but to flee westward, through the mountains of Albania inhabited by hostile tribesmen. They took their 71-year-old king, Peter, with them on a stretcher in a bullock wagon. The three-week retreat left 20,000 Serbs dead by the wayside. When they reached the sea 80 Italian, French and British

WAR IN THE BALKANS

➡ Allied offensives

➡ Central Powers offensives

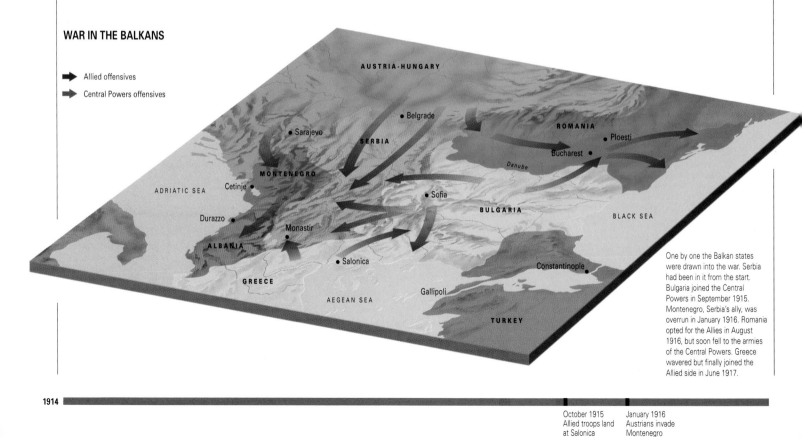

One by one the Balkan states were drawn into the war. Serbia had been in it from the start. Bulgaria joined the Central Powers in September 1915. Montenegro, Serbia's ally, was overrun in January 1916. Romania opted for the Allies in August 1916, but soon fell to the armies of the Central Powers. Greece wavered but finally joined the Allied side in June 1917.

October 1915
Allied troops land
at Salonica

January 1916
Austrians invade
Montenegro

COMING ASHORE French troops land at Salonica in October 1915. Although Greece was officially neutral, the majority of Greeks favored the Allies.

SERBIA'S DEATH MARCH TO THE SEA

A British missionary named Smith described the flight of Serbian children, all boys, who were forced to join 250,000 others fleeing westward after their country's defeat by Bulgaria in November 1915:

"It is impossible to think of the Great Retreat without calling to memory the 23,000 Serbian boys who met their fate on that cruel march. To save them from being captured by the enemy, 30,000 of the boys of Serbia were ordered out of the country. They made part of the great exodus of the nation. They were young boys of 12 to 18 years old and they were unable to stand the cold, the hunger and the physical misery of the march. Fifteen thousand died in the mountains, and those who saw the ships and the sea had nothing human left in their eyes.

"The Italians at Avalona had no hospital accommodation for 15,000 . . . They had the boys encamped in the open country close to a river, and gave them all the food they could spare—army biscuits and bully beef. By the time the ships to convey them to Corfu arrived the 15,000 had been reduced to 9,000. About 2,000 more boys died in the ... journey between Avalona and Vido."

ships ferried the shattered Serbs to Corfu, with the sick and wounded taken to the smaller island of Vido.

In the face of strategic failure, the British and French hunkered down in Salonica. There was no military reason for them to stay, but political reasons dictated that they should. Another retreat would mean a further loss of prestige, on top of the Gallipoli disaster. Besides, it was possible that the final major player in the Balkans—Romania, with its oil fields at Ploesti near Bucharest—would enter the fray one day, and the Allied political leaders hoped to be there to offer help. Instead of pulling out, the garrisons were reinforced with Italians, Russians and the remnants of the Serbian army.

As it happened, there were only two major Allied offensives—in the autumn of 1916 and from March to May in 1917—and they made little impact. After the 1917 advance and retreat over the River Struma, one correspondent noted: "The only forces that hold the Struma valley in strength are the mosquitoes." Thereafter the Allies stayed put behind their lines until 1918.

In the end, Romania did join the conflict, persuaded by Russian promises of support over territorial claims (particularly Hungarian

COAST TO COAST By the end of 1916 trenches stretched from Albania's Adriatic coast to Macedonia's Aegean shore. Here, Bulgarians man their section of the Macedonian front.

August 1916
Romania declares war
on Austria-Hungary

December 1916
Central Powers
take Bucharest

May 1917
Allied offensive
on Salonica front

June 1917
King Constantine of Greece
abdicates; Greece joins the Allies

September 1918
Bulgaria sues
for peace

REFUGEES Serbian peasants, with their goods and livestock, trudge south, fleeing the invaders. Serbia lost 23 percent of its population in the war.

Transylvania) and by the success of Russia's Brusilov offensive in June-July 1916. In August 1916, Romania declared war on Austria-Hungary, with the consequence that Germany, Turkey and Bulgaria became enemies as well. Exhilaration was rapidly followed by disaster and near extinction.

The Romanian Front

Having doubled the size of its army, Romania's position seemed strong. But its troops were poorly armed, with few machine guns, little artillery and virtually no planes. The capital, Bucharest, was almost within reach of Bulgarian guns.

In late August, Romanian forces struck west into Transylvania. Almost at once, the Romanians found themselves under attack from Bulgaria in the south and an Austro-German army in the north. The French and British tried to ease the pressure on their ally by launching another assault on the Somme: it did the Romanians no good. Their poorly equipped troops were no match for their enemies. On the Danube the German commander, Field-Marshal August von Mackensen, seized the fortress of Tutracaia and with it 25,000 Romanians and 115 heavy guns.

When General von Falkenhayn, recently demoted as chief of the German general staff, arrived to take command of the Central Powers forces, the Romanians were stalled and scattered over a 200-mile front. With a daring three-day march through the Bulgarian mountains, Falkenhayn outflanked

them. In October, Austrian and German troops pushed through the Carpathian passes from the north, and in November Mackensen approached over the Danube from the south, driving toward the oil fields of Ploesti. On

THE NINE-DAY WAR

The shortest campaign of the war was the Austrian assault on Montenegro, Serbia's ally. On January 8, 1916, 45,000 Austrians and 5,000 Bosnian Muslims opened a 500-gun barrage, seizing Mount Lovcen, the "Black Mountain" after which the country is named. On January 11, the capital, Cetinje, fell. Six days later Montenegro surrendered. The fighting lasted nine days.

December 6, 1916, the Austrians and the Germans entered Bucharest. The Romanian government fled to the northeast and the Allies lost most of the country. The Central

CHAOS OF WAR Bodies, mud and debris mark the scene of battle near Bucharest. In Germany, the kaiser celebrated the capture of the Romanian capital with champagne.

Powers did not inherit all Romania had to offer, however. The day before their victory, a British politician helping the Romanians, Colonel Norton-Griffiths, organized a spectacular explosion that blew up the oil tanks of Ploesti, destroying 800,000 tons of fuel.

The Salonica Front

Just as the Balkans had sparked the conflagration in Europe, so developments there began to bring it to its close. The decisive action started with an Allied force occupying Salonica, whose position was finally legalized when Greece entered the war on the Allied side in June 1917.

SLAUGHTERED These Romanian soldiers fighting in Transylvania were mowed down by enemy machine-gun fire. Fleeing refugees step around them.

The Allied troops, now 700,000 strong, were restless. The French mutinied briefly at the lack of home leave. Everyone was affected by a blaze that left 80,000 men without shelter, destroyed the quinine supplies and turned the region into a malarial desolation. But their opponents were in trouble, too. In Bulgaria, there had always been widespread opposition to the war. As the months and years passed, shortages and exhaustion reduced the front line to the brink of rebellion.

The crucial step was decided on by chance. The French commander, General Marie-Louis Guillaumat, had been summoned home as a possible national leader in case the Germans took Paris. As it happened he was not needed; he instead took the opportunity to urge action in his old theater, Salonica. Both Clemenceau and Lloyd George agreed, and Allied troops prepared for action.

On September 14, 1918, a six-hour Allied bombardment on the Salonica front cleared the way for a Serbian assault that overran the Bulgarian fortifications. A day later, the Serbs were 20 miles inside their own country, fighting in a Yugoslav ("South Slav")

Division alongside Slovenes, Croats, Bosnians, Montenegrins and Macedonians, all set on eventual independence in a united South Slav state. When a Bulgarian general suggested a separate peace, "Foxy" Ferdinand ordered him to "Go out and get killed in your present lines." But the Bulgarians were not receptive to the idea. Several divisions simply walked away from their positions, ignoring German generals with drawn pistols threatening to shoot them as traitors. With its army in tatters, Bulgaria

IDLE MOMENTS Boredom was an enemy for Allied soldiers in Salonica. These pipes were carved by a private in Britain's Durham Light Infantry.

asked the Allies for an armistice, signed on September 29. King Ferdinand abdicated and fled the country.

Serbia was now once again what it had been at the start—the soft underbelly of Austria-Hungary. On the Western Front, Ludendorff saw the danger at once, knew the end was near, and moved toward an armistice.

THE ITALIAN FRONT

ITALY JOINED THE WAR LATE, HOPING TO WIN TERRITORY IN THE NORTH FROM AUSTRIA, BUT POOR LEADERSHIP LED TO HUMILIATING DEFEATS

For almost a year, the Italians stayed out of the war. This decision temporarily allayed a political crisis, because Italy had previously been allied to Germany and Austria: by remaining neutral, the government gave itself some breathing room.

But, like most nations, Italy had territorial claims, in particular to the South Tyrol and the Adriatic port of Trieste. Supporters of Italian entry into the war—Benito Mussolini, financed by the French, became one of the most extreme and vociferous of these—insisted that the country should assert its status among the "great powers" and complete its unification by intervening on the Allied side. Germany promised the Italians a good deal of what they wanted—to the silent fury of the Austrians—but the Allies promised more: territory, guns, men, equipment. On May 23, 1915, Italy declared war—but only on Austria-Hungary, in the vain hope of avoiding direct conflict with Germany.

OFF TO WAR Allied newspapers, such as this French one, responded enthusiastically to Italy's entry into the war in 1915.

Italy proved to be more of a liability to the Allies than a help. Its armies had enough soldiers—1 million in 1915—but they were mostly unwilling southern peasants with little feeling for the cold and mountainous north. The army had few big guns. Supposedly the "back door into Germany," Italy was, in fact, locked tight by mountains held by the Austrians. Most of the fighting took place in or around a bubble of Italian territory, the boundaries of which ran along the eastern edges of the Alps and then cut across a coastal plain to the Adriatic Sea, following the course of the River Isonzo. The Isonzo was the front line; for the Italians, Trieste, which lay 20 miles beyond it, was the lure.

The Italians hoped that attacks by the Serbs and Russians would sap the strength of the Austrians. But by the time the Italian armies advanced in late June 1915, the Russians were in retreat and the Serbs did nothing, allowing the Austrians to reinforce their positions on the Isonzo. Four times that year the Italians tried to break the Austrian lines, at the cost of 280,000 lives. They had other enemies, too: the mountains themselves, cholera, demoralization and the weather. Private Benito Mussolini, a self-proclaimed socialist and warmonger, was in trenches 6,000 feet up on Monte Nero. "Rain and lice, these are the two enemies of the Italian soldier," he wrote.

MOUNTAIN WARRIORS Italy's crack Alpini see action in 1915 (left and below). The first Alpine companies had been formed in 1872 to defend the country's mountainous northern frontier.

May 1915
Italy declares war
on Austria-Hungary

June 1915
First Battle of the
Isonzo

March 1916
Fifth Battle of the
Isonzo

THE ITALIAN FRONT
1915-18

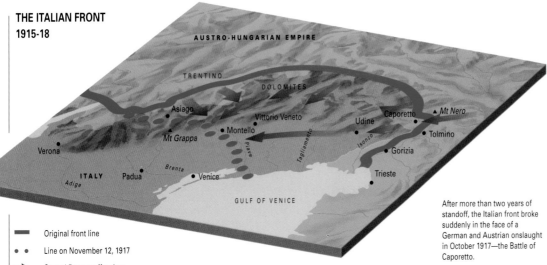

After more than two years of standoff, the Italian front broke suddenly in the face of a German and Austrian onslaught in October 1917—the Battle of Caporetto.

— Original front line

• • Line on November 12, 1917

➤ Central Powers offensives

morale of its troops spiraling downward. They were poorly treated, with only 15 days off a year. In the course of the war, 290,000 men were put on trial for desertion and other wartime crimes, of whom some 4,000 were shot. Some regiments even suffered "decimation" after a collective crime of disobedience, when victims were selected by lot and shot in front of the others. Cadorna sacked some officers for "cowardice" for refusing to "decimate" their troops.

In October 1917, the Italians' weakness was starkly revealed in one of the war's most startling defeats. The Austrians had reported that a 12th battle on

The Italians were unable to make any headway, but nor could the Austrians. In May 1916, Austrian armies attempted an assault on the Trentino front. Despite heavy snow, they forced their way forward, capturing 3,000 Italians. But the struggle was too great to be sustained and they gained a mere 12 miles before the Italians stopped them. The Italians regained the lost ground in June, aided by a wind that blew hydrocyanide gas deployed by the Austrians back across the Austrians' own lines.

Fight and fight again on the Isonzo
In the course of 18 months, from early 1916 to mid-1917, there were no fewer than seven more battles of the Isonzo. In that time, the Italians gained just 10 miles. "If you want to see Trieste," sang their soldiers, "buy a postcard." The Italian commander, General Luigi Cadorna, blamed the failure on the British and French for not sending the men and guns they had promised. For their part, the entente partners would not divert troops to a campaign they saw as a diversion from their efforts on the Western Front.

In June 1917, another assault by the Italians in the Trentino involved fierce battles for six peaks, which were won only to be lost again. Some 23,000 Italians and 9,000 Austrians were killed or wounded, with no change in the position of the front line. So Italy languished within its own borders, the

BUMPER TO BUMPER Austrian troops make their way to the Isonzo front in summer 1916. Good roads were scarce and soon became congested with military and civilian traffic.

August 1916
Italy declares war
on Germany

October 1917
Battle of
Caporetto

June 1918
Battle of
the Piave

October 1918
Battle of
Vittorio Veneto

November 1918
Austria-Hungary
signs armistice

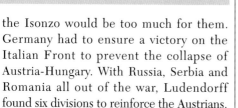

the Isonzo would be too much for them. Germany had to ensure a victory on the Italian Front to prevent the collapse of Austria-Hungary. With Russia, Serbia and Romania all out of the war, Ludendorff found six divisions to reinforce the Austrians.

The plan was to exploit a small bridgehead on the western side of the Isonzo in the mountains at Tolmino. In secrecy, moving at night and using no vehicles, German and Austrian troops crept up through the Alps, carrying 300 guns. Among them was the Alpine Corps, which included the Württemberg Mountain Battalion under Captain Erwin Rommel, the "Desert Fox" of the Second World War. By mid-October, six German and nine Austrian divisions were ready to attack.

DEATH AND WITHDRAWAL Corpses line an Italian trench (right) near Caporetto. Below: Italian Alpini take a rest hour amid the snow.

Cadorna, a remote, austere man who saw cowardice, incompetence and subversion everywhere, knew that something was about to happen from Austrian deserters, but he was not sure what or where and kept his forces spread out. Fatally, his strategy left the 15 miles on either side of Tolmino weakly defended. This stretch of the front had always been relatively quiet, so whereas other sectors had up to eight battalions per mile, it had only two per mile.

On October 24, after a five-hour bombardment through the autumnal mist and rain, the Austrians and Germans moved forward. The foul weather hid the advance, and at one point—in the center of the line, at the town of Caporetto, which gave its name to the battle—four German divisions broke through. This opened the way for the Austrians to the north to pour down the Val d'Uccea, a tributary of the Isonzo leading west.

The result was astonishing: the Italian front collapsed. Rommel's men covered 12 miles in two days and took 9,000 prisoners, for the loss of just six lives. In Alpine valleys where the few roads quickly became clogged with troops, the Italians could do little to stop the advance, and hundreds of thousands of their

SYMBOLS OF RETREAT Dead horses litter the course of the River Tagliamento in autumn 1917 after the Italians had pulled back to yet another line, the River Piave.

men streamed down from the hills, some yelling for joy that the war was over. Between 320,000 and 400,000 Italians were killed, wounded or taken prisoner. Refugees swelled the retreat into a torrent of 750,000. It was a catastrophe that would haunt the Italians for years to come.

Cadorna accepted the inevitable—a retreat for 30 miles to the next line of defense along the River Tagliamento. For a week the new line held, giving the Italians breathing room to plan a third retreat, to the River Piave, another 30 miles to the west. This line, which acted as a second frontier, from the Adriatic into the Alps, was easier for the Italians to defend because it was much shorter.

The succession of defeats had been too much for the Italian government: Cadorna was fired and replaced by Armando Diaz, one of whose major tasks was to restore morale. Diaz took fewer risks with soldiers' lives than Cadorna. The troops were given better rations, and ten more days' annual leave. They responded. It was impossible now to dream of reaching Trieste; they were fighting for national survival and found a self-sacrificial fighting spirit that had been lacking before.

When Conrad von Hötzendorf, the Austrian veteran of the Eastern Front, tried to sweep down from the north, the defenses held. In the mountainous terrain, with few railways and roads, there was no easy way for the Germans to reinforce Hötzendorf, and the attackers, moving ever farther from their bases, found it increasingly difficult to ensure enough supplies. Meanwhile, Italy's allies, France and Britain, finally mustered help. The French plugged a weak point in the Alpine foothills between the Piave and the River Brenta, while the British relieved the Italians at Montello. The Italians were now free to concentrate on holding off the main assaults out of the mountains farther west, around Asiago and Monte Grappa.

The Piave line held, and Italy was saved. A final effort by the Austrians to break through in June 1918 led to the loss of 100,000 men, for no gain. Diaz bided his time. Then, in the autumn, with the Central Powers nearing collapse, the Italians struck back along the whole length of the Piave sector, breaking through toward Vittorio Veneto on October 29. The thrust cut the Austrian forces in two, dividing those on the plain from those in the mountains. There was no fight left in the Austrrian troops anyway, for their empire had collapsed. They deserted in droves, and went home as best they could. Some 500,000 Austrians had been killed, wounded or taken prisoner.

That day, the Austrians asked for an armistice, and Italy's war formally ended on November 4. The Italians had at last gained possession of their original target, Trieste.

GENERAL OF DEFEATS Luigi Cadorna carried out a much-needed reorganization of Italy's armed forces on the eve of the war. As a commander of active troops, he proved less effective.

AUTUMN GLORY

A chaplain with the British forces, E.V. Crosse, described the last offensive against the Austrians on the River Piave in late October 1918 and compared it with his experiences on the Western Front:

"There was something hideous . . . about a trench attack in France. The mud, the duckboards, the dead horses one passed on the way up, the sickening bark and roar of the guns, all combined to produce a sort of uncanny effect which one could only tolerate by suppressing all brooding on the situation. On this occasion, however, the situation was quite different. For months the firebrands in the battalion had been spoiling for a fight. The guns were all silent, the avenues of trees were all decked in the glories of their autumn foliage. Above all, the element of adventure which was involved in the passage of the river, and the fact that we were fighting against an enemy whom we had come rather to despise, combined to free men from the load of oppression which even the stoutest heart had felt a year ago on the Passchendaele Ridge."

WAR IN THE COLONIES

GERMAN FORCES IN AFRICA WON STUNNING VICTORIES AGAINST HUGE ODDS, WHILE ASIA SAW THE MARCH OF JAPANESE EXPANSIONISM

One of many surprises about the First World War was the speed with which it spread around the world. Already, the railroad and the telegraph were turning the world into a "global village," long before the

In Africa, Germany had four colonies: Togoland, a thin strip in West Africa; Cameroon in the Gulf of Guinea; Southwest Africa (today's Namibia) and German East Africa (Tanzania). The Germans in

INTREPID LEADER, INTREPID FOLLOWERS Paul von Lettow-Vorbeck (right) proved to have a genius for guerrilla warfare. He also inspired total loyalty in his askari troops (above).

phrase was coined by Marshall McLuhan in the 1960s. In an age when European nations ruled much of the world, the colonial adjuncts of the great powers were dragged into war instantly and automatically. German settlers in Africa and a scattering of Pacific outposts suddenly discovered that they were at war with British, French and Australian settlers with whom they had no quarrel at all.

THE BOERS: FRIENDS AND ENEMIES

South Africa posed a unique problem for the British at the outbreak of war. Fifteen years before, its Dutch settlers, the Boers, had fought to keep their independence from London. This act of defiance had been of international strategic significance because the Boers had a natural affinity with Britain's main imperial rivals in the region, the Germans in neighboring Southwest Africa. British politicians had feared that, with Boer help, the Germans could somehow make a link across the continent to German East Africa, thus cutting off Britain's northward expansion from the Cape. After a brutal war, the Boers had lost, and the new Union of South Africa was formed by the Treaty of Vereeniging. Moderate Boers became reconciled to British imperial rule and former Boer leaders, such as Louis Botha and Jan Christiaan Smuts, now commanded British imperial armies. But a core of intransigent, embittered, anti-British—and pro-German—Boers remained.

When war broke out and the South African Parliament voted to fund the invasion of Southwest Africa, this disaffected group, seeing themselves as the successors to the guerrillas who had so successfully pillaged British forces in the Boer War, formed an underground society, the Broederbond (Brotherhood), and armed themselves. In October 1914, they went on the offensive to "avenge Vereeniging." Other than the Easter Rising in Ireland in 1916, this was the only wartime revolt against British rule. The uprising was crushed in two months by their own former commander, Louis Botha, though the Broederbond remained a shadowy force in South African politics for decades.

Togoland surrendered to British troops from the Gold Coast and a French force from Dahomey after three weeks. Cameroon was occupied by an Anglo-French force, obliging the Germans to retreat slowly through equatorial jungles into Spanish Guinea. A small contingent of South African troops marched into Southwest Africa soon after war broke out in Europe, and in July 1915 secured the surrender of the German troops there.

Only East Africa proved of strategic significance, thanks to one of the war's most brilliant leaders, Lt. Colonel Paul von Lettow-Vorbeck. In effect, the war in East Africa was his war. He fought for four years, never lost a battle and kept 130,000

August 1914
Japan declares
war on Germany

November 1914
Battle of Tanga
Japanese take Qingdao

February 1916
Allied offensive
against Lettow

PARTITION OF AFRICA

- ALGERIA
- LIBYA
- EGYPT
- FRENCH WEST AFRICA
- ANGLO-EGYPTIAN SUDAN
- GOLD COAST
- TOGOLAND
- NIGERIA
- ETHIOPIA
- CAMEROON
- BRITISH EAST AFRICA
- Mt Kilimanjaro
- BELGIAN CONGO
- GERMAN EAST AFRICA
- Tanga
- Dar es Salaam
- ANGOLA
- L. Nyasa
- NORTHERN RHODESIA
- GERMAN SOUTHWEST AFRICA
- SOUTHERN RHODESIA
- PORTUGUESE EAST AFRICA
- MADAGASCAR
- Zambesi
- BECHUANALAND
- UNION OF SOUTH AFRICA

PARTITION OF AFRICA

- ▇ French
- ▇ British
- ▇ German
- ▦ Portuguese
- ▇ Belgian
- ▦ Spanish
- ▦ Italian
- ▦ Anglo-Egyptian
- ▦ Neutral

Of Germany's four colonies in Africa, Togoland went first. British and French troops had occupied it within the first month of the war. By July 1915 British and South African forces had occupied German Southwest Africa and German East Africa. Cameroon held out for longer.

He had no aircraft and his only artillery were some naval guns taken from a German cruiser. Lacking conventional help, he improvised, recruiting a force that rose to 11,000 askaris and 3,000 Europeans. He turned them into highly mobile guerrillas, experts in bush warfare. Operating mainly in the rugged region around Mount Kilimanjaro, they drove their own cattle with them when possible. When the cattle died, they ate hippopotamuses. They made boots out of buffalo hide, antimalarial quinine out of bark and wove their own uniforms. One key to Lettow's success was his treatment of his askaris, who loved him. He ate with them, slept in their huts and shared his one luxury, a bicycle.

Lettow was such a menace that in February 1916 South Africa's best commander, General Jan Christiaan Smuts, was dispatched against him. Smuts led 43,000 South African troops, fresh from quelling German resistance in Southwest Africa. In numerous encounters, Lettow always managed to slip away, displaying astonishing chivalry. Unwilling to take prisoners with him, he freed them if they promised not to fight against him again. Once, Smuts got a message to him telling him that Germany had awarded him the *Pour le Mérite*, a German

British soldiers who might otherwise have fought on the Western Front tied to Africa. And he did all this with such gallantry that he won the admiration of his enemies.

He was intensely loyal to German East Africa, a patriotism reflected in his first act when war was declared: he kidnapped his own civilian governor to prevent him from surrendering. His aim from then on was to pin down as many British troops as possible. Though his 4,500 askaris and 260 white troops were vastly outnumbered and though he was blockaded by British ships, Lettow seized the initiative by invading British East Africa. The British summoned reinforcements from India. Lettow blackened his face and disguised himself as an African before reconnoitering the British lines. In the Battle of Tanga (November 2-5, 1914) he ambushed British and Indian troops, killing 800 for the loss of 54. By chance, swarms of bees infested the battlefield, lead-

ing his confused and demoralized enemies to claim that he had even mobilized the bees to help him.

With no possibility of receiving reinforcements or equipment, Lettow captured most of his rifles.

LINED UP IN DEFEAT These Sikh soldiers (right) were among Lettow's prisoners after Tanga. Smuts (above right) studied law at Cambridge in England, then fought against the British in the Boer War. After that he became Britain's loyal ally in two world wars.

1919

August 1917
China declares
war on Germany

October 1918
Lettow invades
Northern Rhodesia

November 1918
Lettow disbands
his force

honor. Lettow sent back a message saying he was sure there had been a mistake, as he did not deserve such an award.

Steadily, Smuts pushed Lettow back, taking Dar es Salaam in September. A year later, his army as strong as ever, Lettow retreated into Portuguese East Africa (now Mozambique), fighting his way almost to the mouth of the Zambesi before turning and invading Southern Rhodesia (Zimbabwe). At this moment, the armistice ended the war. In four years, Lettow had lost 7,000 askaris and 2,000 Europeans, mostly from disease, against British losses of 50,000 native troops and 10,000 Europeans. Still undefeated, he disbanded his force and handed himself over to the British.

The story has a postscript. Years later, after the Second World War, Lettow fell on hard times. Smuts heard about his plight and made arrangements to have his old enemy, now his friend, paid a pension.

War in the Far East

Another reason for the war spreading so far so fast was that others joined in for reasons of their own. The Italians wanted to complete their fight for national unity; the Arabs wanted to begin theirs. On the other side of the world, Japan was as eager as Germany had once been to take "her place in the sun" by acquiring colonies.

Japan's imperial ambitions were of long standing. In 1894 it had occupied Korea, formerly a Chinese sphere of influence, precipitating a war that forced concessions upon China—the lease of Taiwan and the Liaodong

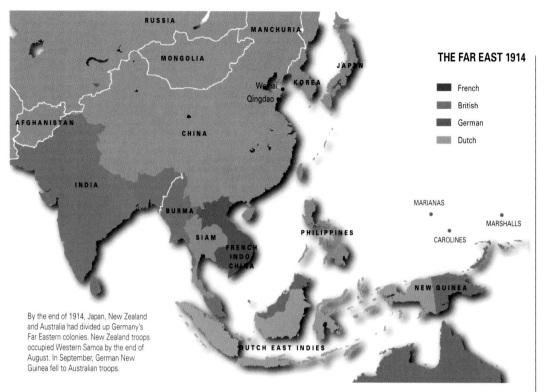

THE FAR EAST 1914

- French
- British
- German
- Dutch

By the end of 1914, Japan, New Zealand and Australia had divided up Germany's Far Eastern colonies. New Zealand troops occupied Western Samoa by the end of August. In September, German New Guinea fell to Australian troops.

peninsula at the tip of Manchuria. All at once Japan had become an international power. Inspired by success, it then seized more of Manchuria, infringing on Russian territory, and defeated Russia's fleet in the Strait of Tsushima in 1905. Industrializing fast, with ever-growing military might, Japan wanted more. Now there was a way: if Germany were defeated, its Far Eastern colonies would become available.

At first glance, the colonies did not amount to very much. Like other European nations (Britain in Hong Kong, for example), Germany had wrung from China a lease to develop the port of Qingdao (Tsingtao), which was a gateway to the densely populated coastal province of Shandong (Shantung). Britain, too, had leased territory there, in the naval base of Weihai.

Elsewhere in the Far East, available territories were mostly occupied by the British, French, Dutch, Portuguese and Australians. Germany had the northeastern part of New Guinea, plus a scattering of islands to the north (the Carolinas, Marianas and Marshalls) and to the east (Western Samoa).

Japan felt secure in its ambitions, because it had the support of Britain. At the turn of the century, both had wanted to define and protect their interests in China, and the two

THE EMPIRE GOES TO WAR Japanese troops march through Shanghai. Japan adopted an increasingly aggressive approach to China.

LONG HAUL Japanese artillerymen transfer their equipment to Qingdao. As the key to the mineral-rich Shandong peninsula, Qingdao was an important prize.

had signed an alliance in 1902. This had survived for 12 years, and now its provisions gave Japan an excuse to enter the war in search of colonial pickings. It declared war on Germany on August 23, 1914.

Determined to seize Qingdao, Japan promptly landed troops nearby on the Chinese mainland, where its force was joined by a small British detachment. It took them six weeks to prepare for the attack, but then a week of bombardment persuaded the garrison to capitulate on November 7.

THE FLAG FLIES A Japanese flag perches on the wreckage of a gun blown up by the Germans before they surrendered Qingdao. With the Japanese soldiers are two British officers.

Qingdao, though, was merely part of a wider scheme. With its power base secured, Japan presented China with the so-called 21 Demands. Among other things, Tokyo demanded all railroad and mining rights in Shandong, which would effectively make the province a Japanese colony, along with concessions in other parts of China. The demands were initially made in secret. When they were made public,

revealing the true scope of Japan's imperial ambitions, a wave of protest within China forced Tokyo to backtrack. Qingdao was Japan's; the rest would have to wait.

Not all Germany's possessions fell to Japan. Australia already had a colony of its own in southeastern New Guinea. As soon as war was declared, Australian troops landed on the shores of New Guinea's Gazelle

BEING JAPANESE IN BERLIN

Japan's declaration of war made little difference in Germany, except to the few Japanese there. In Berlin, restaurants turned away Japanese customers and some Japanese civilians were interned in the buildings of the Ruhleben racecourse; others escaped to Switzerland.

peninsula and the few Germans there capitulated. It was under Australian military administration for the rest of the war. A New Zealand force took over Western Samoa.

Elsewhere in the Pacific, Japan fared better. The coral pinpricks to the north—whose names would later be written in blood during the American advance across the Pacific in the Second World War—were of little interest in Europe. Much to Australia's displeasure, Britain took it upon itself, four months after war broke out, to offer Japan all of Germany's possessions lying north of the Equator, which meant all of its Pacific islands, apart from Western Samoa. Japanese naval forces then landed on several of the islands, and they remained there for the duration of the war.

THE WAR AT SEA

WHILE SUBMARINES PREYED ON MERCHANT SHIPS, THE SURFACE FLEETS SAW MAJOR ACTION ONLY AT JUTLAND, IN SUMMER 1916

Both Britain and Germany had formidable navies in 1914, spearheaded by 20 British dreadnoughts and 13 German equivalents. The First Sea Lord, Sir John ("Jackie") Fisher, had prophesied that these seaborne juggernauts would unleash Armageddon—but this never materialized. The Germans knew that Britain's navy was superior and simply kept their ships in port. They were well-placed to defend their ships, with the Heligoland fringe of islands providing a shield for their ports, and the new Kiel Canal providing a route for naval reinforcements from the Baltic. In addition, two new weapons, the mine and the submarine, conferred effective defenses. As a result, both awaited developments on land before deciding what to do at sea.

PLOUGHING THROUGH THE WAVES German cruisers slice through rough seas off Chile in late November 1914. Just over a week later they were sunk off the Falkland Islands.

Of the two, the British were the more active. The Grand Fleet was gathered in England in the month before war broke out. As tensions rose, it was ordered to Scapa Flow, a huge expanse of water in the Orkney Islands that offered the security of distance, although it did not have anti-torpedo defenses. From here, together with a smaller force based in the English Channel, it secured Britain's sea routes and ensured the safe passage of the British Expeditionary Force across the Channel.

Little happened to upset this deadlock. British cruisers made a foray into the Bight of Heligoland, sinking three German cruisers; German cruisers bombarded British ports; and three old British cruisers were sunk by a U-boat.

The high seas, meanwhile, were wide open. There were eight German cruisers on active service in China, one of which, the *Emden*, played havoc with British shipping in the Indian Ocean for three months during the autumn of 1914. She was hunted by 78 Allied ships before finally being sunk by the Australian cruiser *Sydney*. Several others, notably the *Gneisenau* and the *Scharnhorst*, headed eastward under the command of the admiral Maximilian von Spee. Admiral Sir Christopher Cradock, commanding three cruisers, was ordered to stop Spee. When the two met, off Coronel on the coast of Chile, Spee's heavier ships sank two of Cradock's. Galvanized by this dis-

aster, two battle cruisers were dispatched from Britain. Meanwhile, Spee had decided to raid the Falkland Islands in order to destroy the radio station there. The British ships were coaling at Port Stanley in the Falklands when Spee turned up on December 8. The Germans fled, but were caught and sunk with the loss of four ships and 2,200 lives. From then on, Britain ruled the waves, and Germany's colonies were isolated.

In early 1915, both sides sought to break the deadlock in the North Sea. The British claimed the right to intercept all ships sus-

OCEAN PROWLERS German U-boats line up in the safety of harbor. Their value in picking off enemy shipping was only truly appreciated after the war had started.

pected of carrying supplies to Germany—a strategy that infringed upon the traditional freedom of the seas and drew protests from the United States. The Germans replied with a submarine offensive. This was a novel strategy: before, submarines had been seen as auxiliaries to the main fleets; now, the Germans were proposing to sink merchant ships, even those of neutral nations. Moreover, it was not possible for submarines to give warnings or to rescue passengers: they had to sink ships on sight. It was a strategy that rebounded in spectacular fashion when on May 7, 1915, a German U-boat sank the liner *Lusitania*.

The German submarine campaign continued for a year, with too few vessels to achieve significant results, and too many incidents that provoked American anger. It was finally abandoned after a virtual ultimatum from President Wilson, turning German

December 1914
Battle of the
Falkland Islands

February 1915
Germany begins
U-boat campaign

May 1915
Sinking of the
Lusitania

May/June 1916
Battle of
Jutland

THE SINKING OF THE LUSITANIA

AS THE LUXURY LINER SAILED ALONG THE SOUTHERN COAST OF IRELAND, SHE WAS SPOTTED BY A GERMAN U-BOAT ON THE HUNT FOR MERCHANT SHIPPING

At about 2 p.m. on May 7, 1915, Captain Walther Schwieger in the U-boat *U-20* was cruising the southern Irish coast in search of ships that might be bringing supplies to Britain. Just off the Old Head of Kinsale, he spotted a gift of a target: the luxurious 31,000-ton Cunard liner *Lusitania* on her way to Liverpool from New York.

On board, a Canadian journalist chatting to a friend glanced up and saw the submarine's conning tower and the track of a torpedo. There was a terrible explosion, and the ship went down in 20 minutes, listing and diving into the depths so steeply that few lifeboats could be deployed: 1,198 people died, including 128 Americans, among them millionaire Alfred Vanderbilt.

The sinking, combined with the delight expressed in Germany, caused outrage internationally. There were anti-German riots in Liverpool and London, and German Knights of the Garter had their banners removed from the chapel at Windsor.

The sinking has been a matter of great controversy ever since. The *Lusitania* was indeed carrying weapons—173 tons of rifles and ammunition—and the German embassy had inserted an advertisement in the main New York newspapers warning Americans that "travellers sailing in the war zone on ships to Great Britain…do so at their own risk." Conspiracy theorists have even speculated about a plot by Winston Churchill, then Britain's First Lord of the Admiralty, and the First Sea Lord, Sir John Fisher, to have her sunk to drive the United States toward intervention.

In fact, the atrocity was not planned. Schwieger had no orders to sink her. The *Lusitania*'s captain, William Turner, was ignoring guidelines to zigzag at full speed, avoiding headlands: he was not moving at full steam ahead, and was steering a straight course close to three headlands. Schwieger was lucky, the *Lusitania* unlucky. (Schwieger went on being lucky, accounting for 49 ships, until his own submarine was blown up by a mine in 1917.)

In the longer term, however, the sinking proved unlucky for Germany, for it provoked a wave of sympathy for Britain, and against Germany. President Wilson, though refusing to be rushed into intervention, protested that a continuation of submarine attacks on neutral shipping could force America to abandon its neutrality. The sinking began the slow shift of opinion that culminated in America's intervention in the war two years later.

SETTING SAIL New York crowds watch the departure of the *Lusitania* on what would prove to be her last trip. A French publication squeezes the "crime" for all its propaganda worth.

Collection "Patrie"

GEORGES G.-TOUDOUZE

40c.
Le récit complet illustré.

Le Crime du "Lusitania"

Publié sous le patronage de la Ligue Maritime Française

May 1917
British adopt
convoy system

November 1918
Surrender of the
German fleet

1919

MEN IN CHARGE Scheer (far left) helped to plan the German U-boat offensive. Jellicoe (left), criticized for not winning a clear victory, was an able commander. Below: A German torpedo boat fires at a British cruiser on the horizon.

superior British force—28 dreadnoughts and nine battle cruisers, together with light cruisers and destroyers—under Admiral Sir John Jellicoe steamed out to meet him.

Without radar or aerial reconnaissance, the maneuvers were those of the blind seeking the blind; and the actual contact on the early afternoon of May 31 happened entirely by accident when Admiral Sir David Beatty's

attention once again to the possibility of surface warfare. The result was the war's only battle between whole fleets.

The Battle of Jutland

The battle started with a plan devised by Admiral Reinhard Scheer, who was the commander of the High Seas Fleet. In May 1916 Scheer intended to use the German fleet as a decoy to lure part of the British fleet out of the safety of their harbor and into the range of waiting submarines. As it happened, the weather was so bad that month that the necessary reconnaissance by airships was impossible and the U-boats exhausted their supplies. Scheer decided to go ahead with his plan, using his main fleet rather than submarines, and on May 30

a group of German warships under Vice-Admiral Franz von Hipper set out, with the main fleet following at a distance.

The British knew something of the German plans because earlier, in October 1914, the Russians had sunk a German cruiser in the Baltic and had found on the body of an officer the German naval code book. This they had passed on to the British, who set up a special department in the Admiralty to decipher and pass on the information. As a result, when Scheer set out to sea with a total force of 24 battleships, five battle cruisers, plus light cruisers and destroyers, a

force from Scotland, on its way to rendezvous with Jellicoe, approached Hipper's advance party. Though out of sight of each other, light cruisers in both forces simultaneously saw a Swedish merchant ship blowing off steam. Both turned to investigate—and saw each other looming over the horizon.

Beatty gave chase. Hipper turned, to lead Beatty back into the arms of his main force.

BATTLE OF THE LEVIATHANS These cruisers and battleships represent only a part of Britain's Grand Fleet. Even so, they are an impressive sight at the Battle of Jutland.

JUTLAND: THE BATTLE SHEET

A table of the relative strengths in the Battle of Jutland, the greatest naval force assembled during the war, reveals British superiority:

	Britain	(Losses)	Germany	(Losses)
Dreadnoughts	28	–	24	–
Battle cruisers	9	(3)	5	(1)
Light cruisers	34	(3)	11	(4)
Destroyers	80	(8)	63	(5)
Broadside	332,000 lbs.		134,000 lbs.	

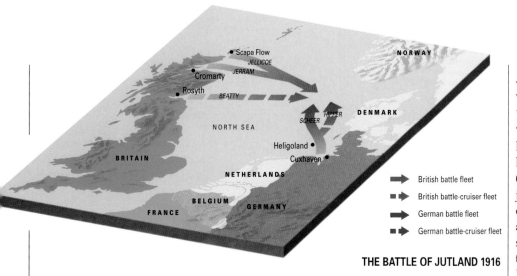

THE BATTLE OF JUTLAND 1916

- → British battle fleet
- ⇢ British battle-cruiser fleet
- → German battle fleet
- ⇢ German battle-cruiser fleet

In what turned out to be a preliminary skirmish, Beatty lost two ships and some 2,300 men. Then, coming upon the main German fleet, Beatty turned and led the Germans back to the main British fleet, of which the Germans were still unaware.

The two fleets met 80 miles off the Jutland peninsula (the Germans refer to the ensuing encounter as the Battle of Skagerrak, the estuary to the north). To bring his broadsides to bear, Jellicoe needed to turn every ship 90° and line them up—but only if the enemy was in the right position. The light was bad, the sky misty, visibility poor. At the last moment, Jellicoe saw where Scheer's ships were, ordered a starboard wheel, brought his ships into line, and thrust across the bows of the German fleet—a time-honored maneuver known as "crossing the T" during which every vessel can unleash a broadside.

The German fleet, meanwhile, executed an about-face and headed for home. There followed a running battle, which lasted until darkness put a stop to it at around 10 p.m. Twice, Jellicoe nearly cut Scheer off; twice, Scheer evaded. During the night, Scheer cut through Jellicoe's wake and found safety in the Heligoland Bight.

What should have been a great British victory ended inconclusively. In London, as Vera Brittain wrote in her *Testament of Youth*, people wondered whether they were "celebrating a glorious naval victory or lamenting an ignominious defeat. We hardly knew." The British losses were greater: some 6,000 British sailors died, compared with just 2,400 Germans. The result revealed several British faults: inferior gunnery, defective armor, bad shell design, and failures in both signaling and intelligence. But all the same, the Germans had fled, and that made Jutland officially a British victory, for never again did the German fleet mount an out-

TAKING CHARGE Falling shells send up huge waterspouts in this painting of Jutland. The battle left Britain in command of the seas.

A BRITISH LEADER SUNK

On June 5, 1916, the British cruiser *Hampshire*, northwest of the Orkney Islands en route to Russia, hit a German mine. The *Hampshire* went down rapidly in the icy waters. On board was Britain's Secretary of State for War, Lord Kitchener, 66, whose face on recruitment posters had summoned millions of British volunteers to arms. Though by this stage of the war Kitchener was regarded as ineffective by his colleagues, he had retained his cult status as a public figure, and his death shocked all of Britain. He was the only leading military figure on either side to come to a violent end during the war.

right challenge. As a result, Britain could go on receiving supplies, and could cut off Germany's. The battle confirmed Germany in the belief that its only recourse was to concentrate on submarines.

Blockade

Through 1916, the effect of the German submarine blockade was partially counteracted by patrols and by the laying of mines that constrained and demoralized crews. But these methods accounted for only 15 U-boats in the second half of 1916, hardly enough to convince neutral nations that the trade was worth the risk. In early 1917, Germany's submarine tactics began to bite. By April, U-boats were sinking one out of four merchant ships leaving Britain. That month, Britain lost half a million tons of shipping, while Allied nations lost another 300,000.

Britain had enough food on hand for only another six months.

The nation's salvation lay in the deployment of convoys. This ancient method of defense had fallen out of favor with naval commanders mainly because it smacked of defeatism, and many arguments were raised against the use of convoys—they needed large numbers of vessels, they were slow, they made good U-boat targets.

These arguments fell apart when convoys were tried across the North Sea. Instantly, losses fell from 25 percent to 0.25 percent. Lloyd George intervened in May 1917 to institute convoys across the Atlantic. Between 10 and 50 merchant vessels would be shepherded by a cruiser, six destroyers, armed trawlers and two torpedo boats with balloons, from which lookouts could spot submarines and torpedoes. They were an instant success. Soon, convoys set out from Nova Scotia, Panama, Rio, Murmansk, Port Said, Gibraltar and Dakar. More than a million Americans were ferried across the Atlantic

in this way, with the loss of only 637 to submarine attacks.

By early 1918, the Allies were building more tonnage than submarines could destroy, and finally shut the door on them by barring their favored exit, the 180-mile passage between the Orkney Islands and Norway, with a string of 70,000 mines.

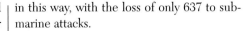

A WOLF IN SHEEP'S CLOTHING

The most dramatic way of hunting U-boats was with "Q-ships," merchant ships fitted with concealed armaments and specially trained crews, which would proceed alone into danger areas, inviting attack. U-boats usually sank small vessels by gunfire from the surface, allowing the crew to abandon ship. On being accosted by a U-boat, a mock "panic party" would stage a rushed exit, while the gun crews remained concealed, awaiting their chance. One commander, Gordon Campbell, described what happened after *U-68* fired a torpedo, just missing his Q-ship:

"He was now about 800 yards off, showing full length, and although the range was a little bit greater than I wished the time had come to open fire before he might touch off our magazines. I therefore blew my whistle. At this signal the White Ensign flew at the masthead, the wheel-house and side ports came down with a clatter, the hen coop collapsed; and in a matter of seconds three 12-pounder guns, the Maxim, and rifles were firing as hard as they could."

U-68 submerged, was forced up by a depth charge and finished off.

CUTTING SUPPLIES
German submarine *U-35* holds up a merchant ship in the Mediterranean. The U-boat offensive threatened British supplies, such as flour from Canada.

AMERICA ENTERS THE WAR

WHEN THE POWERFUL UNITED STATES ENTERED THE WAR IN APRIL 1917, IT TIPPED THE BALANCE DECISIVELY IN THE ALLIES' FAVOR

WRAPPED IN THE FLAG With the rapid build-up of the United States' armed forces in full swing by 1917, President Wilson sets an example of patriotic zeal.

At the outbreak of war, the United States held back in shock. The immediate causes were so obscure that it seemed as though Europe had suddenly been driven crazy by territorial greed and militarism. Overwhelmingly, opinion backed President Woodrow Wilson when he said that the nation would remain neutral. Yet neutrality did not come easily to the nation of immigrants. In 1914, 32 million Americans—one third of the total—were foreign-born or the children of immigrants. More than a million Irish had fled the famines of 1845. Three million Italians had arrived between 1900 and 1914. In 1900 alone, 100,000 arrived from eastern Europe, 133,000 from central Europe and 85,000 from northwestern Europe.

Millions of Americans thus inherited opinions that were anything but neutral about the struggle in Europe. An Irish-American (any one of 4 million) might see Britain as a colonial oppressor, a German American (8 million) as an enemy. To the Progressives, Britain represented the worst aspects of inherited wealth and established aristocracy. On the other hand, millions looked to Britain for their cultural roots, and remembered French support for the American Revolution. Their affinities with Britain and France were strengthened by the fact that Germany had made the first move into war.

No major faction opposed the policy of neutrality, for neutrality worked in America's interests. Business and industry were free to sell to the combatants on both sides. And, as Wilson argued, when peace came, America would be in a strong position to mediate peace, and to guarantee it.

It proved a difficult balancing act, however, for the supposed freedom of the seas soon became a casualty of war. When Germany declared a submarine blockade of Britain in February 1915, Britain responded by claiming the right to seize all ships suspected of carrying goods to Germany. As a result, American trade with the Central Powers dropped from $150 million a year to $1.2 million. Meanwhile, exports to the Allies boomed from $750 million to $3.2 billion. In effect, American businesses had made their nation part of the Allied cause, even while their president had been proclaiming neutrality.

The political tide began to turn when, in March 1915, a German U-boat sank a British

MELTING POT Four men enlisting in 1917—an African American, a man with roots in early America, a Greek American and an Italian American—represent the nation's diversity.

THE ZIMMERMANN TELEGRAM

The telegram sent by the German foreign minister, Arthur Zimmermann, in January 1917 must rank as one of history's greatest diplomatic blunders. In fact, it was Zimmermann's second involvement with telegraphic disaster. As under-secretary in the foreign ministry in 1914, Zimmermann had drafted the telegram that gave Austria-Hungary the nerve to invade Serbia. Now, as foreign minister, he had, in historian A.J.P. Taylor's words, "a bright idea such as only a Foreign Office could conceive."

With America shocked by the German submarine campaign that had killed hundreds of innocent Americans and in turmoil over the issue of whether to intervene in the war, Zimmermann decided it would help Germany if, in the event of war, America were to be distracted by a crisis on its own borders. His plan was that Mexico should be encouraged to "reconquer her lost territory in Texas, New Mexico and Arizona" with "Germany's generous financial support."

The message, sent to the German minister in Mexico on January 19, was intercepted by British Admiralty intelligence, deciphered over the course of the next month, and passed on to President Wilson. It was published in the United States on March 1. Nothing could have been better calculated to reveal German hostility. When the telegram was published, some opponents of America's joining the war discounted it as a forgery, but Zimmermann confirmed it as genuine and Wilson was left with no option. A month later, he opted for war. Far from distracting America's attention, Zimmermann had caught it. Far from saving Germany, he had doomed her.

A PERSUASIVE POSE The artist James Montgomery Flagg used himself as the model for Uncle Sam, in a pose used in similar British posters.

liner, killing an American. Then on May 7, 1915, a U-boat sank the British liner *Lusitania*, killing 128 Americans. Wilson protested, with a threat: call off the U-boats, or we join the Allies. Germany complied, for the moment. But the stance was an artificial one that Wilson feared would end sooner or later. To be prepared, he proposed to take up arms—a suggestion that aroused great controversy until another four Americans went down in a torpedoed French vessel in March 1916.

In February 1917, as Britain benefited from increased trade and Germany approached strangulation, Ludendorff agreed that the only course was unrestricted submarine warfare. This would, almost inevitably, bring the United States into the war, but Ludendorff clung to the hope that victory would follow so quickly that the U.S. would not have time to bring her vast resources to bear.

Wilson, still trying to maintain neutrality, was faced with a dilemma. He could not stop American supplies from flowing to the Allies, which would be to abandon friends and ruin American factories. Nor could he endanger American lives. On February 3, he cut off diplomatic relations with Germany, yet held back from the final, fateful step.

Three weeks later, his hand was forced by an astonishing *coup de théâtre*: it emerged that the German foreign minister, Arthur Zimmermann, had incited Mexico to attack the United States. On April 2, Wilson asked Congress to declare war on Germany to make the world "safe for democracy." Congress approved. On April 6, 1917, Wilson signed the resolution that brought America into the war.

America prepares

American help was not immediate. The commander of the American Expeditionary Force, General John Pershing, left New York for France at the end of May, but he had only a small staff with him. The United States had no army to speak of, few munitions, only 55 aircraft (for training only), and

STICKLER FOR DISCIPLINE General Pershing, commander of the American Expeditionary Force (front row, second from left), with his staff on their arrival in Britain in June 1917.

no big guns. It would take months to build the arms, conscript the men, train them and ship them to France. Meanwhile, Britain and France were near exhaustion, their position made worse by the collapse of their ally, Russia. In April more than a million tons of British and neutral shipping were lost to German submarines.

Through the rest of that year, while the Allies stemmed the losses with convoys and struggled with little success to break the deadlock on the Western Front, the United States flexed its immense industrial muscle.

BOUND FOR EUROPE Troops in New York Harbor prepare to cross the Atlantic to help their allies on the "Old Continent."

May 1915
Sinking of
Lusitania

March 1916
Sinking of *Sussex*
in English Channel

In the war years, the steel industry doubled its production, and a building "crusade" did the same for ships in just two years. By June, 9.6 million men had registered for military service. That month, the first American troops—14,000 of them—arrived in France.

In Europe, while men were dying at Arras, Ypres and Cambrai, there were murmurings of peace. The new Russian democrats called for a peace without preconditions, without annexations and indemnities. The French army had already mutinied. There were strikes in Germany. The Western leaders, however, pulled back from serious negotiations, because talks would mean compromise, and compromise would mean acknowledging that the enemy was not quite as bad as he had been painted; and this, in turn, would show the military and political leadership as weaklings.

Victory still seemed unattainable, however. The first Americans had now been in action, to no effect. On arrival for training in Lorraine, they had only two tanks, built in Washington from French blueprints (they were under the command of a forceful young officer whose experience would make him America's greatest tank commander and one of the nation's greatest generals: George Patton). For artillery, they had to rely on French guns, and mostly French gunners.

On November 2, an American infantry battalion took over from French troops in Barthelémont. Early the next morning, a group of Germans attacked one of their outposts, shot one American, cut the throat of another, smashed the skull of a third, and took 12 prisoners. The survivors were found in shock. An inquiry suggested that the Americans were not well enough trained and

BUILDING UP THE NAVY The Navy had embarked on a substantial shipbuilding program as early as 1916.

TRANSATLANTIC VOLUNTEERS

Until 1917, America remained neutral; but many Americans did not. More than 100 of them joined the 10,000-strong French Foreign Legion in 1914—some of the 32,000 foreign volunteers who joined the French and British, including 1,000 Germans opposed to their own country's aims.

In the ranks of the Legionnaires fighting with the British on the Somme was the Harvard graduate and poet Alan Seeger, who wrote one of the war's best-known poems:

I have a rendezvous with Death
On some scarred slope or battered hill,
When Spring comes round again this year
And the first meadow-flowers appear.

Death kept that rendezvous. Seeger died in a shell-hole on the Somme on July 4, 1916.

Hundreds of American volunteers found a role wherever they could. Dillwyn Parrish Starr, from Philadelphia, served as an ambulance driver with the French before transferring to armored cars at Gallipoli. At 32, as a lieutenant in a British Guards regiment, he was killed on the Western Front in September 1916. On November 23, 1917, a plane was shot down over Bourlon Wood during the battle of Cambrai. The pilot was an American, Lieutenant A. Griggs, serving with an Australian squadron that formed part of Britain's Royal Flying Corps. When Winston Churchill, on a visit to the Ypres salient in 1918, came across Henry Butters from San Francisco, who was a 2nd Lieutenant with the Royal Artillery, he asked him how he had managed to be enlisted. Butters replied candidly: "I just lied to 'em and said I was British born."

November 1916
Woodrow Wilson
re-elected president

January 1917
Zimmermann
telegram sent

April 1917
U.S. enters
the war

May 1917
Conscription
introduced in U.S.

January 1918
Wilson's Fourteen
Points

September 1918
U.S. victory in
St. Mihiel salient

should be taken out of the line. A memorial commemorates the names of the first three Americans to die in France: Corporal Gresham, Private Enright, Private Hay.

In January 1918, President Wilson equated America's war aims with a far-ranging program for world peace. In this—his so-called Fourteen Points—he sought to bridge the gap between the United States, Western Europe and the Bolsheviks, whose anti-imperial stance was, in theory, close to his own position. He called for freedom of the seas, an end to secret diplomacy, and a reduction in military spending. For the post-war years, two suggestions were of particular significance: his insistence on self-determination for all peoples and his proposal for a League of Nations to guarantee self-determination around the world.

ASSAULT!   French tanks lead the way and American troops follow during an offensive on the Somme front.

The reaction in Western Europe to Wilson's proclamation was muted. Of the Fourteen Points, Clemenceau muttered: "The Lord God had only ten." For Britain, self-determination meant the dismemberment of Austria-Hungary, which was desirable, but also the prospect of the end of the British Empire. However, without the United States there would be no victory.

At last, American troops were nearing the end of their preparations. American ships had helped guarantee freedom from submarine attack. Soon, an immense armada would be on its way to Europe.

American troops into battle

To avoid destruction at the hands of the American juggernaut, Ludendorff needed outright victory before American troops could be deployed. Turning from defense to offense, he planned surprise attacks first at the point where the British and French armies joined, on the Somme, and then at

Ypres. In four months, German numbers rose by 30 percent, boosted by men released from the Russian front. Haig, however, was deprived of new men by a government fearful of yet more useless losses. Certain of his defenses, Haig kept his forces around the major battleground, Ypres, ignoring the minor one on the Somme.

It was on the Somme, on March 21, 1918, that the Germans attacked. The lack of a long bombardment ensured surprise, and troops newly trained in infiltration ensured swift penetration. Luckily for the Germans it was a foggy day, which allowed them to get through British lines often undetected. Unused to maneuvering at such speed and deprived of their trench-based telephone system, the British reeled back in chaos. They lost 500 guns to the enemy in the first two days and retreated 40 miles in a week.

But the response was firm. Lloyd George increased transports across the English Channel threefold, and asked President Wilson to provide more help. Haig, in need of support, at last accepted the idea of a joint Allied command, and Ferdinand Foch was named commander in chief of all Allied forces, including the Americans. By controlling the reserves, Foch in effect controlled the events of 1918, allowing the Germans to advance, mounting counterattacks, restoring movement to a war that had been locked in place for almost four years. When the rapid German advance, slowing as it outran supplies, turned northward toward Arras, it ran up against strong British resistance.

Ludendorff now turned on the area south of Ypres, on the River Lys, and forced a hole 30 miles wide, driving the British out of Passchendaele, which they had taken at such

THE FORGOTTEN "HARLEM HELLFIGHTERS"

The United States sent almost 400,000 African-American soldiers to Europe. In 1914, the barriers to black advancement were almost as formidable as they had been just after the abolition of slavery. African Americans were hemmed in by legislation ostensibly confirming their status as "separate but equal." In fact, these laws based voting rights on property and education, condemning black citizens to a state of permanent inequality.

When war broke out, black leaders hoped service would dissolve prejudice and segregation. Far from it. In places such as Spartanburg, South Carolina, there were riots at the presence of "black Yankees" in training. The men and their officers were allocated to labor battalions and given menial chores. There were no black artillery officers or pilots. In France, segregation was imposed. African Americans were not allowed to speak to French women and French officers were told not to meet blacks "outside the requirements of military service."

Yet the African-American soldiers fought as bravely as whites. One unit became known as the "Harlem Hellfighters" for their brave service on the front, led by the heroic efforts of Sergeant Henry Johnson. Several hundred, including Johnson, received the French Croix de Guerre, but none the American Medal of Honor. At home, their contribution

HONORS FROM FRANCE Soldiers of the U.S. 15th Regiment (above), were all winners of the French Croix de Guerre. Sergeant Henry Johnson (left) won the Croix de Guerre for single-handedly routing a unit of 36 Germans.

to the war effort was largely ignored. In President Wilson's Fourteen Points, he asserted a right to self-determination. It was one of the ironies of history that 10 percent of Americans had to wait another 40 years before they could benefit from those ideals.

cost the previous year. A new salient, if too deep, however, could be cut off. The attack was halted on April 25.

Then Ludendorff, trapped as Haig had been by the dream of imminent victory, undertook yet another offensive on the Aisne. There was plenty of warning, but the details came from the newly arrived Americans, and were therefore discounted by the French. Moreover, the general on the spot insisted on massing his troops in forward positions, exposing them as luckless cannon-fodder. As a result, the German

attack, when it came on May 27, was both a surprise and a devastating success. The Germans advanced 10 miles, a success unrivaled since the 1914 invasion itself. They took 65,000 prisoners, a loss that was mitigated, however, by the timely arrival of American forces. Beginning in April, American troops flooded in at the rate of 300,000 a month. By June 3, the Germans were halted, finding themselves back on the Marne, 56 miles from Paris.

Time was running out for Ludendorff, for the Americans were constantly strengthening

the Allied lines. When, on July 15, the Germans struck forward again on the Marne, the French were ready. On one side, east of Rheims, they opened fire first, undermining the German advance. On the other, they fell back. Three days later, a counterstroke in which nine American divisions took part threatened to cut off the advancing Germans, who retreated. On July 24, the Allied leaders all agreed: the time had come for a general offensive to reverse the German gains.

THE FINAL OFFENSIVE

RESHUFFLED LEADERSHIP, THE INJECTION OF AMERICAN MUSCLE AND A NEW ALLIED OFFENSIVE PUSHED THE GERMANS BACK AND BACK

The major German offensive that began on the Somme in March 1918 had the aim of breaking through the British and French lines before the mass of American troops arrived. It was the Germans' last major offensive before the tide of war began to turn decisively against them. In August, the changing balance of power was finally revealed by the British—using their own invention, the tank. In the Battle of Amiens, British, French and Dominion troops put into action the lessons of Cambrai. Preparations were kept secret: troop movements took place at night; local commanders did not know of the attack until a week before, the troops only 36 hours before; and British aircraft harried German reconnaissance planes out of the sky. Steadily, with 290 trains using just two railroad lines, six infantry divisions, nine tank divisions and 1,000 guns arrived to double the strength of the British 4th Army. The reinforcements were carefully spread out as if in a defensive arrangement. Deceived, the Germans did nothing to reinforce the six divisions of the 2nd Army.

When the blow came an hour before sunrise on August 8, surprise was ensured by the lack of a preliminary bombardment. A total of 456 British tanks rolled forward, with artillery opening up behind them and infantry—mainly Canadians and Australians—surging forward with them until they reached the tangled wire and abandoned trenches of the old Somme battlefield. In four days, the 4th Army took 24,000 prisoners, sustaining 20,000 killed and wounded—one-twelfth the rate of losses on the Somme in 1916.

Biding his time in the center, Foch ordered a month-long rain of attacks in neighboring sectors, and the whole 100-mile line between Ypres and Rheims edged forward with names that would be written in blood: Thiepval Ridge, Mametz Wood, Delville Wood. In retrospect, August 8 was the beginning

OFFENSIVE FAILURE German soldiers attack on the Somme front in March 1918. By April 4, the offensive had ground to a halt and Ludendorff was obliged to call it off.

HELP IS ON THE WAY American troops ride in tanks to the battle line in the forests of Argonne, France, on September 26, 1918. The mission through the forests involved 37 French and American divisions and 700 tanks—and cost 120,000 American lives.

enemy territory that stuck out over the River Meuse, south of Verdun around the village of St. Mihiel. Pershing had had his eye on this troublesome salient since June 1917 and had been arguing forcefully that American troops should be deployed under American command, not scattered to fill holes in the British and French lines. He needed an objective of his own, and St. Mihiel was a natural focus for his attention, for Britain was concentrating on areas nearer the Channel to ensure supplies, while the

of the end: the start of the great advance known as the "Hundred Days" that led to the German collapse three months later.

In retreat, the German line remained intact, but their resolve did not. The shock of the British tank advance did more than anything else to show Ludendorff that further fighting would achieve no further advances. He called August 8 "the black day of the German army," and admitted a week later that victory was impossible.

The Americans played an increasing role in Western advances. In their first independent operation, they took on a difficult peninsula of

GUN BOOTY As Allied offensives gained momentum, more German artillery fell into their hands. This "gun park" was located at Amiens.

FOCH: INSPIRING LEADER AND ARCHITECT OF ALLIED VICTORY

Ferdinand Foch (1851-1929), the supreme Allied commander, was one of the few military leaders to serve throughout the war and emerge with his stature enhanced. In 1914, he impressed the French commander-in-chief, Joffre, when he helped halt the German advance. Though as much a believer in France's supposed offensive qualities as other leaders, he soon adapted by supporting the role of artillery. Given the task of coordinating the French, British and Belgians, he famously withheld French reserves in dire situations, to the fury of his colleagues—and released them to good effect in even direr ones. He was fired, like Joffre, after the failure of the Somme offensives in 1916, but coordinated Allied help to Italy and returned to the Western Front as generalissimo in May 1918, at the age of 66. In his words, his job was that of the "conductor of an opera who beats time well." In 1918, he coordinated both the Allied response to the German offensive and the "Hundred Days" of advance that led to Germany's capitulation. He was honored as one of Europe's most respected military and intellectual leaders—marshal of France, marshal of Poland, British field-marshal, and member of the Académie Française.

INTELLECTUAL OF WAR As a college lecturer, Foch had inspired generations of French officers; he was no less effective in the field.

August 1918
Battle of
Amiens

September 1918
Foch's final
assault launched

November 1918
The Armistice
comes into effect

THE GERMAN SPRING OFFENSIVE 1918

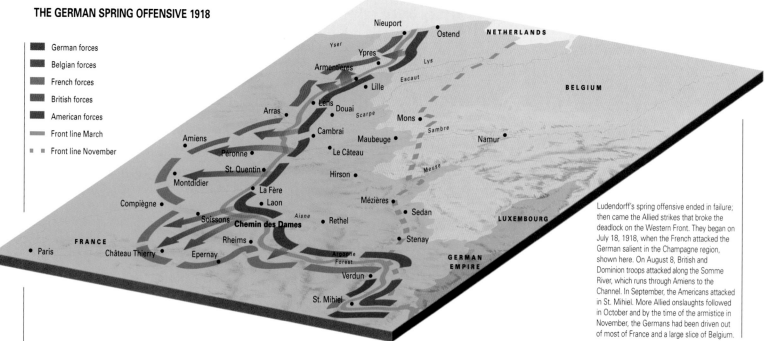

- ▧ German forces
- ▧ Belgian forces
- ▧ French forces
- ▧ British forces
- ▧ American forces
- ── Front line March
- ┄ Front line November

Ludendorff's spring offensive ended in failure; then came the Allied strikes that broke the deadlock on the Western Front. They began on July 18, 1918, when the French attacked the German salient in the Champagne region, shown here. On August 8, British and Dominion troops attacked along the Somme River, which runs through Amiens to the Channel. In September, the Americans attacked in St. Mihiel. More Allied onslaughts followed in October and by the time of the armistice in November, the Germans had been driven out of most of France and a large slice of Belgium.

French were concerned primarily with covering the approaches to Paris. For the Americans, the St. Mihiel salient was conveniently placed opposite their bases on the Bay of Biscay. Moreover, an advance here would serve wider strategic purposes, threatening the whole of Germany's position in France and its industries in the Saarland.

YOUNG "BLOOD AND GUTS" George Patton, later famous for his rapid thrust across France in the summer of 1944, first learned about tank warfare in France in 1918.

The agreed plan at St. Mihiel was for the French to attack the nose of the salient to make sure that the Germans remained engaged on the front line, while 200,000 Americans moved in from either side to pinch off the protruding sector at its roots. It was a massive operation involving 3,000 guns, 40,000 tons of ammunition, 65 evacuation trains for the wounded, all assembled along 15 miles of new road, 45 miles of standard gauge and 250 miles of light-gauge railway. In all, there were 1,483 aircraft under American command.

The Germans had ordered a withdrawal even as the Americans were moving into position on September 12. They were too slow: American artillery fire (with most guns supplied by the French) landed on the retreating Germans, while the American 2nd and 42nd Divisions moved in from the south. Spearheading the advance were Lt. Colonel George Patton's 267 tanks, all supplied by the French. By chance, Patton was not the only future American commander present. Also at St. Mihiel were Douglas MacArthur, commanding the 42nd ("The Rainbow") Division, who later would become a hero of the Pacific theater in the Second World War, and George Marshall, Operations Officer of the 1st Army and the author of the Marshall Plan after the Second World War.

The Americans moved faster than planned.

GOING HOME German troops retreating in August 1918 (above) seem in good spirits. Quick fire is the order of the day as American artillerymen (right) see action in the St. Mihiel salient.

By midday, the advance in the south had covered 5 miles, reaching high ground that was the objective for the end of the next day. There they stopped, awaiting orders. More than 40,000 Germans slipped away along the jammed roads leading westward before the Americans could be urged onward again. Still, it was a remarkable success,

with 15,000 prisoners taken and 443 guns captured. One American sergeant, Harry Adams, saw a German vanish into a dugout, fired at him with his last two bullets, then called on the man to surrender. To Adams' astonishment, his prisoner came out peaceably, followed by another, and more and more, 300 in all, who filed back to the American lines before Adams's empty pistol. After only two days, the French and Americans were in St. Mihiel. The Americans had become the major partner in a stunning victory.

That night, MacArthur saw the lights of Metz, 30 miles away, and was sure that the Americans could roll on right across the Hindenburg Line and begin the great breakthrough. Whether such a new army could have continued to advance so fast, and whether it could have supplied itself, are among the war's great unknowns, for Foch and Haig stuck to their grand strategy.

The great assault

Foch's plan was to launch a huge pincer movement, with the British on the far left, the French in the center and the Americans on the right. In the southern sector—along the Meuse river—this attack would be even more ferocious than St. Mihiel: 37 French and American divisions, spearheaded by 700 tanks, would slice north through the forests of the Argonne toward Sedan, cutting a railway that would be one of the main German lines of retreat. The Americans faced a tough assignment, for they would have to cover 30 miles of difficult country faster than their St. Mihiel penetration, and cross the Kriemhilde Line, as this local section of the Hindenburg Line was called.

The assault on September 26 started off well, largely because the Allies could not afford failure and so limited their objectives to fast, piecemeal advances across land already devastated by every combination of artillery fire—high explosives, mortars and gas. At last, the artillery had learned the advantage of accuracy over mere weight of metal. They perfected the rolling barrage, with shells landing just ahead of advancing infantry so that enemy gunners had no chance of redeploying their machine guns.

On September 28, far to the north, Haig launched the Fourth Battle of Ypres, supported by 500 planes. The next day, the British troops crossed the supposedly impregnable fortifications of the Hindenburg Line, clambering over ramps of earth thrown up by the shells, and crossing the St. Quentin Canal over bridges the Germans had not dared to blow. This was no isolated advance. Along a 30-mile front the British seized 10,000 prisoners, took 200 guns and

CANAL ATTACK Canadian troops cross open ground near the St. Quentin Canal in late September 1918. Caterpillar tracks show where tanks led the attack. At last the war had broken free of the straitjacket of the trenches.

broke through into open country. As a South African, Major Deneys Reitz, serving with the 1st Royal Scots Fusiliers, wrote: "From then onward the evil of the old trench warfare was a thing of the past."

On the far right, the nine divisions of Americans advancing toward Sedan also made a good start, supported by 189 tanks and 800 aircraft. But they owed their initial success to the Germans' fighting retreat. Just as the Americans were becoming disordered by the speed of their advance, and supplies were locked in a logjam of traffic behind the advancing front line, they ran into intense resistance and were forced to a halt. Other hard-fought advances followed

until, on October 10, the Americans were clear of the forest but still dogged by nagging supply problems.

Pershing, pressured by Foch to make progress before winter set in, fired officers, reorganized the million men under his command, created a new army and attacked again, only to see his divisions mercilessly flayed by German machine guns. "They're first-rate troops," noted French Jesuit Teilhard de Chardin, then a stretcher-bearer. "Fighting with intense individual passion against the enemy and wonderful courage. The only complaint one would make of them is that they don't take sufficient care. They're apt to get themselves killed." In their eagerness and inexperience, 120,000 American troops became casualties in the forests of the Argonne.

When the exhausted Americans resumed their advance again on November 1, they prepared the ground with ½-ton shells fired from naval guns mounted on railroad wagons, and with 36,000 mustard-gas shells—the first time Americans had used this weapon. The Germans fell back, and back. Seeing Sedan at last within reach, Pershing wanted the Americans to have "the honor of entering" it, although it was in the French sector. In the end, Pershing's local commander, General Hunter Liggett, invited the French to enter Sedan first, thus allowing France to repossess the town taken by the Germans in

1870. It could not have been a more fitting end to the battle: the day the French entered Sedan was also the day the war ended.

Ludendorff had insisted on September 29 that Germany had to ask for an armistice. The British use of tanks at Amiens on August 8 had shown him the impossibility of victory; and the battles of the St. Mihiel salient, Argonne and Ypres in September raised the possibility of an Allied breakthrough. But it was the collapse of the Central Powers in a different theater entirely that convinced him beyond doubt that he had to seek an armistice. On September 29, Bulgaria had fallen after a 15-day onslaught by the British, French and a medley of Balkan allies moving up from Salonica.

Preparing for peace

The fall of Bulgaria destroyed any remaining hope of help from Germany's allies. In the south, Austria-Hungary was on the point of collapse in its war against Italy. Already the Czechs had declared their independence, and had been recognized by Italy, France and Britain. Now, with the Bulgarians defeated and driven out of Serbia, the Serbs too would be free to fight against their old enemy. With the Austro-Hungarian empire in tatters, Germany had nothing to protect it from invasion from the south. Turkey would be no help, for the Ottoman Empire was a corpse as well, with the British advancing northward from Palestine into Syria.

In his headquarters in Spa (a Belgian town whose curative waters provided the name for

VICTORY AMID THE RUINS Canadian soldiers cross a square in Cambrai, just taken from the Germans, on October 9, 1918. The Germans had held Cambrai since August 1914.

LIFE IN THE PRISONER-OF-WAR CAMPS

FOR THE TENS OF THOUSANDS TAKEN PRISONER ON ALL SIDES LOOMED THE PROSPECT OF SPENDING THE REST OF THE WAR IN SPECIAL CAMPS, OFTEN IN DISMAL CONDITIONS

Between 1914 and 1918, some 8 million prisoners were taken. By August 1915, the Germans held 330,000 British, French and Belgian troops; on the Somme, between July and November 1916, the Allies took 72,000 Germans prisoner. And these figures paled in comparison with the numbers taken in the east. After their victory at Tannenberg, the Germans took 92,000 Russians prisoner in a week.

Despite the unprecedented horrors of industrialized war, all belligerents considered themselves bound by the "rules of war," as defined by a series of conventions agreed to in Geneva and The Hague over the previous decades. Given the bitterness of the combat, however, it is not surprising that in practice the prisoners were often poorly treated, sometimes atrociously. One British captive recorded his journey to camp by rail when he saw "25 of our men all bandaged up about the head and bleeding badly . . . We afterwards learned that the Guard and the loiterers outside the station had set about them with whips, sticks and ropes with steel rings in them and butts of rifles."

LITTER-BEARERS German prisoners carry a wounded Canadian.

Prisoners were often put to work, for which they were supposed to be paid (and sometimes were). One British prisoner at a camp in Tournai had many occupations, "making railways, tramways, emptying coal barges, cleaning streets, removing shells from trucks, carrying German wounded from the trains to hospital." In Russia, 15,000 German and Austrian prisoners joined 45,000 other laborers building the Murmansk-Petrograd railway.

The Russians usually suffered worst. Many of the prisoners from Tannenberg were sent to a camp in Wittenberg, where their daily rations were a 2-pound loaf of black bread shared among ten men and thin soup made from potato flour and beans. Three men sleeping in turns shared a mattress. A British prisoner among the 15,000 inmates noted that the Russians were not allowed to receive food parcels, and soon became "gaunt, of a peculiar gray pallor, and verminous." Many soon died, of hunger, cold and typhus. The administration tried to seal the camp off with dogs and machine guns until protests from abroad forced an improvement in conditions.

In November 1918, a massive repatriation program started. Some prisoners were able to take matters into their own hands. "Even though we were prisoners, we were paid," wrote a British captain imprisoned in Cologne. At the war's end, "They gave us money, debited against our account and it was accumulating all the time . . . The senior officers went to the Cologne Authorities and said 'Look here, can't we contact a boat?', so we chartered a boat down the Rhine."

WOUNDED AND CAPTIVE German prisoners in an English camp scribble notes for their families back at home.

health resorts generally), Ludendorff still did not equate the impossibility of victory with outright defeat. He hoped that an armistice would allow a dignified withdrawal to the heartland of Germany, which would then become a fortress. At least Germany would emerge from the war no worse off territorially than it had been in 1914. His colleagues pointed out that the Allies would object to a Germany still in the hands of its supreme commander, not a civilian. Ludendorff agreed, and the kaiser signed a proclamation establishing a civilian, parliamentary regime.

There was something Machiavellian in Ludendorff's decision. In Germany, unrest was growing and revolution threatened. Ludendorff calculated that it would be better to pre-empt trouble with a "revolution from above" than be rendered powerless by a "revolution from below." Furthermore, if civilians took on the task of negotiating an armistice, then the commanders would take less blame for Germany's defeat.

To head the new government Ludendorff turned to Max of Baden, a 51-year-old prince with impeccable liberal credentials, who had spent the war working for the Red Cross and for the welfare of prisoners of war on both sides. Ludendorff offered to appoint Prince Max chancellor, with the task of arranging an armistice. Max accepted, on the understanding that Parliament, not the kaiser, would have the right to make peace and that the kaiser would no longer have any

ROYAL MEDIATOR Prince Max of Baden, the kaiser's second cousin, was a liberal with a reputation for humanitarian activities.

control of the army and navy. The new chancellor still hoped that delay might lead to a reprieve, until the leading Socialist deputy, Philip Scheidemann, told him: "Better an end to terror than terror without end." On the day after his appointment, October 4, Prince Max opened negotiations with the Allies.

Prince Max appealed to the man whose intervention had made defeat inevitable, and the only Allied leader who had not talked in terms of revenge: President Wilson. In his note requesting a cease-fire, Prince Max accepted Wilson's Fourteen Points. This was an astute move, because it appealed to Wilson's peace-making instincts and offered him the opportunity to impose his ideals on the postwar world. Four days later, Wilson replied directly, without consulting Britain or France, wondering whether he had understood correctly. Would Germany really accept the Fourteen Points? If so, they had to evacuate all occupied territory, and then Wilson would broker a cease-fire with his allies.

Meanwhile, the war was still in progress, and the threat of revolution ever more real. On October 6, the revolutionary socialists and communists called the Spartacists demanded an end to the German monarchy and to the rule of the officers and the rich who had dri-

ven their country to collapse. All along the Western Front, the Allies were pressing forward. On the 10th, a German submarine sank the *Leinster*, the ferry crossing from Kingstown (now Dun Laoghaire) to Holyhead, drowning 176, among them several Americans. This hardened Wilson's attitude. He told Prince Max that the armistice had to be negotiated between commanders. Civilians would talk peace, later. Ludendorff had by now recovered his nerve, believing that military defeat was not inevitable after all.

While the German victories of the spring and early summer had been well publicized,

ONE MAN'S VICTORY

On October 8, in the Argonne forest, American Corporal Alvin C. York won a place in military annals. With his patrol surrounded and outnumbered ten to one, York single-handedly shot 28 Germans and captured another 102 with their 28 machine guns. When his commander asked how many of those he had shot he actually killed, York, who had grown up on a Tennessee farm, said: "General, I would hate to think I missed any of them shots; they were all at pretty close range—50 or 60 yards. It weren't no trouble nohow for me to hit them big army targets. They were so much bigger than turkey heads."

amnesty for political prisoners, 20,000 people welcomed Karl Liebknecht. He was a Spartacist, who had been imprisoned in 1916 for leading a May Day rally calling for the overthrow of the government and an end to the war. Prince Max called a halt to submarine warfare and accepted Wilson's terms.

In Spa, Ludendorff again breathed fire into Hindenburg. Together, the generals prepared a telegram to all commanders, ordering a fight to the finish, then changed their minds—but not before the text of the telegram had been leaked. Prince Max was furious. Who was in control, the chancellor, commander-in-chief or kaiser? The kaiser made clear that it was not Ludendorff. On October 27, Ludendorff resigned. He was replaced by General Wilhelm Groener, who had organized German mobilization in 1914.

The allied commanders and Wilson's representative, Colonel E.M. House, met at Senlis, northeast of Paris, to argue over what they could hope to achieve. Pershing, whose troops were still pushing toward Sedan, was for continuing in order to enforce an unconditional surrender. The others disagreed. There had to be an armistice; but on what terms? The Germans were told to hand over quantities of arms and to withdraw from foreign soil. Britain wanted to end Germany's challenge to the seas by taking possession of the whole High Seas Fleet. The Allies stopped short of demanding the dissolution of the German army, which might yet prove useful as a bulwark against the spread of revolutionary Bolshevism.

The collapse on Germany's eastern and southern frontiers continued apace. Two great empires—Austria-Hungary and the Ottoman Empire—were in ruins. Indeed, on October 4, Austria-Hungary had requested Wilson to arrange an armistice, but was told that the Allies would deal only with the empire's former subjects once they were truly independent. In the last week of October, the Italians were driving Austrian troops

POVERTY AND HUNGER Berliners sift a garbage heap for anything edible. In blockaded Germany people were obliged to eat cats (known as "roof rabbits"), dogs and bread made from potato peelings and sawdust.

the reversals of August and September had been hushed up. The sudden revelation that Germany was so near defeat bewildered a nation already made destitute by food shortages. German troops were still beyond their own borders, as yet undefeated. To ordinary people, it seemed inexplicable that defeat should have come from nowhere. Bewilderment fed anger, and anger fed a spirit of revolt. Berlin had no meat and no potatoes, because there was no transport and no fuel. As Prince Max realized, there could be no further resistance because the German people would refuse to fight. When, in an attempt to stem the rising discontent, the kaiser declared

DISORDER ON THE STREETS Hunger, disillusion with the war and revolutionary agitation were a potent brew. Here, soldiers have been turned against striking workers in Berlin.

NEW MAN AT THE HELM Wilhelm Groener was a moderate conservative, who would later oppose the spread of Nazism.

back toward their own border, while Yugoslavs, Hungarians and Czechs were all on the brink of declaring their independence. On October 27, the Austrians asked for an armistice, and five days later their armistice commission, staying near Padua, signed an armistice with the Allied powers.

In the Middle East, General Allenby forced Mustafa Kemal out of Aleppo, the northernmost town in Syria, while British cavalrymen were advancing toward the Turks up the Euphrates. In an attempt to appease the victors, the Turks released General Townshend, a prisoner since the fall of Kut, and then sued for peace. The armistice with Turkey was signed on board the battleship *Agamemnon*, off the naval base of Mudros (Moudhros), on the island of Lemnos, on October 30. There was nothing now to stop the British sailing

THE END IS NEAR American soldiers pass a border post on their march into Germany in 1918. America's presence helped end the war.

through the Dardanelles and up the Danube.

Germany itself was approaching collapse, socially and politically—though not militarily. The German admirals were as steadfast as Ludendorff, and on October 28 they ordered the fleet, which was based mainly in Kiel, back into action. But the sailors would have none of it. Five times the order to set out to sea was given, and in response the stokers simply put out the ships' boiler-fires each time. Around 1,000 of the 3,000 mutineers were arrested and eight mutineers were killed; but the fleet remained at anchor. Some 20,000 troops joined the mutineers.

The revolt soon spread to Lübeck, Travemünde, Hamburg, Bremen, Cuxhaven, Wilhelmshaven and finally Berlin. As the

COUNTDOWN TO PEACE

British Colonel W.N. Nicholson, attached to the 15th Highland Division, described the last moments of the war:

"The Armistice was timed to commence at 11 a.m. on 11 November and till that hour there was heavy firing from the German lines. A German machine gun remained in action the whole morning opposite our lines. Just before 11 a.m. a thousand rounds were fired from it in a practically ceaseless burst. At five minutes to eleven, the machine-gunner got up, took off his hat to us, and walked away.

"At 11 a.m. there came a great cheering from the German lines; and the village church bells rang. But on our side there were only a few shouts. I had heard more for a rum ration. The match was over; it had been a damn bad game."

socialists and communists sensed imminent collapse, they moved toward an armed uprising. The kaiser even wondered whether he should abdicate in favor of his son. It seemed to Prince Max that the war had to be ended, not to avoid defeat, but to avoid revolution and to save the monarchy.

An armistice commission was set up under Matthias Erzberger, a minister who had long urged a negotiated peace and who had supported democratic reforms. On November 7, Erzberger telegraphed a message to Foch asking for a meeting. He and his small team drove through the night, across the front lines without any assurance that they would not be shot, shelled or bombed, and met Foch in his railway carriage in the forest of Compiègne.

There was little room for argument or delay, for the news from Berlin forced Erzberger to sign as fast as he could. Even as he transmitted the terms by telegraph to his government, that government was metamorphosing into something quite different.

On November 9, with socialists pressing for a republic, Prince Max announced the abdication of the kaiser, who was now at the military headquarters in Spa, Belgium. In Berlin, the newly-released communist, Karl Liebknecht, declared a Soviet republic, while the socialist leader Philipp Scheidemann declared a Socialist republic. Germany was tearing itself apart. The next day, Kaiser Wilhelm left for Holland by back roads. He lived on in retirement until 1941.

In Compiègne, meanwhile, Erzberger did what he could. He had to make peace, and there would be none until he signed. With so little room for maneuvering, he succeeded only in winning Allied agreement that the German army could keep some of its machine guns. He signed the armistice at

5 a.m. on November 11, though fighting would continue for another six hours in order to give time for all commanders to coordinate the cease-fire.

At 10 that morning Canadian troops entered Mons, from which the British had been driven in 1914. After four years and three months of war, the front line had shifted only a few yards. At 10:58 a.m., in the village of Ville-sur-Haine just east of Mons, a Canadian, Private George Price, was standing awaiting the moment of peace. A shot rang out from a German sniper. Price fell dead. He was the last of 60,661 Canadians to die, and perhaps the last of the war's battlefield victims. At 11 a.m., the eleventh hour of the eleventh day of the eleventh month, the guns fell silent at last.

A BUGLER PLAYS THE END TO WAR This French bugler sounded the cease-fire at 11 a.m. on November 11, 1918.

WAR IN WORDS AND IMAGES

THE PATRIOTIC ENTHUSIASM OF POETS AND ARTISTS TURNED TO BITTERNESS AND ANGER AT THE BRUTALITY AND MADNESS OF WAR

AVANT GARDE Guillaume Apollinaire served in the French infantry. Images of war run through his last collection of poems, *Calligrammes*, published in 1918.

Most who experienced the shock of war endured it in silence, seldom able to portray their suffering in words and images. But the war also sucked in writers and artists, figures such as the Cubist painter Georges Braque. When the war broke out he joined up as a sergeant in the French infantry, and was twice decorated for bravery before a severe head wound, treated with trepanation, brought his service to an end in 1915. He spent much of the rest of the war recuperating in the South of France.

On both sides such men threw themselves into the conflict, and many paid for their patriotism with their lives. Just a month after the outbreak of war, the French poet Charles Péguy was shot in the forehead as he stood observing a German retreat through field glasses. At the beginning of November 1914 the Austrian Expressionist poet Georg Trakl died of an overdose of cocaine on the Galician front. It was probably deliberate: he had joined up as a lieutenant in the Austrian army medical corps and had been traumatized by his experiences, including witnessing the agonies of desperately wounded soldiers in his care and the sight of other soldiers being shot for desertion. In March 1916 the German Expressionist painter Franz Marc, a leader of the influential *Blaue Reiter* (Blue Rider) movement, was killed by a shell at Verdun. Weakened by a wound to his head, the avant-garde French poet Guillaume Apollinaire died of Spanish influenza just two days before the Armistice in November 1918.

All of these men experienced the horrors of the war, but it was a group of English-speaking writers who focused particularly sharply on the task of expressing and trying to make sense of them. For an immediate response, verse proved to be the most effective means of expression; poems could be scribbled on the backs of envelopes, many of which were found in the pockets of their dead authors.

For these men, the shock of war was extraordinary. They had grown up in societies in which people knew their places and patriotism was ingrained. In 1914, lines of smiling volunteers had looked forward to a quick victory. Glory, honor, self-sacrifice: nobody had dreamed what dedication to such ideals might mean. For many of the young poets, the war was to be merely another match in the great game of life, a blithe bravado typified on occasions when some young officer led a charge toward enemy lines kicking a soccer ball. A sense of what Wilfred Owen called "new crusades and modern knightliness" was captured by Rupert Brooke, one of the first of the war poets to be

"THINK ONLY THIS OF ME" The blithe patriotism of Rupert Brooke (far left) ensured the success of his *War Sonnets* (1915). The angrier tone of Wilfred Owen (left) was less popular at the time.

THE LOST GENERATION

Some 40 published poets died on active service. They included:

Raymond Asquith	The Somme, 1916
Rupert Brooke	Skiros, 1915
Leslie Coulson	The Somme, 1916
Jeffrey Day	Shot down, 1918
Julian Grenfell	Died of wounds, 1915
W.N. Hodgson	The Somme, 1916
T.M. Kettle	The Somme, 1916
Francis Ledwidge	Flanders, 1917
John McCrae	Died of pneumonia, 1918
E.A. Mackintosh	Cambrai, 1917
Wilfred Owen	Sambre Canal, 1918
Robert Palmer	Mesopotamia, 1916
Isaac Rosenberg	Rifle Wood, 1918
Alan Seeger	The Somme, 1916
Patrick Shaw-Stewart	Western Front, 1917
C.H. Sorley	Loos, 1915
E.W. Tennant	The Somme, 1916
R.E. Vernede	Havrincourt Wood, 1917
T.P. Cameron Wilson	The Somme, 1918

published. He was among the 8,000 who arrived to help to defend Antwerp in October 1914, driving from Ostend in London buses. Brooke welcomed the war in fine romantic form:

Now, God be thanked Who has matched us
with His hour,
And caught our youth, and wakened us
from sleeping.

At that heady moment, drunk with excitement, Brooke could see blood as "the red sweet wine of youth," poured like a sacrifice that would revive a jaded civilization. Brooke seemed the very embodiment of his own sentiments: sporting, well-educated, handsome, talented and admired by most of the other war poets. He died in 1915, and the task of expressing the sheer horror of war fell to others.

Brooke himself had foreseen an end in "some corner of a foreign field that is for ever England." It was one of the war's countless ironies that he died not blown apart or felled on the Western

SHOCKED INTO MATURITY Siegfried Sassoon won a British honor during the war, but later threw his medal away in disgust at the cruelty and waste of the conflict.

Front, but of dysentery and an infected mosquito bite on the Greek island of Skiros, on his way to Gallipoli. He was buried on a hilltop by mourners who included Bernard Freyberg—New Zealand's greatest war hero, who would survive both world wars, winning a string of decorations—and another poet, Patrick Shaw-Stewart, killed in France in 1917.

The poets, the majority of them junior officers, were exposed more than most, and a high proportion of them died—the life-expectancy of a junior officer was about nine months. It is hardly surprising, then, that the war—and the Somme in particular—soon inspired a different type of poetry: of disillusion, anger and sadness, all wrapped in evocations of the noise and stench of trench warfare. If the form of the poetry was rarely innovative, its content was. "My subject is War, and the pity of War," wrote Wilfred Owen, and few had attempted that before. A wagon-wheel crunching over a dead man's face—an image in a poem by Isaac Rosenberg—was not in the tradition of Wordsworth and Keats. But it did capture the truth of the war as mere facts could not.

Title Page reproduced from the edition of the Poem illuminated by Ernest Clegg

"IF YE BREAK FAITH" John McCrae's "In Flanders Fields" was published anonymously in December 1915. He served with the Canadian army medical corps and wrote the poem after days spent tending the wounded.

Indeed, at a time when facts were restricted by censorship, poetry provided insights that would not otherwise have been available.

Wilfred Owen, delicate and dreamy as a boy, was one of those forced into maturity in the trenches. His first experience of the front in January 1917 filled him with horror, outrage and pity for the helpless victims, the boys whose youth and beauty he eulogized. After being shelled in a forward position for days, he was said to have "shell shock" and admitted to Craiglockhart Hospital near Edinburgh, Scotland, where he met two other writers, Siegfried Sassoon and Robert Graves. Tormented by what would now be termed "survivor guilt," he returned to France. "I came out in order to help these boys," he wrote to his mother. "Directly by leading them as well as an officer can; indirectly by watching their sufferings that I may speak of them as well as a pleader can." He pleaded for them by recording in verse the starkest images, the shattered limbs, the blood, the pain:

What passing-bells for these who die as cattle?
—Only the monstrous anger of the guns.
Only the stuttering rifles' rapid rattle
Can patter out their hasty orisons.
No mockeries for them; no prayers nor bells;
Nor any voice of mourning save the choirs, –
The shrill, demented choirs of wailing shells;
And bugles calling for them from sad shires.

Owen died, at the young age of 25, in a hail

April 1915
Death of
Rupert Brooke

December 1915
John McCrae's
"In Flanders Fields"

ABSURD WAR, ABSURD ART

The horrific absurdity of the war and the bourgeois world that had engendered it should be met with absurd art: this was the belief of a group of artists and writers, from different countries but united in their disgust at the war, who had gathered in Zurich in neutral Switzerland by 1916. Led by figures such as the sculptor and painter Jean Arp and the poet Richard Hülsenbeck, they even called their movement by an absurd name: Dada, the French for hobbyhorse.

AGAINST WAR Although Henri Barbusse was twice cited for gallantry, his novel *Le Feu* (1916) was a fierce attack on the war, written from the point of view of an entire squad.

of machine-gun fire on the Sambre Canal, seven days before the Armistice.

Siegfried Sassoon underwent a conversion from Brooke-like naiveté to Owen-like anger. From an intellectual background, he had written lightweight romantic verse before the war changed him. He was a superb officer, but condemned the war in acerbic style:

"Good morning; good morning!" the
   General said
When we met him last week on our way to
   the line.
Now the soldiers he smiled at are most
   of 'em dead,
And we're cursing his staff for incompetent
   swine.
"He's a cheery old card," grunted Harry to Jack
As they slogged up to Arras with rifle and pack.
But he did for them both with his plan
   of attack.

Dozens of others produced war poetry. Americans included Alan Seeger, John Peale

Bishop, Mark van Doren, Edmund Wilson and Archibald MacLeish. The Canadian doctor John McCrae wrote "In Flanders Fields," one of the war's most famous poems, before dying of pneumonia in 1918.

Art as therapy

Artists, too, gave vivid expression to the horrors of the war. Those who fought ranged from the Austrian Oskar Kokoschka to the Frenchman Georges Rouault, the German Otto Dix to the Italian Futurist Umberto Boccioni. The British government even commissioned special war artists including Paul Nash, whose *Menin Road* would become one of the war's most enduring painted images.

In the field of writing, longer works such as novels and memoirs took

time to appear. One novel, *Le Feu* (*Under Fire*), by the Frenchman Henri Barbusse, became established as an anti-war classic during the war itself (Owen

read it while in the hospital). After 1918, works of fiction and personal histories soon numbered in the hundreds. Among the novels, perhaps the greatest was the German Erich Maria Remarque's bitter portrait of the war, *All Quiet on the Western Front* (1929), but there were many others in many languages,

WAR ON CANVAS Like many others, the British artist John Nash took his paint set (above) with him to the front. In the *Menin Road* (left), his brother Paul evoked the desolation wrought on nature itself by the war. Both brothers were official war artists; both also served in the unit known as the Artists Rifles, originally raised as a volunteer corps in 1860.

April 1917
Wilfred Owen
shell shocked

June 1917
Exhibition of Paul Nash
paintings, London

July 1917
Sassoon admitted
to a hospital

November 1918
Deaths of Apollinaire
and Owen

THE WAR THROUGH THE LENS

MAKESHIFT DEVELOPMENTS Men of Britain's Mobile Photographic Section (above) wash photographic plates in a ditch. Right: An Atkin Swan airplane camera.

The First World War was the first major conflict to be recorded in photographs. Before the war, photographers had been hampered by heavy equipment. Now, cameras could be hand-held, and amateurs had pocket Kodaks. Many professional photographers, however, still used glass plates rather than the new, but less sensitive, film, and they did their own developing. The use of film and long lenses proved vital in aerial reconnaissance. Later in the war, thousands of pictures were taken daily from the air, using specially designed cameras such as the Atkin Swan.

On the ground, the new genre was limited by official suspicion—the British armed forces appointed only 16 official photographers, France had about 30, and Germany had 60. Though there were many more accredited Allied photographers—half of them on the Western Front—few recorded front-line action (Captain Charles Bean, Australia's first official correspondent, was an exception).

Major newspapers were slow to use photographs, but the popular press and magazines were hungry for work from professionals and amateurs alike. Photographers such as Britain's Ernest Brooks captured enduring images of the war's grimness and squalor.

from the Czech Jaroslav Hasek's darkly comic masterpiece, *The Good Soldier Schweik* (1920-3), to Ernest Hemingway's *A Farewell to Arms* (1929).

Robert Graves wrote one of the most famous memoirs, *Goodbye to All That* (1929). He later observed: "The memoirs of a man who went through some of the worst experiences of trench warfare are not truthful if they do not contain a high proportion of falsities." His book's truth is that of a novel, not a formal history, the horror heightened with absurdity. In one incident, two men report that they have just shot their company sergeant major:

The adjutant said: 'Good heavens, how did that happen?'

'It was an accident, sir.'

'What do you mean, you damn fools? Did you mistake him for a spy?'

'No, sir, we mistook him for our platoon sergeant.'

TO HELL AND BACK In *L'Enfer* (*Hell*), the French artist Georges Leroux presented a vision of the war that few participants, whether artists, writers or simply soldiers, could quarrel with.

Those who survived never really escaped the war. In 1922, T.E. Lawrence ("of Arabia") wrote to Graves, wondering why so many of their friends could not "get away from the war": "Here are you riddled with thought like any old table-leg with worms; [Siegfried Sassoon] yawing about like a ship aback; me . . . finding squalor and maltreatment the only permitted existence; what's the matter with us all?" These three were typical of millions. The war was the defining event of their lives, the source of nightmares and inspiration and pain for years to come. Writing and painting were attempts to come to terms with the experience. By making their pain public, the artists, poets, novelists and memoir-writers helped men and women rebuild their shattered lives. It is an unending task, as writers today still mine the experience, emotions and effects of the war.

BEYOND THE WAR ZONE

THE DEMANDS OF WAR SEEPED INTO ALL ASPECTS OF LIFE. WITH MEN AT THE FRONT, WOMEN HAD TO TAKE ON MANY OF THEIR JOBS. FOOD SHORTAGES LED TO LONG LINES AND RATIONING. UNREST IN IRELAND LED TO THE ABORTIVE EASTER UPRISING OF 1916. IN 1917 RUSSIA'S TSARIST REGIME BUCKLED UNDER THE STRAIN OF WAR, OPENING THE WAY FOR THE EPOCH-MAKING EVENTS OF OCTOBER WHEN LENIN AND THE BOLSHEVIKS FINALLY CAME TO POWER.

DREAMS OF GLORY

THE FIRST TWO YEARS OF WAR BROUGHT INDUSTRIAL AND SOCIAL TURMOIL THAT CHANGED LIFE IN THE COMBATANT NATIONS FOREVER

By 1914, Europe had become the world's dominant culture, spreading its roots westward to the New World and eastward across Russia to Japan. For 40 years there had been peace, but the time had come when it seemed to those in power that war offered greater opportunities. Those leaders were proved wrong in the most devastating way, for in the following four years they began the process that would, over the coming decades, undermine the dominance of the very culture they represented.

No one foresaw such an outcome. Every national leader thought he was defending his nation's interests, though "defense" almost always meant "attack." To attack, nations called upon developments that were totally new in history—industrial might, speedy transport and mass communication—developments so new that no one except a few visionaries had a clear understanding of them. They thought it would be a matter of a few battles and a rapid conclusion—it would be "all over by Christmas," the British told each other.

The mobilization of British society

In Britain, it was the war minister, Lord Kitchener, who described for his colleagues what modern war might mean. It would not be over in three months, he said in the autumn of 1914. It would take three years and demand millions of men to match the German commitment. When conscription was ruled out as politically unacceptable, Kitchener relied on emotional blackmail to persuade volunteers to join his New Army. From placards across the land, Kitchener's stern features and accusing finger brought home his message: "Your country needs YOU." Another poster, "To the Young Women of London," asked: "Is your 'Best Boy' wearing Khaki? If not, don't

THE BRITISH TOMMY The British private, the backbone of the British army, had the nickname "Tommy" after "Thomas Atkins," the name used on sample army forms at the time of the Napoleonic Wars.

you think he should be?" The campaign succeeded brilliantly: 175,000 men joined up in the first week, 750,000 in the first month, and 2.5 million by March 1916, when conscription ended voluntary enlistment. Many of these volunteers served in "Pals battalions," each made up of men drawn from a particular town, profession or work group. At that time it was the largest volunteer army ever raised. In the first few weeks, the experience of war reflected the structure of British society. The working class—the 80 percent of the population who earned less than the income tax threshold of £160 (about $320) per year—was no worse off than the middle class, the middle 10 and 18 percent of the population.

As the war took hold, however, its effects bit deep, for the needs of Kitchener's New Army were out of all proportion to its supplies. Kitchener, who was also in charge of supply and strategy, was rapidly out of his depth. When the Western Front bogged down in trench warfare, he said despairingly:

SWEARING LOYALTY These office workers, recruited in December 1915, were among the last of Britain's 2.5 million volunteers. In early 1916 conscription was introduced.

"I don't know what is to be done; this is not war." Initially, the army's requirements were supposed to be met by 20 clerks in the War Office's Army Contracts department. Trade unions kept unskilled men and women off the factory floor.

For the first time, the government seized control of national resources. For the manufacture of munitions alone, 20,000 small factories were established, through which poured some £2 billion ($8 billion). The war

March 1915
Appeal for British women
to go into war work

April 1915
First Zeppelin
raid on London

March 1916
Conscription comes
into effect in Britain

MUNITIONS WORKERS Tough work in shell factories brought working-class British women a new sense of power and independence.

effort produced a range of unanticipated effects. Income tax was raised; profiteers became society's new enemies within; the national debt rose tenfold; interest rates on war loans were favorable. Consumer goods took second place, imports were restricted and prices rose. During the war, the pound lost two-thirds of its domestic buying power. Internationally, however, it remained strong, in part because the balance of payments remained favorable, in part because American loans made up for the loans Britain made to her allies.

The demand for workers conflicted with the demand for soldiers—only munitions workers could avoid the imputation of cowardice directed against those who did not volunteer, and later only munitions workers were exempted from the call-up. Even so, some 5 million industrial workers joined the armed forces in the course of the war, a loss that had to be made up mainly by women, by the wounded, and by increased efficiency in production. Despite union militancy, Lloyd George's policy of union conciliation ensured that strikes were kept to a minimum—working days lost during the war (4.2 million) averaged a quarter of prewar losses and just one-tenth of those in 1919-21.

Compliance was also achieved by the growing fear of suffering

November 1916
Government in Germany
handed over to military control

A CLIMATE OF HATRED

In war, it has been said, the first victim is the truth. Xenophobic hysteria certainly accompanied the outbreak of the First World War, in which rumor and the popular press fed each other atrocity stories that had no basis in fact but were, nevertheless, widely believed. This was particularly true in Britain, where the real horrors of war were kept at a distance by the Channel. In their invasion of Belgium, Germans were said to have bayoneted babies and raped nuns. Under the headline "Horrible Stories of German Fiendishness," *The War Illustrated* reported: "British war correspondents in Belgium have seen little murdered children with roasted feet. The tiny mites were hung over a fire before they were slain . . . The things done to Belgian girls and women . . . are so unspeakably dreadful that details cannot be printed." Such stories formed part of a climate of hatred. Long-term residents of German origin were interned on the Isle of Man. Shops with German-sounding names were sacked. There were rumors of people throwing stones at dachshunds, dogs that were seen as German because of their name. One owner protected his pet—as the *Daily Mirror* reported on August 18 —by bedecking it with red, white and blue ribbons and a label proclaiming: "I am a naturalized British subject."

Germans, equally appalled at the consequences of war, were astonished by such crass propaganda. One German wrote later of seeing a French paper showing "an awkward, plain girl, supposed to be a German, gazing enraptured at a slim hand, adorned with two rings, that was cut off at the wrist—allegedly the hand of a French woman."

HORROR This illustration from a French postcard reflects stories of German atrocities that fuelled anti-German feeling.

patriotic, economic and political. Tens of thousands of women took on their husbands' trades, as chimney sweeps, delivery-cart drivers, railway workers, even gravediggers. Some 1.6 million women started working in factories, to which male-dominated unions reluctantly agreed, providing that it was only for the duration. Some 250,000 women went to work on the land, 100,000 joined the armed forces, another 100,000 became nurses. Tens of thousands became voluntary workers in welfare service. Around 200,000

FLOODLIT ATTACK A night-time Zeppelin bombing raid on London was commemorated by a German artist.

and poverty. Sylvia Pankhurst, in her book *The Home Front*, recorded: "Men not medically fit for the Army were to be enrolled at the Labor Exchange where . . . they were nevertheless given the alternative of munition work or the Army. It was assumed of course they would choose the former alternative. As a condition of getting the work which would thus save him from the trenches, each unfit man must 'voluntarily' sign a form binding him to work wherever the

Ministry of Munitions might direct . . . The Orient steamship line threatened to hand over to the military authorities any employee who refused to accept the wage reduction of £1 8s [$3] a month. Few men could resist such pressure. Remember that for the unfit man taken into the Army there was no pension if his health broke down under training; no pension for his family if he died."

As breadwinners vanished to the front, housewives were threatened with destitution. They had no alternative but to look after themselves, and most were eager to do so, for reasons that were

entered government departments, and some 800,000 became engineering workers. In serving their country, women also served their own cause. Fashions became less restrictive, skirts shorter, hats smaller. Women could even be seen buying rounds of drinks in pubs.

For the first time in history, civilians became directly involved in a struggle taking place elsewhere. The first Zeppelin appeared over the British coast on December 29, 1914, and in April 1915 London suffered its first air raid.

HAND-OUT A paper ruler advertises the wages and pensions paid to Australian soldiers, to tempt recruits.

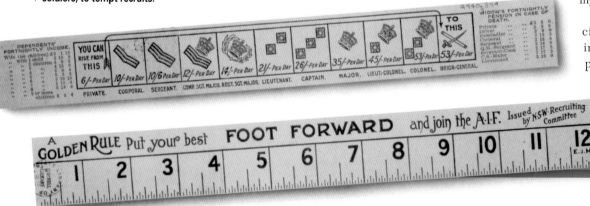

LOTTIE WIGGINS GOES TO WORK

In April 1916 Lottie Wiggins and her friend Polly applied to the munitions factory in Chilwell, and was taken to the Filled Shell Store, which covered 7 acres and could hold 500,000 shells:

"After some controversy about my age, I was only 17 and the authorized age was 18, I was taken on as an over-head-crane driver . . . We could hardly believe our eyes. We had to ascend a ladder to man the crane and descend by way of a rope. I was never very brave but this procedure fairly took the cake. If I failed to mount the ladder I would be out of work, so up I went, but it was some time before I mastered the rope.

"My first impression of that was sheer fright, rows and rows of 8-inch, 6-inch and 9-inch shells, not forget-ting the 12-inch, which reached to my waist and higher. I hardly dared walk near them, but overcame this feeling . . . We were on eight-hour shifts at first, but this was changed to 12 hours, this meant two shifts instead of three. Twelve hours Monday to Saturday, then we changed to 18 hours, going on duty at 6 o'clock Saturday evening and working to 2 o'clock Sunday afternoon when the opposite shift would take over . . . No one would work those long hours today, the Unions would step in. Of course this was war and everyone was out to get results . . . Practically every big shell fired by the British during the Battle of the Somme was filled at Chilwell."

In one notorious raid on the night of September 2-3, 1916, Zeppelins dropped 500 bombs between Gravesend and Peterborough. Only four people died, but Londoners witnessed one of the most dramatic episodes of the war on the Home Front when the massive SL (Schütte-Lanz) 11, over $^{1}/_{4}$ mile long and 230 feet high, was shot down in flames by W. Leefe Robinson in his biplane, a feat for which he was awarded the Victoria Cross.

Germany gears up

Across the Channel, the govern-ments of opposing nations also found that they had to take con-trol of economic life on an unprecedented scale. Old liberal ideas of laissez-faire—allowing market forces to rule supreme—and notions about individual rights were set aside. Where commitment or efficiency failed, society divided against itself and defeat followed. Austria-Hungary, Turkey and Russia all proved too divided to endure under pressure. The British Empire survived as a unit only because its constituent parts made a choice to match Britain's commitment.

In Germany the war was greeted with joy, captured in the memoirs of the chancellor, Theobald von Bethmann-Hollweg: "The memory of that time can only evoke feelings of reverence. It was a time when every self-interest and particularism was dissolved away in a universal corporate consciousness, when, as if by some powerful instinct, one could not help but see in the Fatherland an order of things of a higher and holier kind, deserving of the last drop of blood and the last ounce of treasure."

This unanimity was achieved with the backing of the Socialists who, swept along by the giddiness of war, joined with other parties in a so-called *Burgfriede*, a "fortress peace," by which they agreed not to criticize each other or the government. Here, as elsewhere, men who had spent a lifetime railing against war suddenly gloried in its coming. Wilhelm II declared: "I recognize no parties; I recognize only Germans."

The German economy was well set up to sustain a short, sharp war. The gold reserve was healthy. German iron and steel manufacture exceed-ed that of Britain and France and all their allies. The stock market remained open, as did the banks. The first war loan brought in 4.5 billion marks ($640 million), making it the largest loan to that date. Though the first food restrictions were introduced in late 1914, and Germans began to substitute pota-to flour for grain flour, there was no lack of bulk or nutrition. Hotels, restaurants and shops did good business. Anyway, Germans were happy to tighten their belts, as long as it was only a notch or two. For a while, asceticism was chic. *Wanderredner*, travelling

GERMAN REACTION A German poster asks "Who is the Militarist?" Bottom: Volunteers in Berlin join up.

OFFICIAL SCAVENGERS German children in Brunswick, members of the local AVG (Abfall-Verwertungs-Gesellschaft or Rubbish Utilization Society), collect potato peelings.

lecturers, instructed eager audiences on methods of chewing food for maximum nutrition.

But there were weaknesses in the economy. Germany's rich agriculture depended on imported fertilizer, its iron and steel industries on imported ore, and its economy on a host of metals, chemicals and materials, such as manganese, chromium, molybdenum, asphalts, phosphates, rubber, cotton, silk, petroleum, nitrates, sulphur, graphite, and asbestos. When German vessels were hounded from the seas, all imports except those that could be brought in slowly and in small quantities by road and rail suddenly dried up.

The German government at once gave army commanders civil powers. It was not enough. Within a few weeks, and as the war turned from one of movement to one of stagnation, as its scope widened to include Central Europe and the Middle East, Walther Rathenau was put in charge of providing raw materials for state corporations and of devising a system of strict priorities. Rathenau, inheritor of the huge AEG industrial combine, a scientist, writer, industrialist and statesman, was Germany's Lloyd George: practically single-handed, he made it possible for his country to endure for four years. In April 1915, Rathenau declared that supplies were secure.

But organization, requisition and centralized buying could not fulfill requirements. New industries had to evolve. For instance, Germany had a 50 percent shortfall in nitrates, of which it had consumed 1.4 million tons in 1913. Now the army clamored for nitrates, which were vital for the manufacture of explosives. Germany had developed a means of making nitrates out of atmospheric nitrogen, but it was expensive. New plants were pressed into service. The army's consumption of nitrates increased from 12,000 tons per month in 1914 to 40,000 tons in January 1916, and eventually to 100,000 tons a month.

By the winter of 1915, scarcity was starting to bite. Cotton, wool and leather were becoming rarities in the stores. Housewives learned to scrimp and patch. People clattered about the streets in clogs. Housewives became used to substitutes: margarine, artificial coffee, gravy tablets, dried soups, clover-meal, chestnut flour.

The following year, the increasing shortages and the growing demand from the front line created a munitions crisis, at the same time as Britain was resolving its own shortages. In November 1916, the government set up a Supreme Command (Oberste

THE VICTIM WHO FORGAVE

Edith Cavell, the daughter of a Norfolk clergyman, became the first nationally acclaimed heroine and female war martyr. A professional nurse with a long career behind her, she was in 1914 the 49-year-old director of the Berkendael school of nursing in Brussels. When the city fell to the Germans and her institute became a Red Cross hospital, she remained at her post and decided to help Allied soldiers caught behind enemy lines, aiding some 200 to escape into neutral Holland. Her actions, however, were in contravention of military law and she was arrested, tried by a German military court, found guilty and sentenced to death. The sentence was considered an outrage by the Allies because she was condemned only for humanitarian aid, not espionage.

On the night before her execution on October 12, she told the American Legation chaplain: "This I would say, standing as I do in view of God and eternity: I realize that patriotism is not enough. I must have no hatred or bitterness towards anyone." The next morning, after pinning her long skirt tightly around her ankles so that it would not lift as she fell, she was shot.

Her death was seized upon by the Allies, for whom she became a symbol of bravery and innocence in the face of Prussian barbarism. Her execution led to an upsurge of anti-German feeling in Britain and the U.S., fuelled by a rumor that she had fainted in front of the firing squad and had been shot while unconscious by the officer on duty.

FRENCH SHELL-MAKERS In France, as in all belligerent countries, women made up the bulk of the work force in munitions factories.

Heeresleitung, or OHL) to place all industry at the service of the war effort. Under the regulations of the so-called Hindenburg Program, every civilian male between 17 and 60 was compelled to serve in industry. Women were urged to volunteer for munitions work, children were led out to scavenge for waste paper, old rubber and scrap metal. It was an unprecedented effort to mold a society toward a single end: victory. In the end, after imposing much suffering, it could not prevent the opposite: defeat, and its offspring, collapse and revolution.

France on the front line

France bore the brunt of the war in the West. When the German advance was halted, Germany held the 6 percent of France that included most French resources of iron and coal, and some of its best agricultural land. Moreover, most French soldiers came from the countryside—of the 3 million who

HELPING THE TROOPS In a makeshift sweatshop, French women repair soldiers' uniforms.

mobilized in 1914, almost half were peasants. In the last months of 1914, France was left with its industrial base eroded, much of its richest lands occupied, and few men to work the remainder. Of 125 blast furnaces, 95 lay in war zones. French farms, relying by necessity on women and children, never supplied enough grain, sugar or meat.

The burden of industrial work was carried in part by women. "If the women working in the factories stopped for 20 minutes,"

General Joffre once remarked, "France would lose the war." But the role of women in France differed from that in other European nations. Already before the war, about 40 percent of women went out to work —a higher percentage than in any other European nation. France had twice as many married women in work as England. In 1914, half of the female workers were on farms, and a quarter in industry, where they formed half the work force (the rest were in

domestic service, commerce and the professions). This balance remained constant through the war. As a result, the war changed life less for lower-class women than for the daughters of the middle class.

Another peculiarity of France was the power of the military over the civilian authorities. Since the front line was on French soil, the army controlled a good deal of the territory, a power base reinforced by the government's flight to Bordeaux for three months at the end of 1914. For three years, the military remained dominant, under Joffre, as attack followed fruitless attack and casualties mounted. It was only the rising tide of casualties that finally brought the downfall of Joffre, and it was not until Clemenceau came to office in late 1917 that the civilian authority seized full control.

The Russian Home Front

Russians, too, united to rejoice at the onset of war. On August 2, 1914, in St. Petersburg, 300,000 stood outside the Winter Palace, hoping for a glimpse of Tsar Nicholas II.

RUSSIAN HOSPITAL In Suwalki, eastern Poland, a Russian doctor redresses the leg of an amputee, with no attempt at sterilization.

FACE OF STARVATION A Russian peasant weakened by disease and hunger is tended by his wife and daughter.

Inside, the tsar repeated the oath that Alexander I had made in 1812: "I shall not make peace so long as a single enemy remains on the soil of Russia." When he stepped out onto the balcony, the vast crowd went down on its knees. All parties swore devotion to Holy Russia, to the tsar, to the cause of victory.

For a few weeks, the promise of that joy seemed fulfilled. Factories were fat with government contracts and wages rose. But the good times did not last. With 5 million called up—15 percent of the male population—industries soon declined, revealing the underlying weakness of Russian economic and political institutions. With the Baltic and western frontiers closed, imports dried up. The Trans-Siberian railway was open to Vladivostok, but it was single track and 4,000 miles long. Murmansk in the north was ice-free, but it lacked a rail link until 1916. Russia was isolated, and spiralled downward. By the second year of war, even the simplest tools, such as axes and spades, were hard to come by. At the front, men deserted, causing one minister to report: "The men are saying, 'Why should we perish of hunger and cold, without boots; the artillery is silent, and we are killed like partridges. The Germans are better off. Let us go.'"

In a collapsing society unable to supply its army, a vital role was played by voluntary organizations, the *zemstvos*. News of defeats were censored, but no one could censor the trainloads of wounded who arrived behind the lines, badly bandaged and unfed. One senior politician, Mikhail Rodzianko, President of the Duma, described how, after the Battle of Lodz, he came across a station where 18,000 men lay in mud and slush, awaiting attention from just 15 Polish volunteer doctors and nurses. When he went to the Carpathian front in November 1914, he noticed that soldiers were marching and fighting barefoot. It was the *zemstvos* who found, bought and delivered the boots.

In 1915, the *zemstvos* deployed their own purchasing agents, depots, warehouses, kitchens, orphanages, homes for widows, even military equipment—anything to make up for the inadequacy of the military authorities. It was the volunteers who cared for the refugees, fought the epidemics, countered starvation. Finance came in part from fundraising, but in large measure from the government, who thus obtained good, cheap services, and avoided the problems their policies created. That such organizations existed, arranged by the people for the people, was a terrible indictment of the bureaucrats and politicians, and provided fertile ground for the coming revolution.

THE DEPTHS OF SUFFERING

DURING THE SECOND HALF OF THE WAR, THE PEOPLE OF THE BELLIGERENT NATIONS ENDURED UNPRECEDENTED AGONIES

By 1917, all the fighting countries were suffering as never before. The French had sustained 3.3 million casualties, the Germans some 2.5 million, and the British over 1 million. It had become clear that if Germany did not starve Britain, Britain would starve Germany.

Attrition on the German Home Front

In mid-1916, Germany faced the grim consequences of extended war. Verdun had failed to break France's spirit; and there had been no great breakthrough to justify hopes of victory. The only possibility now lay in breaking Britain, which by German estimates had no more than 12 weeks' supply of food left. Ordinary people suddenly became experts on Britain's weaknesses, and the press demanded action. After the peace overture of December 1916 had fallen on deaf ears, the German government decided in January 1917 to return to unrestricted submarine warfare. The decision cleared the log jam in the land war, but not in the way Germany had intended. Britain did not collapse, and America was dragged into the war, introducing another great—and untried—industrialized power into the equation. Instead of the blockade lifting, it intensified. Instead of guaranteeing victory, Germany had guaranteed its own destruction.

For ordinary Germans, life became utter misery. On October 1, 1916, 30,000 people gathered in Frankfurt to demand peace, and the winter of 1916-7 became known as the "Turnip Winter," after the turnip flour used in place of wheat flour. Official food rations in 1917 were 1,000 calories a day, under half the subsistence minimum as defined by the health ministry. In the war years, the birthrate halved and infant mortality rose by 25 percent. In 1917, the average three-year-old was 2 pounds, 3 ounces underweight; and tuberculosis, in particular, took an increasing toll.

The suffering of the German people was mocked by the growth of the black market. People forced to face starvation were confronted by the sight of the influential obtaining supplies—*hintenherum*—by the back door. Carriages full of supplies disappeared, only to turn up in certain hotels and restaurants, or for sale on side streets at exorbitant prices. Up to 30 percent of all milk, butter, cheese, meat, eggs and fruit went on the black market at prices 10 times prewar levels.

After new food restrictions came into force in April 1917, suspicion and bitterness stalked the country. The bureaucracy that controlled rationing was so complex and so unfair that ordinary people were, in effect, invited to break the law in order to survive. The British were perceived as a lesser enemy than the man who could feed his family—the seedy character selling scarce goods or the bureaucrats in Berlin. That April, 125,000 workers in Berlin and Leipzig struck in protest. Unrest threatened to spread, not only over the issue of peace and shortages, but also over voting rights in Prussia, where returning soldiers had been deprived of the vote by a three-tier system that favored the privileged. There was no more *Burgfrieden*, or political truce, now. Opposition to the war was fomented by

HARD TIMES *Gulaschkanone*, vast vats of soup, were provided on street corners for Berliners. Germans also had milk ration cards (above).

a breakaway group of Social Democrats and revolutionaries who called themselves Spartacists, and peace was preserved in part only because the kaiser, in his Easter Message of 1917, hinted that he would reform the Prussian voting system.

But with the war continuing, there could be no improvement

PROPAGANDA IN THE CLASSROOM

German teachers were encouraged to play their part in sustaining support for the war. With so many teachers away at the front, a class was likely to have around 80 students. Typical lessons, as revealed by teacher-training documents in southwest Germany in 1917-8, might have been organized as follows.

The first lesson was German. The class analyzed a story in which two boys volunteer, because "we want to fight courageously so that the French cannot come into our homeland and destroy our village." A discussion about the story brought in a description of mobilization and uniforms. Religion followed, with the story of the two fishes and five loaves. The teacher tried to explain to his hungry class the importance of eating sparingly and sharing. The moral of the story was: "We should not say that we don't like the K-bread [war bread], that would be ungrateful to God. God blessed the bread so that a very small quantity was enough for many people."

Finally came the arithmetic lesson. The teacher would have the class calculate British ship losses, the costs of war, war loans, and the pensions of the wounded. A problem one teacher posed was: "In the Battle of Neuve Chapelle, the British have advanced and conquered a small strip of land 2 miles long and 3,000 feet deep. This success has cost them 25,000 dead. How many soldiers do they have to sacrifice in order to liberate the entire French territory under German occupation?" The children arrived at the answer: 195,600,000. "That's impossible," said one. "Yes," said the teacher, "and that's why they can't win the war."

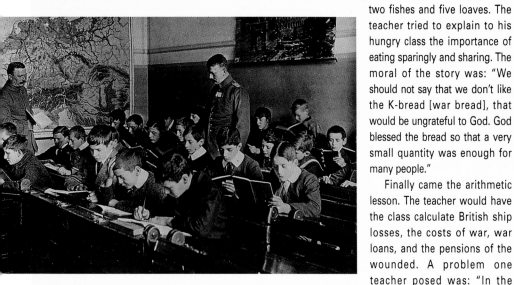

LESSON OF WAR   German officers, acting as schoolteachers, supervise a neat and compliant class.

for ordinary people. In 1918, insurance companies reported that the death toll in November 1918 was 184,896—over twice that of 1913—more than half being due to malnutrition. Civilians took to eating dogs and cats (nicknamed "roof rabbits"). A bitter parody of a middle-class recipe captures the feeling of the times: "Take a meat card, turn it into an egg card and fry until nice and brown in a butter card. Cook the potato card and the vegetable card and add the flour card. To cook it quickly and under high heat, lay the coal card and the liquor card underneath and light them. For dessert brew the coffee card and add the milk card to it. Gourmets dissolve the sugar card in it. After the meal, one washes oneself with the soap card and dries oneself with the ration coupon."

Town turned against country, class against class, people against government. In January 1918, munitions workers went on strike. Some 250,000 workers took to the streets in Berlin, and comparable numbers in Bremen, Hamburg, Essen and Leipzig. A strikers' directorate in Berlin demanded the lifting of food restrictions, an amnesty for political offenders, the restoration of the right of assembly, and—above all—peace. Only by placing the seven biggest industrial plants in Berlin under military control was the strike broken and revolution avoided . . . for the time being.

The blockade of Britain

Britain, meanwhile, had acquired a dictator of her own: Lloyd George, who became prime minister in December 1916. Lloyd George ruled by the moment, by intuition, guile and dynamism, always looking, in his words, for "a way round." He exercised command through a war cabinet of half a dozen, who controlled the country's economic and political mainsprings—shipping, labor, food, national service and food production. Over the next two and a half years,

all merchant ships were requisitioned, prices controlled, ration books introduced.

Besides managing the war, Lloyd George's greatest problem was to manage the economic difficulties imposed by Germany's all-out submarine warfare. Between January and March 1917, 470 British ships were sunk; and in April, one ship out of four leaving British ports never returned. New building could replace only 10 percent of the losses. The failure of coal barges to arrive from Norway drove the British coal industry,

URGING SELF-SUFFICIENCY   A British poster of June 1917 exhorts people not to depend on foreign wheat carried by vulnerable convoys.

along with its mine-shafts, to the brink of collapse. Food and fuel ran low. The food controller, Lord Devonport, issued a mass of regulations that seemed somehow reassuring in their triviality: window displays were not to flaunt goods; sweets were to cost no more than such-and-such; buns were to be made in this or that way; one day a week was to be meatless in hotels and restaurants. More seriously, Lord Devonport put the country's flour mills under government control and restricted beer production.

Even so, April and May 1917 brought the country to a point of near-collapse. In April, the country had just six weeks' supply of

butcher and grocer, with every disappointment fuelling the fear. In early 1918, in a typical London district, police reported over half a million people lining up every day. Only with the introduction of rationing, applied in February to meat, butter and sugar, and extended to most major food-stuffs in June, did the lines begin to melt away. It was a tribute to the success of government poli-cy—of rationing, of equitable dis-tribution, and of increases in efficiency that raised domestic wheat production by 60 percent during the war years—that the population faced insecurity with

wheat left (not that the public knew this), and sugar was practically unobtainable. The public was exhorted to consume a quarter less bread and to avoid flour in pastry. A Cultivation of Land order turned over every unoccupied urban lot to the Food Production Department—the start of a great British insti-tution, the allotment. And men experienced with traction engines were exempted from military duty to work on farms.

Devonport's health collapsed under the strain, and the mantle of "Food Dictator" fell upon Lord Rhondda, an experienced busi-nessman and administrator, who set up food commissioners and committees that ensured equitable distribution. At the end of the war, the food ministry, the commissioners and the committees together employed some 27,000 people and controlled 94 percent of

NEW SOUP KITCHEN Lord Rhondda, the food controller, opens an East London soup kitchen. He introduced ration books (right), which ensured equal distribution of food.

everything eaten and drunk in Great Britain. The ministry bought up surpluses of Canadian cheese, Australian wheat and American bacon; it requisi-tioned home-produced meat, butter, cheese and potatoes; and it fixed prices right through from stockyard, barn or ship to the store counter.

Though the convoy system had success-fully countered Germany's sub-marine campaign by the end of 1917, the winter of 1917-8 saw shortages of almost everything, everywhere, and the government introduced two meatless days per week for everyone. A sort of mass hysteria threatened to undermine public stability, and people began to hoard food, lining up at every

such equanimity. Much of the credit must go to Rhondda, whose skill and openness won him the support of the press. But the strain took its toll. He died in July 1918.

Occupied France

Uniquely among the major belligerents, France was in part an occupied nation for four years, and those in the ten occupied *départements* experienced unique wretched-ness, offering a foretaste of what defeat might mean. In the main towns of Lille, Roubaix and Tourcoing, Germans billeted troops, requisitioned men to dig trenches, and seized cash and supplies. The only news from "unoccupied France" came from news-papers that were published by the Germans. The French could hear the guns and see the jousting planes, but never knew the truth of

GROWING THEIR OWN The British were encouraged to "Dig for Victory" by cultivating waste ground, or "allotments," a right they have valued ever since.

1919

October 1916
Peace demonstration
in Frankfurt

February 1917
Germany resumes unrestricted
submarine warfare against Britain

May 1917
Convoy system
introduced by Britain

August 1917
Antiwar demonstrations
in Turin

January 1918
Strike by German
munitions workers

June 1918
General food
rationing in Britain

CONSCIENTIOUS OBJECTORS IN BRITAIN

THOSE WHO DARED DEFY THE CALL-UP ON POLITICAL OR IDEALISTIC GROUNDS FACED DERISION, OR WORSE—IMPRISONMENT AND HARD LABOR

From the start, the war was opposed by those who objected to war in principle, and their opposition gave currency to a newly coined term: pacifism. Politically, the pacifists found a voice through the Union of Democratic Control, but there were many others who acted out of religious or political conviction. A socialist journalist, Clifford Allen, called for a Labor protest

HARD LABOR The camera brings smiles to the faces of conscientious objectors (COs) digging seed-trenches on Dartmoor. Men in civilian garb wore armbands (right) to show they were not "Conchies."

against the war, and many staunch Christians held similar views for different reasons. Though widely reviled as cowards, they received support from writers and artists, among them the philosopher Bertrand Russell.

In March 1916, when compulsory military service came into effect, the rights of pacifists were acknowledged. Men who found it against their conscience to fight could ask for exemption at tribunals set up to test the genuineness of people's objections. Some 16,500 tough-minded idealists—mostly politically inexperienced young men— withstood the legal and social pressures to join up. Of these, over half agreed to perform non-combatant service, such as medical or agricultural work. Some 6,000 refused to accept the authority of the tribunals and were detained, most of them eventually agreeing to the conditions of the tribunals.

However, 1,300 "absolutists" refused all service, on a variety of religious, philosophical or political grounds. These people were imprisoned repeatedly, until they recanted. Among the 1,000 or so who remained adamant and were given hard-labor sentences in Dartmoor prison was Stephen Hobhouse, a Quaker from a wealthy family who had renounced his inheritance and devoted himself to working with the poor in London's East End. Another, Henry Firth, succumbed to the appalling conditions and died in February 1918. Clifford Allen, President of the Non-Conscription Fellowship, was sentenced to consecutive, and increasing, terms of hard labor. After 16 months of this, he emerged a broken man, and died before he was 50. Some conscientious objectors were drafted anyway, and could then be sentenced to death by courts martial: 41 were actually sent on active service to France for a month, until the prime minister, Herbert Asquith, had them brought home.

Those who supported the conscientious objectors found themselves pressured and ridiculed. Bertrand Russell was fined £100 ($400) in 1916, deprived of his lectureship at Trinity College, Cambridge, and in February 1918 he was sentenced to six months in prison for publicly advocating a German offer to open peace negotiations. For COs, the war against war did not end with the arrival of peace. In 1918, COs were disenfranchised for five years, a strange punishment for their idealism.

what was happening; for example, bells were rung only for German victories.

The diary of a Roubaix shopkeeper, David Hirsch, reveals the torment caused first by the lack of information, then by the growing privations. "Normally, Roubaix could get along with two grave diggers," he scribbled in June 1916. "Now, there are six." As the German economy declined, pressures in the occupied areas increased. In April 1918, Hirsch wrote: "Nine hundred men taken by railway—to cut wood in the forests? To plant potatoes? Or to be taken into Germany?" In all, 2,000 people were forcibly deported as "voluntary" workers.

In the rest of France, through 1916, conditions worsened. The cost of living had risen by 40 percent, and the harvest that year was poor. Flour was scarce, sugar a luxury. In 1917, the government prescribed two pastryless days, two sweetless, and two meatless days per week. Restaurants and hotels were limited to two courses per meal. However, the greatest impact on French society, during the war and after, was caused by the toll of war victims—1.3 million men dead and over 2 million wounded. Already before the end of the war, the *mutilés de guerre* were a common feature of French life, and a potent argument for peace.

Nevertheless, French society did not collapse. The people endured privation as the only alternative to total defeat and occupation.

WORKING WOMEN PROTEST Parisian *midinettes*—clothing workers—on strike in May 1917.

Unions remained compliant and opposition among civilians remained marginal (though in the ranks it sparked mutiny).

During the summer and autumn of 1917, the task of government was assailed by a number of scandals focusing on the issue of negotiation. French Socialists, who had attended two international socialist conferences in Switzerland in 1916, set up a committee that was openly pacifist, inspiring the government to refuse passports to anyone wishing to attend unofficial international meetings. A pacifist Paris paper, *Le Bonnet Rouge*, was suppressed when its director Miguel Almereyda, and its manager Emile-Joseph Duval, were arrested for accepting payments from French industrialists and from Germany. Almereyda was reported to have committed suicide in prison a few days after his arrest. Duval was executed for treason in 1918. An international adventurer, Paul Bolo, was arrested after he was found to have several million francs earmarked for pacifist propaganda.

These scandals were minor problems, however, compared to the incidents of industrial unrest. Twice, in January and May 1917, women in the clothing business, the *midinettes*, took to the streets to demand higher wages. And in one place, near the industrial area of St. Etienne 30 miles southwest of Lyons, protests became violent, with

THE JOY OF SURVIVAL French women who endured German occupation rejoice with British troops after liberation.

the threat of a Bolshevik-style revolution. The causes lay in the same weariness that had sparked the army mutinies, combined with spiralling prices. In November, metalworkers in the Loire struck for higher wages, and won. Then in early 1918, union activists began demanding both higher wages and peace. One, Clovis Andrieu, was ordered back to his regiment—like many workers called up in 1914, he had subsequently been sent back to work in war production. He refused to go back, and over the next few months established a strong power base among the factory's work force. When the local commander tried to force Andrieu into obeying orders, the 4,000 men at his factory, the Holtzer metalworks in Firminy, went on strike, inspiring 100,000 workers to close all the other factories in the region as well, with speakers openly calling for rebellion. In ten days of intense negotiation, May 18-28, the government carefully avoided a violent confrontation. Then, as the German offensive of May 1918 hardened the country's resolve and it became apparent that revolution would not spread, fresh troops arrived. Andrieu and other leaders were arrested. The possibility of a major stoppage, which would have virtually ended France's war effort, was over.

Italian society under strain

Italy came into the war late—in May 1915, against Austria-Hungary—and did not declare war on Germany until August 1916. In a country only recently

DEATH ON THE RAILWAYS

On May 22, 1915, three trains collided at Gretna Green, killing about 227 people (the exact figure was never established because bodies were dismembered). The majority of the dead were soldiers leaving Scotland to join the army in Gallipoli. This was the worst rail crash in British history. It did not compare, however, with the crash of December 12, 1917, in Modane, France. Two French troop trains returning from Italy were combined, and ran away down a gradient. Sparks from the brakes caused a fire that derailed the 19 coaches, killing 543 men.

DEATH AT GRETNA Rescue workers douse burned-out carriages at Gretna Green on May 22, 1915.

unified, the war was not welcomed with the crusading zeal of the other belligerents. Peasants and industrial workers alike looked for a fair return for their goods and labor, and showed no readiness to accept the sudden extension of state power demanded by mass mobilization. Though industrial mobilization came under tight military control, the 900,000 workers were not easily managed. The 200,000 women who went to work in factories, many of them peasants, objected to working on Sundays, and the work force in general (under the watchful eyes of *caribinieri*) came to realize its own importance—and its power.

Initially, factory conditions improved and wages rose, but so, inevitably, did prices. Soon shortages and rising prices created food lines, a novel experience in Italy. A worried

WOMEN AT WORK Filling positions left vacant by men serving in Europe, American women tend factory machines, right. Above, a recruiting poster from the First World War.

official from the Ministry of Arms and Munitions reported: "There is serious discontent among the working classes who are absenting themselves . . . in a manner exceedingly dangerous for the industrial economy and the battle on the Home Front." The government coped by introducing ration cards and identity cards, assurances that food would be distributed equably. Volunteers formed local welfare groups, known as *fasci* (bundles)— a word as yet without any ominous political connotations.

Steadily, though, conditions worsened. With 5.9 million Italian men in uniform during the war, several million families, deprived of their breadwinner, fell back on charity. Around 100,000 deserters roamed country areas, living off the land, sometimes forming gangs. Family life broke down, heavy drinking increased among young people, and teenage crime rose.

In 1917, northern Italy was swept by demonstrations against the shortages, the most serious occurring in Turin in August. What had begun as a protest against bread shortages turned into an antiwar demonstration that did not end until the army intervened with force, leaving 50 dead and 200 injured. Only the prospect of defeat unified the country.

American society stirs

By 1917, America had already gained much from the war. In two years, trade with the Allied Powers had quadrupled, largely due to American loans, on which Britain, France and Italy would pay interest; dollar loans would eventually reach $3 billion. Despite President Wilson's neutrality, America was tied ever more closely to the Allied cause, its economy prospering as the British, French and Italians relied on American products. America's entry into the war in April 1917 was an added stimulus to an already booming economy.

America was not geared up for war. To mobilize the nation—to produce the ships and weapons, and to train and equip the men who would cross the Atlantic to fight in Europe—President Wilson created the War Industries Board, which was eventually headed by Bernard Baruch, who had made a fortune speculating on Wall

STARS OF STAGE AND SCREEN

The war inspired some freer forms of entertainment to replace the serious-minded realism of the prewar theater. In London, revues, which directly involved the audience, injected new zest; and in the bars of Paris, Munich and Zurich, cabarets added an acerbic political edge to nights on the town.

After a long day's travel from the Western Front, British soldiers on leave could find release from war in London's theaters. The stuffier among them admired J.M. Barrie's *Dear Brutus*, but most sought easier fare. The great days of the music hall were over and, increasingly, theatergoers flocked to the new form of stage entertainment that had recently arrived from the United States: the revue, a miscellany of music, song, dance and comedy, all shot through with a new style of music, ragtime. Harry Lauder, the singing, dancing, kilted Scot, became a living legend after he braved enemy fire to bring entertainment to the front line. He lost his own son in the war. George Robey and Violet Lorraine made a lasting hit with "If you were the only girl in the world" in *The Bing Boys*, and an unpretentious musical, *Chu Chin Chow*, established a record run.

In Paris, the opening night of *Parade* caused a sensation. Written by Jean Cocteau and danced by Diaghilev's company to music by Erik Satie, it introduced the surreal to the stage. Parisians also flocked to see the aging Sarah Bernhardt, who decades before had been an actress of great beauty and talent. She had injured a leg jumping from battlements in *Tosca* and had to have it amputated. At 73, she returned to the stage to great acclaim.

SCOTTISH ICON With songs like "I love a lassie" and "Keep right on to the end of the road," Harry Lauder became a legend.

work and wages. White women who had previously been domestic servants or textile-workers entered the factories. Black males streamed up from the South for jobs as railroad workers, meat-packers and coalminers. Between 1910 and 1920, Cleveland's black population tripled, and Detroit's rose sixfold.

Not everyone favored the war, however. Socialists who condemned the war as a "crime against the American people" made impressive gains in the state and local elections of 1917. Antiwar protesters staged rallies; many refused to register for the draft.

In response, Wilson passed the Sedition Act to "prohibit any disloyal, profane, scurrilous or abusive language" about the government, the constitution, or the armed forces. He set up a Committee on Public Information, headed by George Creel, with the job of disseminating anti-German propaganda. Creel succeeded all too well: Pittsburgh forbade the playing of Beethoven, and German Americans were widely reviled. But America held firm, and the tide of battle turned.

Street. The board was the keystone for an administration that controlled not only raw materials, but also railroads, shipping, fuel and prices. A Food Administration Board, headed by the future president, Herbert Hoover, responded to Britain's pleas for help by asking Americans to adopt "meatless" and "wheatless" days and restaurants to replace beef and fish with whale and shark, in order to create a surplus. Farm production increased, and prairie lands were ploughed up. France alone received enough food to feed 12 million of her people for 18 months.

The effects of this effort were astonishing. In 1919, the United States shipped three times as much food to Europe as it had before the war. The steel industry doubled its prewar production. And from 1914 to 1920, GDP rose over 20 percent every year.

The boom had a tremendous social impact. With almost 3 million men drafted into the armed forces, factories needed labor; as a result, Americans by the hundreds of thousands moved across the country in pursuit of

THE WAR AT HOME American girl scouts collect peach stones, the seeds of which provided an edible oil.

You Save Peach Seeds They Will Save Soldiers Lives

THE RUSSIAN REVOLUTION

IN 1917, RUSSIA'S DESPAIR GAVE COMMUNISTS THE CHANCE THEY
NEEDED TO SET ABOUT REMOLDING THE NATION—AND THE WORLD

By early 1917, Russia was ruined by war. Throughout the summer, under the increasingly shaky leadership of a provisional government, the country advanced, lost ground, and finally collapsed into Bolshevik hands in October. Only then did Russia cease to fight.

The forces that were to remove Russia from the war first removed its royal dynasty, the Romanovs. Tsar Nicholas had promised democratic reforms after the revolution of 1905, and had not delivered. Wave after wave of strikes among Russia's growing industrial proletariat were met by oppression. Soon after the outbreak of war, undermined by military and economic disaster, Nicholas attempted to rally his people by taking personal command of the army, but this merely attracted the blame for Russia's military failures. The tsarina, Alexandra, was determined that her son would inherit a throne as absolute as always. As the country and the monarchy drifted toward collapse,

she retreated into mysticism under the influence of the monk Rasputin.

In early 1917, strikes and food shortages brought increasing chaos. A police report in February noted that "the proletariat in the capital is on the verge of despair. It is believed that the slightest disturbance, on the smallest pretext, will lead to uncontrollable riots with thousands of victims. In fact the conditions for such an explosion already exist . . . Even if wages are doubled, the cost of living

has trebled. The impossibility of obtaining goods, the loss of time spent lining up in front of stores, the increasing mortality rate because of poor housing conditions . . . all these conditions have created such a situation that the mass of industrial workers is ready to break out in the most savage of hunger riots."

The final collapse of the monarchy began in Petrograd (St. Petersburg) with a food

LINING UP FOR FOOD In a provincial town, Russians line up for scarce supplies outside a pastry shop.

BOLSHEVIK SOLDIERS Soldiers from the Petrograd garrison supported the revolution, February 1917.

COMING COLLAPSE Amid protests in Petrograd, above, the government wavered. Kerensky (right, second from right) almost brought stability.

blocked at Pskov. On the evening of the 15th, two delegates of the Provisional Government met him at Pskov, and he abdicated in favor of his brother, Grand Duke Michael, who for a few hours held the fate of the monarchy in his hands. Grand Duke Michael said that he would not accept the throne unless asked to do so by the government. No one asked him, and the dynasty fell.

crisis. On March 8, lines of people besieged bakers' shops; the next day, police fired on crowds; factories and schools stopped working as people took to the streets. The tsar, at the front, ordered repression. On Sunday March 11, police shot about 100 demonstrators, who were joined by soldiers. Troops arrived at the Duma (Parliament) offering support to the crowds; together they created the Petrograd Soviet of Soldiers' and Workers' Deputies.

On the 12th, the Duma appointed a provisional government under Prince Georgi Lvov, whose idealistic liberalism did not suit him for firm administration. A message was telegraphed to the tsar: "The last hour has come." There was no reply. On the 14th a socialist, Alexander Kerensky, was appointed minister of justice. All the generals were telegraphed, and returned promises of support.

The tsar had simply been removed from the decision-making process. He tried to return to Petrograd, but the railway line was

Now the forces that were to create the Soviet Union and dominate world affairs for 70 years gathered strength. The man who ensured their success was Vladimir Ilyich Lenin, who had for years been campaigning in exile in Western European capitals for a Marxist uprising in all advanced industrial nations. Since 1903, Lenin had been the

LENIN ARRIVES AT PETROGRAD'S FINLAND STATION

On April 16, 1917, Lenin was met at Petrograd's Finland Station by a crowd of several thousand organized by the Petrograd Soviet, whose members, transported in armored cars, prepared a triumphal reception.

Sukhanov, one of the non-Bolshevik leaders of the Soviet, described how, as a band played, "Lenin walked, or rather ran, into the 'Czar's Room' in a round hat, his face chilled, and a luxurious bouquet in his arms. Hurrying to the middle of the room, he stopped in front of Cheidze [first president of the Petrograd Soviet] as though he had run into a completely unexpected obstacle." Cheidze, with a melancholy look, delivered a tedious little speech of greeting. Lenin "stood there looking as though what was happening did not concern him in the least, glanced from one side to the other, looked over the surrounding public, and even examined the ceiling of the 'Czar's Room,' while rearranging his bouquet (which harmonized rather badly with his whole figure)," then ignored Cheidze and his committee of welcome, and addressed the crowd directly, ending: "Long live the worldwide socialist revolution!"

The soldiers insisted that Lenin climb on one of the armored cars, and he was carried through the dusk, past crowds of workers, soldiers and sailors to a palace. There, in Trotsky's words, Lenin "endured the flood of eulogistic speeches like an impatient pedestrian waiting for the rain to stop." With a forced smile, he kept glancing at his watch. Then it was Lenin's turn. He spoke for two hours. "I will never forget that thunder-like speech," wrote Sukhanov. "Startling and amazing not only to me ... but also to the faithful, all of them. I assert that nobody there had expected anything of the kind ... 'We don't need any parliamentary republic!' he said. 'We don't need any bourgeois democracy. We don't need any government except the Soviet of workers', soldiers', and farmhands' deputies!' ... I came out onto the street feeling as though on that night I had been flogged over the head with a flail."

MAKER OF REVOLUTION
Lenin, Russia's new leader, addresses a Moscow crowd in 1917.

dominant force of the Bolsheviks, a group that owed its name to the fact that it had once held a majority in the old Russian Social-Democratic Workers' Party.

The Bolshevik coup

When the tsar abdicated, Lenin was in Zurich, where he found himself trapped, unable to return home across war-torn Europe. With the tsar gone, he was certain that the time had come for universal revolution, and was bitterly opposed to the provisional government's determination to continue fighting. If only Russia withdrew from the war, he urged, workers on all sides would rise in revolt, throw out their war-mongering leaders, and initiate a new era of universal peace.

Lenin's views were anathema to Britain and France, who refused to allow him to cross their territory. The German general, Ludendorff, however, was happy to grant him passage through Germany, on the grounds that if he could be injected into Russian politics, he might take Russia out of the war. In April, by secret agreement, Lenin and his entourage were spirited across Germany, Sweden and Finland into Petrograd, where the soviets—the socialist workers' councils—ensured widespread support for the Bolsheviks.

At once, a second revolution began to foment. Lenin rejected cooperation with the provisional government, reasserting that the coming revolution would not be led by the bourgeoisie but by the workers, spearheaded by the Bolsheviks. There was no room in his view for compromises that would dilute the Bolsheviks' aims. The party's greatest theorist and orator, Leon Trotsky, who had also been in Switzerland, arrived a few weeks later. Soviets elected by soldiers and workers sprang up in many places, looking to the Supreme Soviet in Petrograd for guidance.

Throughout May and June, workers and deserting soldiers in the thousands joined the Social Democrats, and Prince Lvov found that he could not rule at all without the cooperation of the soviets. But the soviets were increasingly Bolshevik, and intransigent. As the first All-Russian Congress of Soviets was in session, half a million workers parading through Petrograd almost took over the capital, failing to do so only because the Bolsheviks believed the revolution they wanted was premature. Trotsky was arrested and Lenin fled to Finland. In July, Prince Lvov resigned, his place being taken by Kerensky. Tensions multiplied, with military reversals in the south, and demands for greater independence from the Ukraine and other minorities.

Later that summer, when a German advance in the north threatened Petrograd itself, General Lavr Kornilov, Kerensky's commander in chief, decided to seize control of the government. In early September, he sent a corps of cavalry to Petrograd, but Bolsheviks harangued the soldiers until they gave up the plan to attack their countrymen. Kerensky had Kornilov arrested, and on September 14 declared Russia a republic.

FOUR-MONTH PM Prince Georgi Lvov was Prime Minister from March to July of 1917, when he resigned, giving way to Kerensky.

ERUPTING VIOLENCE Government troops fire into a Petrograd demonstration in July 1917. The Bolsheviks decided to delay their coup until another opportunity arose.

arrived, there was no time to plan revolution before the Second Congress of Soviets, due to begin on the 20th. But on October 17 (old style), the opening was postponed to October 25 (Russia used the old Julian calendar until after the Revolution; the Gregorian or "new style" calendar was back-dated to cover "old-style" dates, but the events of October were of such significance that it is remembered as the October Revolution). This provided the Bolsheviks with the opportunity they needed. In the Bolshevik headquarters in the Smolny Institute, a former convent school for girls on the outskirts of Petrograd, workers' and soldiers' soviets voted 10:2 to seize power.

It was not Lenin but Kerensky who dictated the timing of the October Revolution. On the night of the 24th, news came that the provisional government intended to arrest the Bolsheviks in the army. A cruiser, the *Aurora*, at anchor on the River Neva, was ordered to put to sea to join the rest of the fleet. Government troops closed down the press that printed the new Bolshevik paper, *Pravda*. "A piece of official sealing-wax on the door of the Bolshevik editorial rooms—as a military measure that is not much," wrote Trotsky later. "But what a superb signal for battle!" A man and a woman ran to

Kerensky, however, could hardly claim to be the victor. Instead, the Bolsheviks could counterclaim a greater moral force: they had saved the day, peacefully, and argued that the country was being torn apart by two factions, both equally incompetent to rule. The people seemed to agree, for by now 2 million soldiers had deserted, and peasants had begun to seize the great country estates. Lenin, still in Finland, decided that the moment for action had come. The Congress of Soviets was due to meet again, and Lenin wished to present a fait accompli. "History will not forgive us if we do not take power now," he claimed on his return from Finland. The timing was crucial. Once Lenin

SEIZING POWER Red Guards (below) pose outside the Smolny Institute. The institute (right), the Bolshevik HQ in Petrograd, was heavily guarded.

March 1917	April 1917	July 1917	August 1917	October 1917		July 1918
Abdication of Tsar Nicholas II	Return of Lenin and Trotsky to Russia	Lenin goes into hiding	Attempted coup by General Kornilov	Overthrow of provisional government		Murder of the imperial family

PROPERTY OF THE PEOPLE

The American journalist John Reed was in Petrograd in 1917. In *Ten Days that Shook the World*, his account of the Bolshevik revolution, he described the storming of the Winter Palace:

"Carried along by the eager wave of men we were swept into the right-hand entrance, opening into a great bare vaulted room, the cellar of the east wing, from which issued a maze of corridors and staircases. A number of huge packing cases stood about, and upon these the Red Guards and soldiers fell furiously, battering them open with the butts of their rifles, and pulling out carpets, curtains, linen, porcelain, plates, glassware… One man went strutting around with a bronze clock perched on his shoulder; another found a plume of ostrich feathers, which he stuck in his hat. The looting was just beginning when somebody cried, 'Comrades! Don't take anything. This is the property of the People!' Immediately twenty voices were crying, 'Stop! Put everything back! Don't take anything! Property of the People!' Many hands dragged the spoilers down. Damask and tapestry were snatched from the arms of those who had them; two men took away the bronze clock. Roughly and hastily the things were crammed back in their cases, and self-appointed sentinels stood guard. It was all utterly spontaneous. Through corridors and up staircases the cry could be heard growing fainter and fainter in the distance, 'Revolutionary discipline! Property of the People!'"

THE WINTER PALACE SEIZED In a U.S. magazine illustration, Soviet soldiers, bemused by the opulence, stage their restrained occupation of the main government building.

Smolny and asked for help, where-upon the soviets ordered Bolshevik soldiers to open the plant again.

Meanwhile, sailors on the *Aurora* asked what they should do. They were told by the Bolsheviks in Smolny to use their radio to broadcast the news that the revolution had started. Throughout the day, Smolny was turned into an armed camp. That evening, a volley of blank shots from the *Aurora* gave the signal for action. Within hours, every strategic building—railway stations, the telephone exchange, the state bank—fell into Bolshevik hands. Kerensky fled in a car borrowed from the American

GUARD DUTY Revolutionaries warm themselves while controlling a Petrograd street, October 1917.

embassy, claiming that he would be returning in a few days with reinforcements. Instead, he fled west, ending up in America, where he died in 1970.

The main government building, the Winter Palace, occupied by a few government ministers and 1,000 nervous troops, was sealed off by a crowd of 18,000. The building's river flank was covered by the *Aurora*, and late on the 25th, the cruiser fired some blanks, followed by live rounds, to scare those inside into submission. In the early hours of the 26th, the besiegers stormed the gates, bursting through the doors, overwhelming the occupants and taking ministers prisoner.

That night, when the Second Congress of Soviets opened in Smolny, Lenin received a political gift. The other two socialist factions—260 of the 650 delegates—walked out in protest at the Bolsheviks' seizure of power. "To those who have gone out," Trotsky concluded, "We must say, 'You are pitiful isolated individuals; you are bankrupts; your role is played out. Go where you belong from now on—into the rubbish-can

SOVIET HERO An adulatory painting of 1930 shows Lenin proclaiming revolution from his armored car.

of history.'" The Bolsheviks were able to claim that they alone represented the will of the people.

When Lenin, the new ruler of the Russian capital, appeared the following day, he was greeted by an ovation lasting many minutes. As the applause died, he said simply: "We shall now proceed to construct the socialist order." He announced that the new government would at once make peace with Germany and that landowners would have their estates seized without compensation, thus ensuring himself of popular support in the countryside.

It had been an astonishing few days, and remarkably free of violence. That began to change two weeks later when, in elections planned under Kerensky, the Bolsheviks won only 25 percent of the seats. Lenin quickly quashed the results, saying that they were the product of a discredited regime and that the soviets represented "a higher form of

THE RED ARMY In 1918 Leon Trotsky, military commissar, reviews the new Red Army that would eventually win the civil war.

democratic principle." To fulfil these high principles, in mid-January 1918, the members of the new Constituent Assembly were invited to disperse under the steely gaze of machine-gunners.

Constructing the socialist order

The Bolsheviks had seized the mainsprings of power and made peace with Germany. But these were merely the beginnings of a task that would keep the new Russia—not yet federated with would-be independent republics into the Soviet Union—convulsed with violence and ground down by economic catastrophe for another three years. In industry, the promise of pay irrespective of production undermined productivity, which sank to one-sixth of its wartime capacity. The ending of private enterprise destroyed the distribution system, exacerbating food shortages. Banks were closed, church property seized, houses confiscated.

Naturally, those dispossessed of power, in particular the officer class, objected. Several set up so-called White armies and emerged briefly into the limelight: Kerensky's old rival, Kornilov, in the south; Colonel Nicholas Semenov in Siberia; General Yudenitch in Belorussia; Denikin and Wrangel in the

RASPUTIN: THE MAD MONK

Empress Alexandra always welcomed mystics. A French spiritualist, Philippe of Lyon, who had wielded influence at court during the Russo-Japanese War, was succeeded in 1905 by Rasputin, a Siberian self-styled holy man who combined depraved habits—"Rasputnik" means "libertine"—with supposed powers of clairvoyance. With his hypnotic gaze, he preached that physical contact with him could work miracles. At first, the empress lent on him during crises in the health of her son, Alexis, a hemophiliac who lived in constant danger of sudden death. Over nine years, Rasputin survived criticism and scandals (including rumors that he was the empress's lover). The empress would hear nothing against him, however, referring to him as "a man of God" and "Our Friend." Since his position derived from that of the royal family, he supported autocracy, and was welcomed into the royal household as a spokesman of the Russian peasantry.

The chaos of war gave him renewed opportunity. In July 1914, he foretold defeat, and was proved right by the Battle of Tannenberg. It was partly his pressure on the empress, and hers on the tsar, that persuaded the tsar to make himself commander in chief. Then, with Nicholas at the front, the empress's domestic influence increased—with Rasputin behind her. He influenced her to have several ministers dismissed. When a general devoted to the tsar brought to royal attention a police report of Rasputin's debauched behavior, the general was dismissed. When the empress considered replacements, her chief consideration was whether "he venerates our Friend."

Rasputin finally became a government within a government. Through his own protégé, Boris Stürmer, he controlled the ministries of the interior and foreign affairs, and the premiership. He recommended officials, promoted financial schemes, interfered with food supplies, and demanded to know military plans. All this was reported, and widened the gulf between the tsar and his people.

With revolution threatening, a group of extreme conservatives decided to assassinate Rasputin to save the monarchy from its own folly. On the night of December 29/30, 1916, Prince Felix Yusupov, husband of the empress's niece, and Vladimir Purishkevich, a right-wing member of the Duma (Parliament), lured him to Yusupov's house and poisoned him. When this had no effect, they shot him and still he did not die. They then bound him and threw his body into the River Neva, and he drowned. The tsar refused to heed even this warning, however, and remained virtually isolated. He was forced to abdicate three months later.

FATAL ADVISOR   The mesmerizing Grigory Novykh, known as Rasputin, worked his way into royal favor.

Vladivostok, prompting the Bolsheviks to set up an independent buffer state in Siberia.

Among the victims of these convulsions were the tsar and tsarina, their son Alexei and their four daughters, Olga, Tatiana, Maria and Anastasia, who had all been shipped off to western Siberia. In April 1918, they were removed to Ekaterinburg (now Sverdlovsk) in the Urals. In order to prevent the possibility of a rescue by local Whites and the approaching Czechs, their captors murdered them on July 16, burned the bodies, dowsed them with acid and cast them into an abandoned mineshaft.

No one had forseen such misery and chaos. According to Lenin, once "the people" took power, imperialism and capitalism would simply crumble away. Instead, the Bolsheviks found that to stay in power they had to institute an autocracy far more ruthless than anything contemplated by the tsars. Opponents were assassinated en masse. The

ROYAL MURDERS   The royal family was shot in July 1918 in the cellar of the house where they were kept captive.

Caucasus—all had to be fought off and crushed in a series of actions by Trotsky's new Red Army. The Ukraine declared itself independent, concluded a separate peace with Germany, and was not reconquered until 1920.

Such opposition drew support from the Western nations, incensed by what was seen as a betrayal of the Allied cause. The result was a rash of foreign interventions, all aimed at undermining Bolshevism. In the summer of 1918, British and French forces landed in northern Russia, holding Murmansk and

Archangel for a few months, and threatening to wage war on the Bolsheviks. In a bizarre epic, a legion of Czechs, ex-prisoners of war from the Austrian armies, struggled eastward across the whole country by train, aiming to work their way around the world and rejoin the war in Europe. Conflict with Bolshevik forces in Siberia inspired the Czechs to seize the Trans-Siberian Railway and link briefly with the local Whites. In Omsk, Admiral Alexander Kolchak made himself briefly "supreme ruler of Russia." The Japanese seized

Bolsheviks could not have achieved their aims, however, if the previous regime had not so alienated the population that there was a universal longing for revolution, whatever the cost. In the words of one historian: "Lenin appeared to the young generation like Moses descending from the mountain with the tablets of the new law." In contrast, nothing united the opposition except self-interest.

HOME RULE OR HOME FRONT

AS OFTEN, ENGLAND'S DIFFICULTY WAS IRELAND'S OPPORTUNITY, AND IRISH NATIONALISTS SEIZED THE MOMENT AT EASTER 1916

When war broke out, the political situation in Ireland was delicately balanced. Britain's Liberal government had passed a Home Rule Bill that received the royal assent in September 1914. It was an act of devolution by which Ireland would have its own parliament, though remaining part of the United Kingdom. However, although the act became law, it was put on hold for the duration of the war. Meanwhile, Catholic and Protestant Irishmen flocked to join up— some 180,000 in all. Great southern regiments—the Connaught Rangers, the Munster Fusiliers—marched off to the killing fields of Flanders with Ulstermen.

MAKERS OF REVOLT Left to right: Patrick Pearse, Tom Clarke and James Connolly unleashed the uprising that ended in the shelled ruins of central Dublin (background).

Given the immense events unfolding elsewhere and the ready support of Irishmen for Britain's war effort, it seemed in London that the "Irish problem" could be safely ignored—for the time being at least. In fact, the coming of war merely papered over violent disagreements within Ireland. In the north, the Ulster Volunteers had been founded in January 1913 to oppose Home Rule, by force if necessary. In April 1914 they had been armed with 24,000 rifles and 3 million rounds of ammunition smuggled in from Germany. In the south, the Irish Volunteers had been founded in December 1913 as a nationalist answer to the Ulster Volunteers and were similarly gathering arms. Although many nationalists joined up when war broke out, a hard core refused to get involved.

The turning point when it came was the work of diehard Dublin nationalists who had

no intention of waiting until the war ended before they attained Home Rule. Many were militant republicans who wanted outright independence, not just Home Rule within the United Kingdom. They looked back to the 18th-century father of nationalism, Wolfe Tone, and to uprisings in the 1860s by the Irish Republican Brotherhood, also known as the Fenian movement. One of these men was Tom Clarke, who ran a tobacconist's shop in the center of the city. A veteran of the Fenian movement, he had spent 15 years in a British jail for setting off bombs on the mainland and then lived for many years in the U.S. before returning to Ireland in 1907. Around him gathered others equally committed to the freedom of a united Ireland— men like Patrick Pearse, a poet and teacher, and the trade unionist James Connolly.

Remembering Wolfe Tone

When an old Fenian, Jeremiah O'Donovan Rossa, died in America in 1915 after 40 years of exile, Clarke and his colleagues organized a funeral for him under the innocent-sounding auspices of the Wolfe Tone Memorial Committee. This was a front: they were really planning an eye-catching display of nationalism. On the day of the funeral, thousands of onlookers saw Irish Volunteers fire a volley

PATRIOT OR TRAITOR? Sir Roger Casement arranged a German arms shipment for the republicans, and was later executed. A French newspaper illustrates a gun-running scene, with Irish republicans preparing to receive arms from a submarine.

over the coffin, and heard Pearse rail against the British government: "The fools! The fools! The fools! They have left us our Fenian dead, and while Ireland holds these graves Ireland unfree shall never be at peace." It was a brilliant publicity coup—a small group of militant republicans had proclaimed their agenda to the public.

James Connolly, who commanded another brigade, the Irish Citizen Army, persuaded Pearse to work toward an uprising for Easter Sunday—April 23, 1916. The timing was just right. Pearse had a mystical faith in the value of a "blood sacrifice" and a resurrection for his oppressed people. More practically, a consignment of 20,000 rifles was on its way from Germany, organized by a former British consular official, Sir Roger Casement. Using planned maneuvers by 10,000 Irish Volunteers as a cover, the nationalists would seize strategic strong points in Dublin, dominating the main roads, the station, the harbor and the four army barracks housing some 2,500 British troops. The headquarters would be the General Post Office in Sackville (now O'Connell) Street.

This grand scheme degenerated into near farce. Casement, fearing that the uprising would fail and hoping to postpone it, was put ashore by a German submarine. He was arrested soon afterward. The German arms shipment was intercepted by the British. And the leader of the Irish Volunteers, Eoin MacNeill, cancelled the maneuvers. British intelligence learned of the planned uprising, and the government moved to disarm both the Volunteers and the Citizen Army and arrest their

Le Petit Journal illustré

Le Sous-Marin Fantôme

leaders. However, because of the Easter weekend with highly popular horseracing at Fairhouse on Easter Monday, and because trouble seemed unlikely anyway with the maneuvers cancelled and the arms intercepted, action was delayed until Tuesday. Meanwhile, Pearse and Connolly cancelled MacNeill's cancellation, declaring that the maneuvers would go ahead 24 hours later than originally planned: on Easter Monday, April 24. Thus disaster, chaos and pure luck combined to create a window of opportunity for the rebels.

Meeting at Liberty Hall

In any event, only about 1,000 men turned up on Easter Monday at Connolly's trade union HQ, Liberty Hall, most of them totally unaware that there was to be a rising. One group of 50 who did know (their commander's brother was one of the ringleaders) arrived by bus, having held up the driver at gunpoint while everyone crowded on, then paid their fares in full. They joined officers and men of the Volunteers and Citizen Army, and members of the youth and women's groups.

While some went off to occupy buildings of lesser strategic importance, Connolly, Pearse and Clarke marched the main body to the General Post Office. There, Pearse read out a proclamation on behalf of the "provisional government" of the Irish Republic: "Ireland, through us, summons her children to her flag and strikes for her freedom." As the rebels set about stuffing mailbags in

AN IMPERIAL RESPONSE During the rising, British troops man a makeshift barricade held together with barrels and bits of furniture.

September 1914
Irish Home Rule Bill
receives royal assent

April 1916
Easter Rising

May 1916
Executions of
Rising's leaders

THE AFTERMATH Curious Dubliners gather outside the gutted shell of the General Post Office, rebel HQ during the uprising.

fired by two 18-pound guns, awaited a general rising across the country. Nothing much happened, other than an ambush at Ashbourne, County Meath, in which 16 policemen died.

By Friday, the Post Office was on fire, and the rebels were forced out. Some—among them James Connolly, wounded in the ankle—fought their way across the road to set up a new HQ in nearby houses. On Saturday evening, Pearse surrendered and was driven to Kilmainham jail. Other outposts followed suit. The dead amounted to 220 or more civilians, 64 rebels and 134 troops and police.

Next morning, the prisoners were marched to Richmond Barracks where the leaders were separated. Many rank-and-file members of the rising were sent home. Others were marched down to the harbor for internment in Britain. The leaders were held for courts martial.

There was no great show of support from the people for a week of violence that had started as a fiasco and apparently ended in failure. Yet the small force had done something unprecedented: taking arms against a government in wartime and holding out for a week. As people stared at the smoking ruins, a feeling grew that there was heroism as well as madness in the rebels' actions.

Executing vengeance

Still, it might all have dissolved if the British had been less vengeful. Seventy-seven men were condemned to death. Although most were reprieved, the leaders were not. The executions continued through May until 15 had died, the last of them being James Connolly, shot in a chair because with his wounded ankle he could not stand.

It was the executions that changed the Irish people's hearts and minds. The rebels went from being heroes to martyrs. Popular support swung away from Home Rule to republican nationalism. Politically, this meant growing support for Sinn Fein, particularly in the U.S. Since America was on the brink of entering the war, the British government was forced to listen. Several hundred insurgents were released for Christmas 1916, and more, including De Valera, in June 1917, with consequences that were to take on a momentum of their own when the war ended.

order to blockade windows, a body of British Army cavalry came riding along Sackville Street, apparently unaware of trouble until the rebels opened fire, killing four soldiers. The cavalry beat a hasty retreat.

The British response was slow. Only about 400 troops were on duty, and these went to defend Dublin Castle. Some 1,600 cavalrymen arrived in the city on Monday afternoon, but little happened until Wednesday, when two infantry brigades landed at the harbor. Early that morning, they marched into town where they were greeted by women with tea and biscuits. One column was fired on from an outpost in a bakery, Boland's Mill, commanded by Eamon De Valera, then a mathematics teacher but soon to become a towering force in Irish politics. It took the soldiers the whole afternoon to take the mill.

Meanwhile, artillery and infantry had cordoned off the city center, where rebels and British troops exchanged fire for two more days. The action killed a dozen civilians, but none of the 200 republicans in the Post Office. There, the rebels, sheltering from shells

MAKER OF MODERN IRELAND Crowds listen rapt (above) to Eamon De Valera (right) after his release from prison in June 1917.

June 1917
Eamon De Valera
released from prison

WAR AND EMPIRE

THE EMPIRES OF BRITAIN AND FRANCE—THE TWO GREATEST IMPERIAL POWERS—MADE IMMENSE AND REMARKABLY WILLING CONTRIBUTIONS TO THE WAR EFFORT

Britain's self-governing dominions lost no time in rallying to the cause. London had scarcely declared war before the dominion governments were offering to send expeditionary forces. These became so important that the British War Cabinet transformed itself into the Imperial War

ALL HANDS ON DECK Chinese workers were brought in to work alongside the women in this French armaments factory.

Cabinet, giving leaders such as the Canadian Sir Robert Borden, the Australian William Hughes and the South African Jan Christiaan Smuts the power to influence policy and assert their nations' interests. Others, too, came in their hundreds of thousands from other parts of the empire—Africans, Indians, Polynesians and Chinese, dying for a few yards of Flanders mud. From India alone, 230,000 troops went to France in the first months of the war, distinguishing themselves in the battles of Neuve Chapelle and Loos. In all, some 1.3 million Indians fought in France, Mesopotamia, Palestine, Gallipoli, Egypt, Cameroon and China. Some 37,000 of them died. India gave $400 million to the war effort, lent another $292 million and provided stores and equipment worth $320 million.

Yet the war also encouraged unrest. In the Punjab, a nationalist party, the Ghadr, backed violent revolution, which German missions in Bangkok and the Dutch East Indies tried to encourage. Among politicians, India's war effort inspired a movement toward Home Rule, as a step toward full independence. In 1917, Britain committed itself to the "gradual development of self-governing institutions."

INDIAN GUARDIANS Bengal Lancers on parade in London display loyalty to the imperial cause.

France, meanwhile, was no less reliant on its colonial troops. During the war, it recruited or conscripted some 600,000 colonial soldiers, of whom roughly half came from North Africa. They served in all the major theaters including the Western Front, Salonica and Gallipoli. Around 70,000 lost their lives.

Most joined up with good will, especially the Muslims of North Africa; the most decorated unit in the French armed forces was a Moroccan regiment. France's West African subjects were less eager, and the first black African member of the National Assembly in Paris, Blaise Diagne, was dispatched to West Africa in 1917 to bolster conscription levels. Even so, one Senegalese soldier would later recall: "We all had the same ambition, which was to beat the enemy. France's victory meant our victory." A contingent of Annamites from Indochina played their part in such struggles as the defense of Verdun.

Although the handful of Africans with French citizenship went into the French metropolitan army, most of the rest went into the colonial army. Many of the colonial units had proud traditions such as the Senegalese *tirailleurs* ("skirmishers") who had fought against the Germans in the Franco-Prussian War of 1870-1. Colonial troops earned only half the pay of citizen soldiers, and on discharge their pension was a third that of citizens. They did, however, enjoy one benefit denied to other soldiers: they were sent to the South of France in winter. They had special camps where they were fed their native food, and Muslim soldiers were instructed in their religion by *marabouts*, holy men. They were certainly never segregated in the way that black American soldiers were.

THE AFTERMATH

THE ARMISTICE USHERED IN THE PROBLEM OF THE PEACE. WITH MORE THAN 8 MILLION DEAD AND MANY MORE WOUNDED, THE HUMAN COST OF THE WAR WAS IMMENSE—CHILDREN LEFT FATHERLESS, WOMEN HUSBANDLESS, SURVIVORS MAIMED IN BODY AND MIND. EMPIRES HAD TUMBLED; GERMANY STOOD ON THE BRINK OF REVOLUTION. NEW NATIONS AROSE AND MAPS WERE REDRAWN AS THE WORLD'S STATESMEN THRASHED OUT THE VERSAILLES SETTLEMENT.

THE ARMISTICE

THE ARMISTICE MEANT THE END OF FIGHTING, BUT THE START OF ENDLESS DEBATE ON THE SHAPE OF THE POSTWAR WORLD

The Allied commanders, gathered in a railway carriage in the forest of Compiègne, northeast of Paris, had a delicately poised problem to resolve. They were there to sign the armistice with German delegates. But Germany's army was as yet unbroken and might fight on if presented with conditions that were either too harsh to accept or too lenient to guarantee peace.

Foch veered toward harshness. Germany was to hand over a third of its artillery (5,000 pieces), half of its machine guns (25,000), 5,000 railway engines, 150,000 railway cars, 5,000 trucks and all of its captured ships. Its armies were to pull back behind the German Empire's prewar frontiers, with the Allies in

THE VICTORS Foch, with cane and kepi and (on his right) Admiral Sir Rosslyn Wemyss, the chief British representative, prepare to meet the German delegation at Compiègne.

occupation of the Rhineland and a few bridgeheads over the Rhine to ensure compliance. It would have to pay reparations. The British Admiralty, protective of Britain's naval power, suggested seizing the whole German fleet. Lloyd George moderated this proposal to the surrender of all 150 submarines and the internment of 16 of Germany's most powerful ships—10 battleships and 6 battle cruisers—as well as 8 light cruisers and 50 destroyers.

With Allied forces gathering strength in France, with revolution at home in Germany and with the other former Central Powers, Austria, Bulgaria and Turkey, out of the war, the leader of the German delegation, Matthias Erzberger, had no alternative but to accept these humiliating terms. All he could do was protest. The terms, he said, would lead to famine and anarchy. As soon as he had signed, early on November 11, he handed over a declaration ending: "A nation of 70 million people suffers, but it does not die."

"*Très bien*," replied Foch dismissively, and left the carriage without shaking hands.

All quiet on the Western Front

When the guns fell silent later that morning, the German army on the Western Front was still in much the same positions it had occupied at Christmas 1914. This laid the foundation for a great myth that would sustain those Germans who could not accept their country's defeat: that the army, poised for victory, had been "stabbed in the back" by its civilian leaders who lacked the will to continue.

The truth was just the opposite. Ludendorff himself had declared that the war was as good as lost and, backed by Hindenburg, had demanded an immediate armistice. By a curious paradox, left-wing unrest at home, by making further resistance

CELEBRATING PEACE With their men still at the battlefront, women dance in London's East End (top), while West End young men party in the Ritz Hotel (above).

VIVE LA PAIX! British, French and American soldiers join French civilians cheering the Armistice in central Paris.

among the crowds in Trafalgar Square lit a bonfire at the base of Nelson's Column, while Buckingham Palace was mobbed by people waiting to see King George V and Queen Mary. When they appeared, the king's words were lost in the noise. A band struck up "All People That on Earth Do Dwell" and "Home Sweet Home" as the crowd roared out the words. "It was this that touched the crowd really," wrote one of those present. "It was solemnly sung, almost with a sob, and I felt it a moment never to be forgotten. After that the English reserve gave way and they sang 'For He's a Jolly Good Fellow!'" As night fell, the celebrations continued, becoming more riotous as the beer flowed; after three days the police intervened to restore order.

The problems of peace

All over Europe, the effects of the last four cataclysmic years echoed and re-echoed. The Allies had won, but peace brought a whole new set of problems. There were millions of restless soldiers to be brought home. Americans in France, impatient to be back with their friends and families, mutinied, as did British troops in Folkestone—they were calmed only by the arrival of one of the war's most popular politicians, the demagogue and Member of Parliament Horatio Bottomley. At Rhyl in North Wales, Canadians turned to violence in which six were killed.

On a much larger scale, desperate populations across the Continent needed help. In Russia, different anti-Bolshevik forces were trying to establish alternative governments. Nationalists in the Ukraine and the Baltic states struggled for independence. The Allied blockade of Germany and Austria remained in force, pending the conclusions of a final peace treaty. With the emergence

impossible, had saved the army from outright defeat, thus ensuring the survival of the very forces the left-wingers opposed.

The myth that branded the peacemakers as the "November criminals" became a key element in the mind of a man for whom the capitulation was "the greatest villainy of the century." Adolf Hitler was in a military hospital northeast of Berlin that November when he heard the news. "Everything went black again before my eyes," he wrote later. "So it had all been in vain. In vain all the sacrifices and privations . . . in vain the death of 2 million . . . Did all this happen only so that a gang of wretched criminals could lay hands on the Fatherland?"

On the front, the news of the Armistice was greeted with a sense of relief by Allied soldiers. "There was no cheering or demonstration," wrote a New Zealand artilleryman. "We were all tired in body and mind, fresh from the tragic fields of battle, and this momentous announcement was too vast in its consequences to be appreciated or accepted with wild excitement." Allied prisoners simply walked out of POW camps and made their way back home or to their own lines.

In London, where November 11 was a cloudy, still day, the news was greeted with gunfire, sirens, church bells and car horns. Hundreds of thousands abandoned their work and took to the streets, shouting, whirling rattles, making a noise with anything they could. Girls draped themselves in Union Jacks, and soldiers on leave crammed on to taxis and buses. Canadian soldiers

November 1916
Death of Emperor
Franz Josef

November 1918
The Armistice
comes into effect

THE GREAT INFLUENZA PANDEMIC

In the winter of 1918-9, the death toll was vastly increased by the onset of a virulent form of influenza. In Europe, it was known as "Spanish influenza," because it was believed to have been brought from Asia to the Iberian peninsula. In its onset and speed, this ferocious strain of "flu" was as frightening and inexplicable as the Black Death had been in the 14th century, for the influenza virus was not identified until 1933. Fever lasted some three days, and then either dissipated or led to bronchial complications and death. There was no treatment, and it struck anywhere and everywhere, killing as easily in the booming U.S. as in undernourished and war-torn Europe or the rural backwaters of India.

According to one estimate, some 20 million died worldwide, of the 1 billion who fell sick. In India estimates of deaths ranged between 7 and 16 million. It killed over a million in West Africa, reducing Accra to a ghost town. An estimated 20 to 25 percent of the Pacific Islands' population died. In Britain, three-quarters of the population came down with it, and 150,000 died.

Among the victims were the 28-year-old Expressionist painter Egon Schiele, who died in Vienna, and the French poet Guillaume Apollinaire, who died two days before the Armistice. His burial added to the bittersweet mood in Paris: peace, yes, but so many dead, and so many still dying.

ANTI-FLU MASK   Believing that flu spread through the air, some sought protection . . . in vain . . . with filters like this.

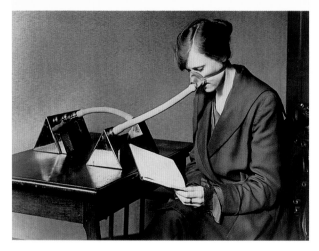

HELP FOR THE POOR   German Red Cross workers collect discarded clothing that they will later distribute to the poor.

of Soviet Russia as an inspiration, revolution was never far below the surface. Between October 1918 and spring 1919, revolutions broke out briefly in Germany, Austria and Hungary. In Moscow, the Bolshevik leaders eagerly awaited universal revolution, which Lenin sought to foment by founding the Third International in March 1919.

In central and southern Europe, new nations began to emerge. In November 1916, the 86-year-old Habsburg emperor, Franz Josef, had died in Vienna, ending a 68 year reign, the longest of any monarch in European history. After that, the unravelling of his multi-ethnic realms became virtually inevitable. On the same day the Western Allies were celebrating the Armistice, his successor and great-nephew, the Emperor Karl, issued a proclamation in which he recognized the right of the Austrian people to choose their own form of government; he did the same for Hungary two days later on November 13. Although he never renounced his hereditary titles, Karl's action effectively brought to an end more than 600 years of history during which his Habsburg forebears had ruled in Austria. Hungary and Austria went their separate ways as republics; Karl went into exile in Switzerland in March 1919.

Meanwhile, on December 1, 1918, the Croats and Slovenes, also formerly ruled by the Habsburgs, had declared their solidarity with the Serbs in a southern Slav kingdom, later known as Yugoslavia. On December 21, Dr. Tomás Masaryk, who had been campaigning for a separate Czechoslovak state throughout the war, arrived in Prague. The Romanians redrew their western border by seizing the Hungarian province of Transylvania. Bulgaria—whose king, "Foxy" Ferdinand, had abdicated in October 1918 in favor of his son Boris—would have to be punished for Ferdinand's pro-German policy during the war.

No one yet knew what to do with Germany's colonial possessions in Southwest Africa, East Africa, the Far East and the Pacific, where Australia and New Zealand were already demanding an extended role. In Turkey's former empire, the different Arab lands that had thrown off the Ottoman yoke would have to be divided up and administered. Britain was committed to helping the Jews establish a homeland in Palestine. All of these developments would

need international discussion, agreement and confirmation.

At the heart of the matter lay Germany. In early December, British and American troops crossed the border, finding to their surprise that behind the lines, with their shell-riddled wastelands, blasted trees and shattered villages, there lay neat agricultural lands untouched by the conflict. But beyond that, in the cities, Germany was in a state of economic and social collapse. A German-born Zionist, Arthur Ruppin, wrote in his diary: "Never, indeed, in the history of the world has a people been confronted with such terrible armistice terms . . . although its armies are still deep within the territories of its enemies. The simple man in the street cannot understand what has happened so suddenly, and feels completely lost."

On November 9, the country had suddenly become a republic, though what this meant was an open question. The republic was proclaimed almost on a whim by the Socialist leader Philipp Scheidemann, shouting out of the Reichstag window. His aim was to forestall the emergence of a Soviet-style state that the revolutionary Spartacists, Rosa Luxemburg and Karl Liebknecht, were urging in the streets below. Two hours later, Liebknecht proclaimed a rival republic. For two months, nobody paid much attention to Liebknecht's

STRUGGLING FOR PEACE Philipp Scheidemann proclaimed Germany a republic, but resigned rather than sign the peace treaty.

proclamation. Then, on January 1, 1919, the Spartacists declared themselves the Communist Party of Germany, and on January 11 the two leaders, gambling on widespread workers' support, led the seizure of several public buildings. They never had any hope of success because they never controlled any of the centers of power that, despite a Social Democratic government, remained in the hands of long-established bureaucrats. After four days of fighting and the deaths of about 1,000 people, Liebknecht and Luxemburg were arrested and taken to the headquarters

RED FAILURE Militiamen display their captive—a supporter of Kurt Eisner's short-lived, left-wing Bavarian republic.

of one of the paramilitary groups that had crushed the uprising. They were then clubbed and shot to death. Some attempt was made to bring the ringleaders responsible for this atrocity to justice. One, however, was spirited into the Netherlands; the other received a two-year sentence—though he would later get a gratuity from the Nazis by way of thanks.

The Spartacists were not the only revolutionaries in Germany. In Bavaria, a kingdom within a kingdom, the Wittelsbachs had gone the way of the Hohenzollerns, and a popular Jewish writer, Kurt Eisner, had proclaimed a "People's State." Eisner was assassinated in February 1919 by a right-wing student, and workers set up a short-lived Soviet republic. This was crushed in May by paramilitary Freikorps volunteers from Berlin, who killed several hundred people.

Meanwhile, on January 19, 1919, elections had taken place for a Constituent Assembly to work out exactly what form the new German republic would take. This met for the first time on February 6 at Weimar, once the home of Germany's greatest writers, Goethe and Schiller. But the liberalism and humanism evoked by the name Weimar failed to make much impact. At the polls, more than 50 percent of the electorate had voted for conservative parties. The new constitution was promulgated in August; although it was democratic, it left much power in the hands of the old guard—army officers, paramilitary groups, the civil service, semi-feudal landlords, industrial magnates, the judiciary, and the police.

War in the east

Three months after the end of hostilities, Allied leaders assembled in Paris to start the talks that would bring about a final peace treaty. Since President Wilson had opted to head the U.S. delegation, the leaders of all the other participating nations did the same: Lloyd George came from Britain, Vittorio Orlando from Italy, Clemenceau from France, Saionji Kimmochi from Japan. But even as the Allies began to wrestle with the present

HITLER'S SWEET VENGEANCE

For Hitler, the Allied victory over Germany was so humiliating that when his moment came—the Nazi victory over France in June 1940—he was determined to get his revenge. He would impose his terms in exactly the same circumstances that the Allies had imposed theirs on Germany in 1918.

The site was the railyard in the forest of Compiègne, 40 miles northeast of Paris. The railway car in which Marshal Foch and other Allied generals had met the German representative, Matthias Erzberger, had been preserved there in a museum. A granite monument nearby proclaimed that "here succumbed the criminal pride of the German Empire."

Hitler had the museum walls torn down and the carriage pulled into a siding in a glade of elms, oaks, cypresses and pines. On the afternoon of June 21, 1940, a glorious summer day, Hitler arrived in his Mercedes with other Nazi leaders and walked into the clearing. He read the granite inscription, snapped his body into a brief gesture of defiance, entered the carriage and sat in the very chair occupied by Foch in 1918.

The French delegation, without prior warning of this humiliation, was brought in five minutes later in a state of shock. Hitler left after a few minutes, leaving his subordinates to go through the terms. All French objections were overruled, and they signed the following day. The granite block marking the spot was blown up three days later at Hitler's command, and the carriage itself was carried off to Berlin, where it was destroyed in an Allied bombing raid.

HUMILIATION REDRESSED Hitler leaves the carriage in which he imposed terms on the French.

the support of both the Allies and the Czechs, and dissension and defeat followed. He pulled back, along the Trans-Siberian Railway, as far as Irkutsk, where he was seized by the Czechs, handed over to the Bolsheviks and shot in February 1920.

Such issues marked the emergence of a new global society. It was to confront them that the leaders of the victorious powers began their deliberations in Paris in January 1919.

ANTI-SOVIET FORCE Czechs like these legionnaires posing by the Trans-Siberian Railway (above) supported the 14 month regime of Admiral Kolchak (right).

and future problems of peace, the ripples of war continued to spread.

Soviet Russia, in particular, had come under attack from four anti-Bolshevik forces: the Western Allies, the White Russians, a group of Czechs, and the Japanese. Eager to undermine an ideology they regarded as dangerous, the Western Allies sought to buttress the White Russian forces in the civil war of 1918-21. British, French and U.S. troops landed in the northern ports of Archangel and Murmansk, ostensibly to guard ammunition dumps once destined for Russia and now destined for anti-Bolshevik forces, of which the most formidable was led by Admiral Kolchak in Siberia.

A few days after the war had ended in the west, Kolchak set himself up as ruler of an independent Siberia, and for a few months the Allies had great hopes for him. Kolchak was aided by a legion of 4,000 Czechs—former prisoners of war who had been cut off in Russia at the start of the revolution in 1917. The Czechs were now a powerful force in Siberia. Travelling along the Trans-Siberian Railway, they had captured the Russian gold reserve in Kazan and placed both their troops and their cash at the disposal of Kolchak. On June 29, 1918, some of them reached the

port of Vladivostok. A few days later, at President Wilson's suggestion, some 12,000 Japanese were dispatched to help them. For the Japanese, this was a chance to expand their mainland empire, while for the Allies it was an opportunity to help the Czechs, and thus Kolchak's anti-Bolshevik forces. By the time of the Armistice, there were 75,000 Japanese in Siberia, scattered between Vladivostok and Irkutsk, and poised to seize as much of the Soviet Far East as they could.

Kolchak advanced westward and northward, aiming to link up with the British in Archangel. However, his brutality lost him

THE BIRTH OF A MYTH

A year after the armistice, Germany's military leaders, unable to accept the consequences of their own capitulation, seized on a phrase that became an inspiration for Hitler: the "stab in the back." The military historian John Wheeler-Bennett pinned down the origin of the phrase, describing an evening in 1919 when Major-General Malcolm, head of the British Military Mission in Berlin, was dining with Ludendorff: "Ludendorff . . . with his usual turgid eloquence was expatiating on how the High Command had always suffered lack of support from the Civilian Government, and how the Revolution had betrayed the Army. In an effort to crystallize the meaning of Ludendorff's verbosity into a single sentence, General Malcolm asked him: 'Do you mean, General, that you were stabbed in the back?' Ludendorff's eyes lit up and he leapt upon the phrase like a dog on a bone. 'Stabbed in the back?' he repeated. 'Yes, that's it exactly. We were stabbed in the back.'"

On November 18, Hindenburg declared before a Committee of Inquiry of the National Assembly: "As an English general has very truly said, the German Army was 'stabbed in the back.'" It was a phrase that would enter the psyche of Germans set on redeeming their country by force of arms, and would become a central part of Hitler's psyche and Nazi ideology.

THE HUMAN COST OF WAR

THE BALANCE SHEET OF THE WAR WAS HORRENDOUS, BUT ITS TRUE COST WAS TO BE FOUND IN SCARRED BODIES, HEARTS AND MINDS

Perhaps the most poignant losses of the war were of men who remained genuinely lost—those who simply vanished and of whom relatives and friends could find no trace on the battlefields or in the hospitals. Of all Britain's war memorials, the most moving was that of the Unknown Warrior.

The driving force behind this was a British lieutenant-colonel, Henry Williams. At the end of the war 5,000 men were given the job of exhuming those buried on battlefields, identifying them if possible and then reburying them in cemeteries. As a member of the Imperial War Graves Commission—

HONORING THE DEAD Britain's Unknown Warrior is carried through Boulogne (below). Right: coffins arrive at Douaumont in preparation for selecting France's *Soldat Inconnu.*

established in 1917 to bury or commemorate the war dead of the British Empire—Williams was asked to command them. He was struck by the numbers who were unidentifiable or missing, presumed dead: the 3,888 graveless British soldiers killed during the retreat from the Marne, the 56,000 unknown dead at Ypres, the 20,763 men who had died in Gallipoli with no graves. Backed by Sir Fabian Ware, the head of the Commission, he suggested that one unidentifiable body should be interred in Britain as a symbol of all those who had no grave. It took a year for the War Office to agree that there should indeed be a memorial to the Unknown Warrior.

Once the decision was made, a body was chosen, and the Unknown Warrior began his journey

home in a coffin of oak cut from a tree in the grounds of Hampton Court Palace. In memory of the joint losses of the two wartime allies, Britain and France, he was escorted through northern France by French cavalrymen and carried across the Channel on a British destroyer with a French name, the *Verdun.*

On November 11, 1920, two years to the day after the war had ended, the Unknown Warrior, his coffin now

February 1915
Term "shell
shock" coined

THE EMPTY TOMB Britain's most famous architect of the day, Sir Edwin Lutyens, designed the Cenotaph, here being unveiled in 1920.

adorned with a British soldier's "tin hat" and a crusader warrior's sword, was taken from Victoria Station down Whitehall. There, on the last stroke of 11 a.m., the king unveiled the new Cenotaph (from the Greek for "empty tomb").

The former war correspondent Philip Gibbs wrote in the *Daily Chronicle*: "It did not seem an Unknown Warrior whose body came on a gun-carriage down Whitehall . . . He was known to us all. It was one of 'our boys'—not warriors—as we called them in the days of darkness lit by faith . . . To some women, weeping a little in the crowd after an all-night vigil, he was their own boy who went missing one day and was never found till now . . . To many men wearing ribbons and badges in civilian clothes, he was a familiar figure, one of their comrades."

After two minutes' silence and the singing of "O God, Our Help in Ages Past," the procession continued on its way to Westminster Abbey where the body was interred. The burial service was read, and the king scattered French soil on the coffin.

Meanwhile, the French had acquired their own *Soldat Inconnu*, chosen by their youngest decorated soldier who was blindfolded and asked to point at one of six caskets brought to a special vault at Douaumont, Verdun. At the same time as the service in Westminster Abbey, France's Unknown Soldier was buried with similar pomp in the Arc de Triomphe.

Other memorials to the missing began to be unveiled wherever men had fought, along with tens of thousands of marked graves. Up and down the Western Front today are post-war cemeteries. In Gallipoli, at the southern tip of Cape Helles, overlooking the landing beaches, a tall obelisk stands as the Helles memorial to the missing. In July 1927, the Menin Gate, a huge memorial to the missing, opened on the road out of Ypres. To this day, money raised in Britain pays for a bugler of the Ypres fire brigade to sound taps every evening. Across France and Britain, villages, towns, schools, factories and offices, all raised war memorials recording the names of former neighbors, husbands, sons, students or colleagues who had laid down their lives.

Other nations, too, adopted the motif of the Unknown Warrior. Germany has its *Unbekannte Soldat*, Italy its *Milite Ignoto*. The U.S. Unknown Soldier has his memorial in Arlington National Cemetery on the banks of the Potomac opposite Washington. Australia's memorial to the Unknown Soldier of the 1914-8 war was opened in Canberra in 1993.

No memorial, however, can do more than hint at the terrible waste of the Great War. The Allies lost 5 million men. Great Britain alone lost 743,000 dead. France suffered almost twice as many casualties—just under 1.4 million dead. Of the Romanians who fought, 44 percent were killed. The Central Powers lost more than 3 million on the battle-field. In all, more than 8 million soldiers died as a result of the conflict.

Counting the cost

A high proportion of these men fell between the opposing walls of artillery and machine guns, which acted like the jagged wheels of mincing machines. It was the terrible effectiveness of these killing forces that left so many tens of thousands of men mutilated beyond recognition. This made the task of assembling accurate figures almost impossible—a task further complicated by the onset of other no less destructive events, such as the influenza pandemic of 1918-9.

As with the human cost, the material cost of the war far exceeded the damage done by any previous war. According to some estimates this amounted to around $270 billion, including the damage done by the war and the costs of raising and equipping 65 million soldiers as well as the costs of lost production and war relief.

Such losses were staggering, unprecedented, almost unimaginable. Yet the true cost of the war lay not just in the statistics of death and destruction, but also in the minds of men and women. Hearts and minds bore

THE GRIEVERS In this war memorial at Lodève in the South of France, the emphasis is on the women and children left behind to mourn.

THE CASUALTIES

Estimates of casualties vary hugely. The following are conservative figures based on the best modern scholarship:

	Total forces mobilized	Dead	Wounded
Allies			
Russia	12,000,000	1,700,000	4,950,000
France	8,410,000	1,357,800	4,266,000
Italy	5,615,000	650,000	947,000
Britain	4,970,900	743,000	1,662,600
U.S.	4,355,000	48,000	204,000
India	1,440,400	65,400	69,000
Canada	995,400	56,600	149,700
Japan	800,000	300	900
Romania	750,000	335,700	120,000
Serbia	700,000	45,000	133,000
Australia	420,600	59,300	152,100
Belgium	267,000	13,000	45,000
Greece	230,000	5,000	21,000
South Africa	136,000	7,100	12,000
New Zealand	124,200	16,700	41,300
Portugal	100,000	7,000	14,000
Montenegro	50,000	3,000	10,000
Colonies	12,000	500	800
Newfoundland	11,900	1,200	2,300
Central Powers			
Germany	11,000,000	1,774,000	4,216,000
Austria-Hungary	7,800,000	1,200 000	3,620,000
Turkey	2,850,000	325,000	400,000
Bulgaria	1,200,000	87,500	152,000
Totals (approximate)	**64,238,000**	**8,501,000**	**21,189,000**

far deeper scars than anything recorded in statistical tables.

In Britain, more than 1.5 million were left wounded in body or mind, or both—one in eight of those who served. For the first time in human history, medical advances meant that men involved in the war were as likely to die in action as of disease. Every European village witnessed firsthand the effects of the war. Britain, France and Germany together had some 280,000 cases of a lasting form of injury that was hard to ignore: severe facial disfigurement. As a French textile worker remarked: "The agricultural workers came back as amputees, blind, gassed, or as 'scar throats,' as some were called because of their disfigured, crudely healed faces . . . What a crowd! What a rude shock at the railway station, where the wives went to meet their husbands, to find them like that—crippled, sick, despairing that they would be of no use any more."

In Britain, a special 1,000-bed hospital was set up in Sidcup to cope with the flow of broken faces. Here, new techniques of plastic surgery were developed, with masks—"tin faces"—for those too disfigured for further treatment. Around 11,000 operations were performed between 1917 and 1925.

The lives of thousands were as shattered as their faces, as an orderly at a London hospital recorded: "To talk to a lad who six months ago was probably a wholesome and pleasing specimen of English youth . . . is something of an ordeal. You know very well that he has examined himself in a mirror. That one eye of his has contemplated the mangled mess which is his face—all the more hopeless because "healed." He has seen himself without a nose. Skilled skin grafting has reconstructed a something which owns two small orifices that are his nostrils; but the something is emphatically not a nose. He has every reason to bless surgery. And yet . . . Surgery has at last washed its hands of him; in his mirror he is greeted by a gargoyle."

With France's greater proportion of casualties, disfigurement was a particularly French problem. Many men were scarred beyond recognition. One blind veteran, named Lazé, returned home, only to hear his young son running away screaming in fear, "That's not Papa!" Lazé told his nurse: "Having once been a man, having once understood the meaning of this word and wanting nothing more than just to be a man, I am now an object of terror to my own son, a daily burden to my wife, a shameful thing to all humanity." He committed suicide. Others found a new life only because of the work of their own charity, the Union of Disfigured Men.

Post-traumatic stress

The war also saw the emergence of a new ailment, the psychological and emotional collapse of men in the face of its unexpected horrors. Only in the 1970s was the condition recognized by psychologists and given a name: post-traumatic stress disorder (PTSD).

AN EYE FOR AN EYE Disfigurement inspired original remedies, like this French mask to disguise the loss of a right eye.

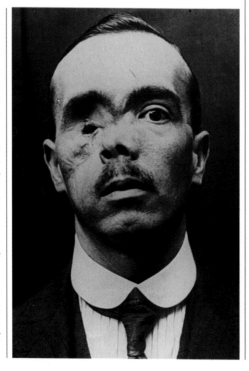

The symptoms are listed in many medical papers—nightmares, flashbacks, guilt at having survived when others died, uncontrolled weeping, an inability to function in normal society—and the causes are now well understood. In part, PTSD is a response to the shock of seeing life torn apart in hellish circumstances. But such experiences have been a commonplace of war for centuries, and men have adapted. Not so in 1914-8. In this war, something more fundamental was at stake.

In February 1915, a paper by Dr. Charles Myers in *The Lancet* gave the condition a name: shell shock. Before knowledge of the term became widespread, the condition was dismissed as a personality defect—cowardice, loss of nerve. That attitude put down deep roots among officers, as if all a man had to do was "pull himself together" or "get a grip." Anyone who could not do this risked being labelled SI—"self-inflicted wound"—and disciplined.

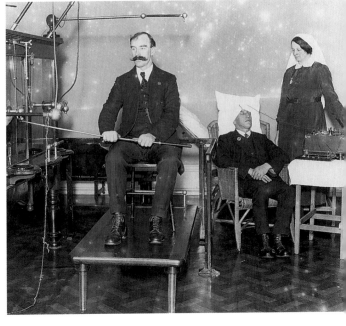

REHABILITATION Sound in body but bruised in mind, two shell-shocked soldiers undergo different forms of treatment in a British hospital.

event most often men—asks "why?" and receives no answer. Often, a professional soldier needs no other answer than the survival of his group, whether the group is a six-man platoon or a nation. But many men need a larger purpose. On the Western Front, often, suffering had no greater purpose. Soldiers—in increasing numbers as the professionals became swamped with volunteers and then poorly trained conscripts—saw no meaning in a universe of destruction.

By 1918, 50,000 British soldiers had collapsed with shell shock, or "war neurosis," as it was sometimes called. After the war, the suspicion arose that some of the 346 British soldiers shot for capital offenses, desertion, cowardice or refusing to obey orders were in fact suffering from this ailment. Yet the psychological effects of war were never truly acknowledged. A Shell Shock Committee met for two years but failed to provide further insight. Men whose minds remained blasted by war had to live with the fear that they would be branded as cowards, a wound of the spirit that was carried into civilian life.

Even when a man came through the war still able to function emotionally, he was not unscathed. "The man who really endured the war at its worst was everlastingly differentiated from everyone except his fellow soldiers," wrote the poet, Siegfried Sassoon, reduced to a wreck by his war-time experiences.

Lasting consequences

The emotional impact of the war hit the societies of all belligerent countries, and it lay at the root of many postwar changes. Across Europe, for instance, people came to believe that there had to be better ways of living than those of the old

SELF HELP A poster publicizes France's Association of War Wounded, which helped men like this Senegalese amputee (right).

Only in the aftermath of Vietnam did American psychologists identify PTSD and its core cause, which many psychologists now agree is loss of meaning. A man or woman subjected to pain, horrific sights and probable death needs to feel that there is a purpose in the suffering, if it is to be endured with fortitude. In Vietnam, and in the First World War, all too often the victim could see none. He—victims are by the nature of the regimes. The mood turned against royalty, and toward republicanism and democracy.

Germany suffered the most. The Allies were left with the comfort of having won the war, and thus were able to believe that something had been gained. But German society suffered from a national case of post-traumatic stress disorder. The Allied blockade continued until peace was signed in late 1919. Millions of fathers returned not as victors, but as victims. Children were growing up surrounded by disease, poverty and shattered homes, all sufferings imposed by outsiders. Parents were torn by grief, not only because of their losses, but because they were riven by a terrible dilemma: they had believed that their sons were fighting for a good cause, in defense of the Fatherland, but now they had come to believe that the sacrifice was for nothing, that the older generation had in effect betrayed the younger.

It was an agony captured by the Berlin artist Käthe Kollwitz, whose son Peter was killed in October 1914. She had been proud when he volunteered, yet later saw "only the madness of war" and her own guilt in helping to unleash it. Fourteen years after the war's end, she stated her agony in a statue for the Roggevelde German cemetery in Belgium. It is of two old people on their knees, begging the forgiveness of the dead around them.

For many of the older generation, life had become meaningless. Others—the reac-

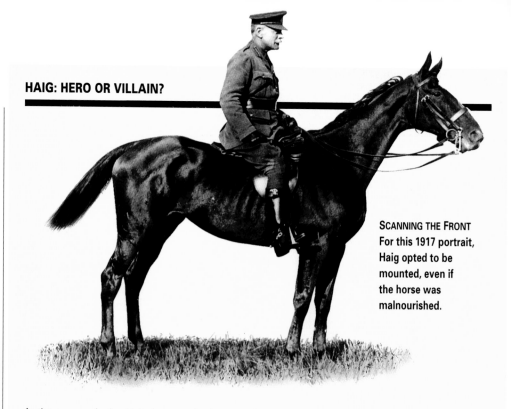

HAIG: HERO OR VILLAIN?

SCANNING THE FRONT For this 1917 portrait, Haig opted to be mounted, even if the horse was malnourished.

As the commander in chief who supervised unprecedented slaughter, and as the commander who saw the British army through to final victory, Sir Douglas Haig has been criticized for heartlessness and lack of imagination, and praised for his fortitude. Historians still work to balance the two.

Haig, a methodical Scot, was not an attractive personality, nor brilliant; he had failed his staff college exam. But he had ambition and drive. He eagerly assumed the burden of leadership in 1916, and never thought of setting it aside until the problem of breaking through the German lines had been solved. It was this obstinacy that drew criticism, for he did not allow ever-rising casualty lists to deter him. But that does not equate with heartlessness. "Why waste your time with me?" he said testily to the portraitist Sir William Orpen. "Go and paint the men. They're the fellows who are saving the world, and they're getting killed every day." He made a point of touring the front often; and after the war, his devotion to veterans was unstinting.

Haig's fault was that of all commanders on either side—he did not understand what trench warfare involved: the impossibility of taking trenches by assault, the dominance of the machine gun, the need for massive artillery and for some new, as yet unknown, means of breaking the deadlock. He learned the rules of this warfare as quickly as anyone and saw, with greater insight than many, that they were ruthless. That realization threatened his emotional stability—he developed attacks of asthma and nervous twitches, tugging at his moustache. But he endured. In the end, industrial production and weight of firepower—backed by the tank—prevailed. Historians accept that, once committed to war and final victory, vast losses were inevitable. Many agree that Haig—dour, unimaginative, plodding—was just the man to command so grim an endeavor.

REMORSE IN STONE Statues by the German Käthe Kollwitz show the sculptress and her husband, Karl, kneeling at the grave of their son, Peter, in Belgium.

tionaries and the young —sought meaning by embracing myths, like the notion that "true" Germans had been betrayed, and that meaning could be found in what had just been endured: in violence. Only by violence and revenge could they hope to avoid the ultimate assault: a complete loss of identity. Such humiliation might have been salved by political stability and economic revival, as happened after the Second World War. After 1918, there would be no revival, with consequences that would prove dire. A few foresaw the catastrophe that such stress engendered. In 1919, the economist John Maynard Keynes, in his *Economic Consequences of the Peace*, posed the question: "Who can say how much is endurable, or in what direction men will seek at last to escape from their misfortunes?"

It was a question that would be answered, tragically, in 1933, when the Nazis came to power in Germany, and in 1939 when another world war broke out.

RESHAPING THE WORLD

THE VERSAILLES PEACE TREATY LARGELY DEFINED THE WORLD FOR THE REST OF THE CENTURY—BUT LEFT MANY PROBLEMS UNSOLVED

A young economist, John Maynard Keynes, summed up the mood at the peace conference that convened in Paris in January 1919: "We are at the dead season of our fortunes. We have been moved beyond endurance, and need rest. Never in the lifetime of men now living has the universal element in the soul of man burnt so low."

Rest and resurrection were to be granted in some measure by the peace, the widest-ranging treaty since the defeat of Napoleon and eclipsing even that in its scale. Though the participants did not call this a world war—to them it was the Great War—it had encompassed the world, and the peace would have to do the same. In all, 27 nations would be parties to the main treaty, and 17 of these would be non-European. One of them was the United States, another Japan. For the first time, East and West met to help to remold the world, supposedly in the image of new ideals. The war was to become the war that ended all war.

Authority at the talks reflected a combination of economic power, military power and ambition. President Wilson had all three. The war had blessed America. "Only" 48,000 men had died in battle—some 6 percent of British deaths—and from the carnage in Europe, America had emerged as the world's greatest power. Wilson had played such a crucial role in molding the Armistice that he was able to dictate an agenda, based on his Fourteen Points, which he wanted to be the foundation for a new world order.

But everyone brought his own agenda, and the actual talks became a confusion of international and domestic interests, of idealism and hatred. Composing the inner circle of Great Power leaders were Wilson, France's Georges Clemenceau, and David Lloyd George, who brought much of the British government from London to Paris with him. Sometimes the inner circle expanded to include Vittorio Orlando of Italy and Saionji Kimmochi of Japan. Together, the prime ministers and foreign ministers of these five countries formed a Council of Ten, with lesser powers hovering at the door—delegates from the dominions and from the new nations of Eastern Europe.

Wilson arrived with the idea of a League of Nations at the top of his agenda. It was at his insistence that the formation of the League became one of the first items to be included in the peace treaty. A second Wilsonian principle was that colonial claims should be adjusted so that the interests of the populations concerned would be considered equally with the claims of the governments. In effect, all peoples should be granted equality—an extension of democracy to the international order. The world, as President Wilson said, was to be made safe for democracy. These were ideas that subject races found particularly inspiring, and they would influence international relations from then on.

Differences of opinion

From the start, the great ideals were obscured by old-fashioned nationalism. France, which had suffered most from German occupation, saw peace in terms of a humbled Germany. Clemenceau had lived through the German occupation of Paris in 1871; the president, Raymond Poincaré, came from Lorraine, which Germany had annexed in 1871; and the commander in chief, Marshal Foch, knew how close France had been to collapse in 1918. Their idea of peace was to keep Germany as weak as possible. There was even a move to annex the left bank of the Rhine with its

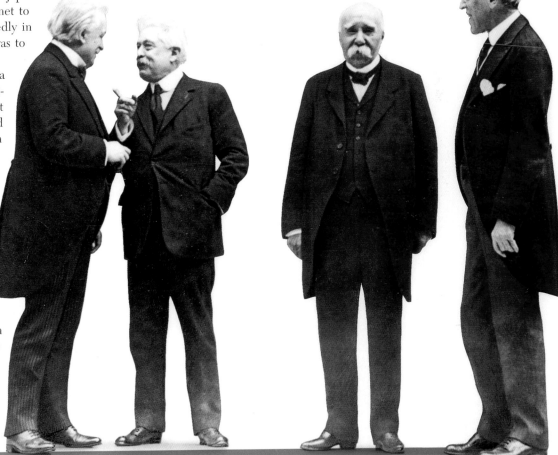

BIG FOUR The leaders of Britain, Italy, France and the U.S.—from left to right, Lloyd George, Orlando, Clemenceau and Wilson—dominated the conference.

rich coal and steel resources. Lloyd George, too, was in no mood to be generous toward Germany. He had recently promised his electorate to "squeeze Germany until the pips squeaked." Since these sentiments were not at all what Wilson had in mind, he spent a good deal of time and

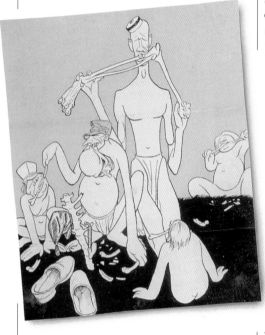

CONSUMED BY REVENGE A German cartoon in the satirical magazine *Simplicissimus* shows the Allies as cannibals devouring Germany.

effort in moderating the punitive impulses of France and Britain.

There then emerged a difference between the French and British views. France was wedded to the idea that Germany, previously the economic powerhouse of Europe, should make reparations for the war and thus be kept weak. "*L'Allemagne paiera!*" —"Germany will pay!"—insisted the French. Britain soon realized, however, that a ruined Germany would be unable to buy British products.

Already, the grand idea of self-determination for all had proved an ideal better honored in words than in practice. America itself had been part of the Allied attempt to unseat the Bolsheviks in Russia, despite the

SQUEEZING GERMANY French soldiers guard German coal in the Ruhr, occupied in 1923 after Germany had defaulted on coal deliveries imposed at Versailles.

Bolsheviks' espousal of an ethic that was as uncompromisingly anticolonial as America's. And what, in the end, defined a nation that was not yet a nation? Everything depended on the clout of those wanting to become nations and the prejudices of those around the table at Versailles. Poland was to be blessed with nationhood; the Jews, too, should qualify, even if this meant that the Arabs would not qualify to quite the extent they had been promised. No one took seriously the idea that non-whites should have the same rights conferred upon them as whites. Japan tried to have racial equality written into the treaty as a principle, and failed.

Nationhood and colonies

Britain, as an imperial power, was not yet ready to adopt Wilson's anticolonialism. There was no denying that the so-called white dominions—Canada, Australia, New Zealand, South Africa—should qualify for nationhood, after their contribution to the war effort. However, no one even raised the possibility that the South African blacks, the Maoris of New Zealand, the Australian Aborigines or the Canadian Indians should have a voice in their countries' government.

Indeed, all nations but the U.S. still seemed to regard the possession of colonies as proof of nationhood. Japan was eager to take over German possessions in China. South Africa wanted German Southwest Africa (present-day Namibia), and Australian and New Zealand delegates demanded control of Germany's colonies in the Pacific.

Wilson did his best to infuse his anticolonial ideals into the Australian premier, William Hughes. At one point Wilson shouted at Hughes, who was very deaf: "Is Australia prepared to defy the appeal of the whole civilized world?" Hughes replied: "That's about the size of it, President Wilson."

Wilson gave up, though a new word, "mandate," was invented to replace the politically incorrect "colony." Thus, Australia was granted a mandate over New Guinea, New Zealand got Samoa, and Japan was given Germany's Pacific islands as well as taking over its concessions in Shandong, China.

IMPERIAL OVERSTRETCH

The war shattered Britain's economy and marked the beginning of the end for its empire. Ironically, though, because of the new mandates awarded at Versailles, the British Empire emerged from the war larger than ever before. In geographical terms, it reached its peak in 1919-22, when British direct or indirect rule reached a quarter of the world: some 40 mainland territories, several hundred islands and 450 million people.

Negotiations centered on the problem of Germany. The Germans had sued for peace because they could not win the war. But nor had they lost it. As time dragged on and the Allies demobilized, the Germans, with their army still largely intact, appeared increasingly strong. This reinforced German expectations that, with the kaiser gone, they would be accepted on roughly equal terms. The Allies had no such intention in mind. Wilson, Clemenceau and Lloyd George could not acknowledge that there were any good Germans, however democratic and liberal their stated aims.

January 1919
Peace conference convenes

June 1919
Treaty of Versailles
—with Germany

September 1919
Treaty of Saint-Germain
—with Austria

November 1919
Treaty of Neuilly
—with Bulgaria

THE LOSERS The leader of the German delegation, Count Ulrich von Brockdorff-Rantzau (third from right), poses grimly with his staff.

In May 1919, the treaty was presented to the Germans, whose delegates had been kept under humiliating conditions of virtual house arrest in Paris. Their head, Count Ulrich von Brockdorff-Rantzau, was appalled. "Those who sign this Treaty," he said after reading it, "will sign the death sentence of many millions of German men, women and children."

At the time, an elected Assembly in Weimar was drawing up a new constitution for Germany. A bitter debate followed among its leaders, but the Allies were adamant. In June, they presented Germany with an ultimatum: sign, or hostilities would be resumed. It was in response to this crisis that the Germans scuttled their own fleet held by the British at Scapa Flow. To avoid invasion

Terms would be harsh. Germany was to be disarmed, deprived of an air force, heavy guns, tanks and a navy. The army was to be limited to 100,000 volunteers. Though the French demand to occupy the Rhine's left bank was watered down, the area would be a neutral zone, occupied by Allied troops for 15 years. France would be allowed to exploit the coalfields of Saarland for 15 years, in compensation for wrecked coalmines in territory Germany had occupied during the war.

In small ways, the principle of self-determination worked in Germany's favor. A plebiscite gave Silesia to Germany, and the Polish port of Danzig (Gdansk), with its majority of German speakers, became a Free City. But in one major instance, the principle of self-determination was ignored. Now that Austria-Hungary was no more, the Austrians —Germans in speech and culture—had proclaimed their freedom as German-Austria and demanded *Anschluss* (union) with Germany. But, the victors argued, it would clearly make a nonsense of victory if Germany emerged from defeat larger than ever. *Anschluss* was forbidden.

The most controversial question was that of reparations. In theory, the Germans were supposed to take the blame for starting the war and were therefore supposed to pay for the damage they had caused. But no one actually suggested that Germany could do this, since the German economy was in ruins. In any case, it was impossible to work out the extent of the damage caused by the

war or what the Germans might be able to pay. The Allies settled for a statement of principle. Germany was proclaimed as the guilty party, and the level of reparations was left to be decided by a special commission.

THE END OF THE GERMAN FLEET

The German fleet had been seized by Britain after the Armistice, and the 74 warships were anchored in the sweeping 15 by 8 mile inlet of Scapa Flow in the Orkneys, with skeleton crews of 1,800 under the command of Rear-Admiral von Reuter. Britain was eager to take possession of the ships, but had to wait until the other Allies agreed.

On June 21, 1919, von Reuter heard that the Versailles Treaty was about to be signed and guessed that the ships would be handed over to the British. In response to orders issued in 1914 that no ship was ever to be surrendered, von Reuter decided on a grand gesture of defiance: he ordered the ships to be scuttled.

First to go down, shortly after midday, was the battleship *Friedrich der Grosse*. Quickly the rest followed. The British sailors on the few guardships tried to stop the Germans abandoning their vessels by opening fire, killing eight Germans, but to no effect. By late afternoon, all the ships were gone except four that were towed ashore

RELIC OF WAR The remains of a German ship at Scapa Flow.

by British ships. Last to sink was the *Hindenburg*, which vanished beneath the grey waters at 5 p.m. The wrecks were later raised, broken up and sold for scrap.

April 1920
Treaty of Sèvres
—with Turkey

June 1920
Treaty of Trianon
—with Hungary

" THE TREATY OF VERSAILLES

The British diplomat, Harold Nicolson, recorded the moment the German delegates arrived to sign the treaty:

"And then, isolated and pitiable, come the two German delegates, Dr. Müller, Dr. Bell. The silence is terrifying. Their feet upon a strip of parquet between the savonnerie carpets echo hollow and duplicate. They keep their eyes fixed away from those two thousand staring eyes, fixed upon the ceiling. They are deathly pale. They do not appear as representatives of a brutal militarism. The one is thin and pink-eyelidded: the second fiddle in a Brunswick orchestra. The other is moon-faced and suffering: a *privat-dozent* [lecturer]. It is all most painful.

"They are conducted to their chairs. Clemenceau at once breaks the silence. '*Messieurs*,' he rasps, '*la séance est ouverte*.' He adds a few ill-chosen words. 'We are here to sign a Treaty of Peace.' The Germans leap up anxiously when he has finished, since they know that they are the first to sign. William Martin, as if a theater manager, motions them petulantly to sit down again. Mantoux translates Clemenceau's words into English. Then St. Quentin advances towards the Germans and with the utmost dignity leads them to a little table on which the Treaty is expanded. There is general tension. They sign. There is a general relaxation. Conversation hums again in an undertone. The delegates stand up one by one and pass onwards to the queue which waits by the signature table . . .

"We kept our seats while the Germans were conducted like prisoners from the dock, their eyes still fixed upon some distant point of the horizon." "

and further suffering from the blockade, the Assembly accepted—as a man may sign his soul away with a gun at his head.

The threat of war lifted, and the blockade ended. But acceptance marked the start of another round of bitterness. Whatever was agreed immediately, the treaty's absurdities were so obvious that there could only be one long-term aim for Germans: rejection.

The formal signing was arranged in the Hall of Mirrors in Versailles—a symbolic setting, for it was here that the German Empire had been proclaimed after Germany's victory over France in 1871. On June 28, all the leaders signed the 200-page treaty, and then, amidst fusillades of gunfire and playing fountains, the public celebrated the formal end to the war.

Ideals and reality

High hopes were soon shattered by cold realities. There were still many loose ends to be tidied up, and these were discussed in several other palatial venues around Paris through the autumn, and into the following summer. Peace was signed with the other former enemies: with Austria at Saint-Germain in September, with Bulgaria at Neuilly in November, with Turkey at Sèvres in April 1920 and with Hungary at Trianon in June 1920. But these treaties were formalities. By the time the negotiations started, the states in question, except for Bulgaria, had changed out of all recognition since the leaders of Habsburg Austria-Hungary and Ottoman Turkey went to war as the Central Powers.

The treaties recognized the new nations, but could not resolve the issues lurking behind their emergence—the demands for self-determination. Indeed, in this large patchwork of countries, self-determination could never be guaranteed by frontiers, because the peoples and cultures formed a smaller-scale patchwork. In all the nations of eastern Europe, pockets of minorities remained,

MAKING PEACE In a painting by the war artist Sir William Orpen, the Big Four watch the German delegates sign the treaty in the Hall of Mirrors, Versailles.

resentful of being cut off from their fellows. German-speakers in South Tyrol were now under Italian rule; a third of Poland's inhabitants did not speak Polish; an enlarged Romania contained formerly Hungarian Transylvania, with over a million Hungarians.

ENEMIES NO LONGER Delegates from Hungary arrive under French escort to sign the Treaty of Trianon on June 4, 1920.

Czechoslovakia was a collection of minorities, its 10 million people comprising 3 million Czechs, 2.5 million Slovaks, 1 million Hungarians, half a million Ruthenians and over 3 million Germans. The principles of self-determination, strictly applied, would have redistributed all but the Czechs to other countries. The nation was recognized as it was largely through the force of personality of its Czech leaders, Tomás Masaryk and Eduard Benes.

On the Dalmatian coast, Fiume (present-day Rijeka in Croatia) had been variously Austrian, Hungarian, Croatian and Austro-Hungarian, but never Italian. Nevertheless, its main section had a majority of Italians. Italy was anxious to own it, and took up an inordinate amount of conference time asserting its claim. The secret treaty of London, signed in April 1915, had backed many Italian claims in the event of Italy's entering the war. In the case of Fiume, however, Wilson thought that it should go to the new Kingdom of Serbs, Croats and Slovenes—effectively an enlarged Serbia, renamed Yugoslavia in 1928. On the other hand, Italy was an ally and one of the Great Powers. The conference could not decide. In response, the self-publicizing right-wing poet, Gabriele D'Annunzio, seized Fiume in September, 1919. Three months later Italy agreed with Yugoslavia that Fiume was to be a free city and threw him out.

One of the great flaws of the Versailles conference was its failure to include the new Soviet Russia. At a stroke, the treaty with Germany annulled the Treaty of Brest-Litovsk, which Soviet Russia and imperial Germany had signed in March 1918, but nothing took its place. The Polish-Russian border was defined by the British foreign minister, Lord Curzon. For a while, the Great Powers intervened in Russia's Civil War, hoping to unseat the Bolsheviks. When they failed, they ignored them. Thus they ensured the creation of that which they most feared: an introverted state intensely hostile to the outside world.

NATIONALIST FLOURISH The flamboyant writer Gabriele D'Annunzio (left) briefly cut the Gordian knot of Allied diplomacy when he arrived to seize Fiume for Italy (below).

Article 8 of the League's Covenant—that everyone would eventually disarm down to the level of Germany. The subject of disarmament took up much League time in the years to come, with nothing to show for it. In the end, it was shown to be suicidal when Hitler came to power in 1933, and all nations rearmed to ensure their own security.

Another idea that foundered was that of reparations. In April 1921, the Reparations Commission finally reported that Germany should pay more than 132 billion gold marks ($33 billion). The Allies demanded a billion marks by the end of May, backed by the threat of occupying the rich industrial zone of the Ruhr. Germany complied by borrowing the money in London. It took 10 years, ruinous inflation in Germany and a worldwide depression to make the Allies back away from their insistence on reparations. By then it was too late.

A new map for the Middle East

In the Middle East, the collapse of Turkey created a hydra of new problems. By the Treaty of Sèvres, Sultan Mehmed VI had renounced all claims to non-Turkish territory.

The League of Nations, meanwhile, with its headquarters in Geneva, got off to a weak start. In many ways it was an exciting venture: here, for the first time, was an international authority that was not an empire, but the beginnings of a world organization—42 nations, of whom 26 were non-European. However, Wilson's vision was not supported by politicians back home. America refused to join, and the League proved unequal to the intricacies of postwar international relations.

One of the ideals embodied in the League was disarmament. Although the French assumed that German military weakness, imposed at Versailles, would allow France to remain strong, Wilson and other League members held an opposite view, based on

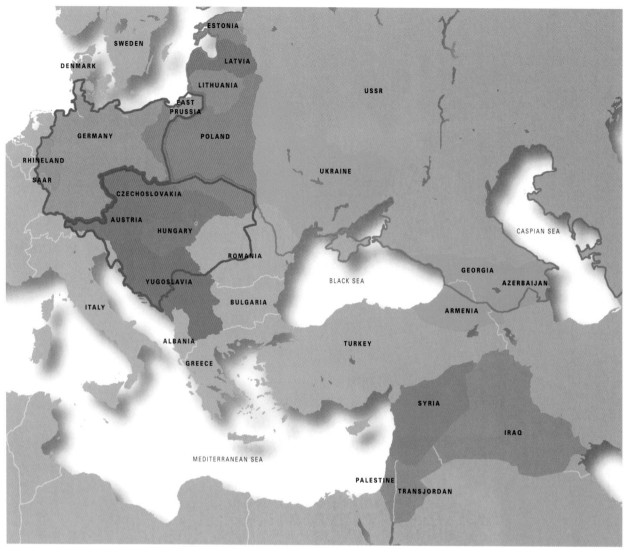

POSTWAR EUROPE

━━ Frontier of German Empire 1914

━━ Frontier of Austro-Hungarian Empire 1914

━━ Frontier of Russian Empire 1914

▆ British Mandate 1920

▆ French Mandate 1920

On Germany's western frontier, the Rhineland became a neutral zone to be occupied by the Allies for a term of 15 years, and the Saar was placed under League of Nations control, with the French allowed to work its coalfields. In central Europe, Estonia, Latvia and Lithuania were given complete independence from Russia. Poland was reconstituted as a state with territory from Germany, Russia and the former Austro-Hungarian Empire. Several new states were created from the Austro-Hungarian Empire: Austria and Hungary were separated; the new state of Czechoslovakia was formed. Serbia became the core of a new state, eventually known as Yugoslavia. Italy, Romania and Greece gained new territory. The Ukraine, Georgia and Azerbaijan, all part of Russia in 1914, briefly became independent republics, as did Armenia; by 1924 they had been forcibly incorporated into the new U.S.S.R. In the Middle East, lands that had previously been part of the Ottoman Empire were divided between British and French spheres of influence.

This allowed the emergence of two rival forces, Arab and Jewish, both conjured on to the stage by the British.

During the war, Britain had supported the cause of Arab nationalism, hoping to undermine the Turks from the south, and in 1916 it recognized its main ally, Hussein, as king of the Hejaz (now the Western Province of Saudi Arabia). But British influence was offset by the presence in Syria of the French, there as the result of a secret Anglo-French agreement in 1916, dividing the Ottoman Empire into spheres of influence.

Arab nationalist aims were in direct conflict with another British commitment that had little to do with the war, but which played a crucial role in the peace: Britain's backing of Zionist aspirations for a Jewish state. In 1903, Britain had offered to back the establishment of a Jewish homeland in Uganda—an idea that inspired an acrimonious debate among Zionists and was turned down by the majority. British support culminated in a declaration by the Foreign Secretary, Arthur Balfour, in 1917, favoring "the establishment in Palestine of a national home for the Jewish people" as long as the civil and political rights of the non-Jewish Palestinians were protected. British motives, though rooted in a feeling that Biblical realities should be restored, were influenced by geopolitics. The French would assert their claim to Syria, and would thus control territory uncomfortably close to the Suez Canal. A Jewish national homeland would provide a useful buffer.

Thus, at Paris, when Turkey's empire came to be divided up, Britain in effect gained

TOWARD THE UNITED NATIONS The committee appointed to devise the new League of Nations included delegates from Japan, Greece, Serbia, South Africa and China.

all the Arab lands apart from Syria. It divided ancient Palestine between a new Jewish area on the west bank of the Jordan and an Arab state on the east bank, Transjordan. A third state, Iraq, rounded off these mandates. Britain hoped for the compliance of royal kinsmen, two sons of Hussein—Abdullah who became King of Transjordan (today's Jordan), and Feisal, who became King of Iraq. But the new nations seethed with discontent. In the Hejaz, Hussein himself was ejected in 1924, and later Saudi Arabia came into existence under a new king, Ibn Saud.

The consequences of peace

Versailles confirmed and extended what the war had already established: a new Europe and a new order that would define world politics from then on. Four empires had vanished—those of the Habsburgs, the Hohenzollerns, the Romanovs and the Ottoman sultans—and new nations emerged, most of which survive to this day. Wilson's principles of self-determination formed the agenda for colonial peoples everywhere.

REPRESENTING ARABIA Arab delegates at the conference included Hussein's third son, Feisal (at front), accompanied by Colonel T.E. Lawrence (middle row, second from right).

ECHOES OF WAR IN CENTRAL ASIA

The war that gave birth to the Russian Revolution had effects even farther afield, in the grasslands of Mongolia. This vast expanse, peopled by nomads whose way of life had changed hardly at all since Genghis Khan led them to a brief imperial glory 700 years before, had been Chinese until China's weakness allowed the Mongolians to break away in 1911. Now a brief resurgence of Chinese power from the south came into conflict with rival Red and White Russian ambitions to the north.

Mongolia had broken from China in 1911 to become a Buddhist monarchy, similar to the Dalai Lama's Tibet, led by the Jebtsundamba Khutukhtu, "Living Buddha." It was retaken in 1919 by a notorious Chinese warlord known as Little Hsu, and then taken over in February 1921 by a psychotic, anti-Semitic White Russian baron, Roman von Ungern-Sternberg. The "Mad Baron," with a piercing stare and wild hair, was from a German Baltic family. Baron Ungern, as he was known, had been a naval officer in the Russo-Japanese War, and then joined the Trans-Baikal Cossacks, planning to turn this band into a clan of Buddhist warriors who would combat what he believed to be the forces of darkness and destruction: Communists and Jews. But Baron Ungern was prepared to extend his range. In exchange for $3 million, paid by the Living Buddha, Ungern agreed to support the Buddhist monarchy and drive the Chinese out, on the understanding that he could use Urga (present-day Ulan Bator) as a base for an assault into Siberia. He then embarked on an orgy of destruction that turned all but his immediate entourage against him.

Baron Ungern's murderous five-month regime ended in July 1921, when Mongolia's national hero, Sükhebaatar, brought in Red Army troops to drive out the Mad Baron and the Chinese alike. Mongolia became the world's second Communist nation, with a Russian presence that ended only with the collapse of communism 70 years later.

Ironically, one lobbyist at Paris was a 25-year-old Vietnamese, eager to assert his people's rights over those of their French imperial masters. Years later, the same man would assert those claims by force of arms, first against France, then against the U.S. The man would become known as Ho Chi Minh.

The most disastrous consequence of the peace was the continued impoverishment of Germany—a country crucial to Europe's well-being. From political weakness, economic ruin and inflation unmatched before or since sprang the demon of Nazism, driven by Hitler's burning desire to avenge the humiliation of the peace. When Hitler came to power, reparations had all but been abandoned, but the territorial awards remained, as did the military restrictions. His first tasks in reversing Versailles were to rearm, seize the Rhineland, unite with Austria and then dismember Czechoslovakia.

It was not until 1945 that the lessons of the First World War were truly learned. Only then did the world, with the League reborn as the United Nations and America accepting the role its influence demanded, adopt President Wilson's principles of reconciliation and cooperation. Only then, and in the decades following, could it be said with some truth that the supreme sacrifice of more than 8 million lives had not, after all, been in vain.

TIMECHART

1914

JANUARY

23 In Panama, George Washington Goethals, army engineer in charge of building the **Panama Canal**, is appointed Governor of Canal Zone.

MARCH

20 In the **Curragh Mutiny**, British cavalry officers say they will resign if ordered into Northern Ireland to support Irish Home Rule.

MAY

25 The British House of Commons passes the **Home Rule** for Ireland Bill.

JUNE

23 The British prime minister Herbert Asquith modifies the Home Rule Bill to allow the **exclusion of Ulster**.

28 In Sarajevo, the assassination of **Archduke Franz Ferdinand**,

THE COLLECTIVE BOOT This French postcard of 1914 reflects the Allied belief that the Triple Entente of Britain, France and Russia would deal with the kaiser and Germany.

heir to the Austro-Hungarian throne, sets the world on the road to war.

JULY

5 Germany promises to support Austria in the event of conflict with Serbia.

10 Ulster's Unionist leaders reaffirm their determination to resist Irish Home Rule.

23 Austria issues an **ultimatum** to Serbia.

25 Serbia **mobilizes** and gives an evasive reply to Austria. Austria mobilizes against Serbia.

28 Austria **declares war** on Serbia.

30 Russia orders mobilization in support of Serbia.

31 Germany sends an **ultimatum** to Russia, demanding an end to war preparations. Germany also refuses to guarantee that it will respect the **neutrality of Belgium**. Austria starts a general mobilization.

AUGUST

1 France and Germany both **mobilize**. Germany declares war on Russia. A German-Turkish treaty is signed in Constantinople. Italy declares its neutrality.

2 Germany invades **Luxembourg** and demands permission from Belgium to cross its territory. The demand is rejected. Russia invades East Prussia.

3 Germany **declares war** on France.

4 Germany declares war on **Belgium**, and invades. Britain declares war on Germany, and establishes a naval blockade in the North Sea. President Wilson declares **U.S. neutrality.**

ROADSIDE REFUGEES Belgian peasants, made homeless by the advancing Germans, take a rest.

5-6 In a night attack, the Germans pass the fortifications of **Liège**, which are then destroyed by artillery.

6 Austria-Hungary **declares war** on Russia. Serbia declares war on Germany.

7 The British and French invade **Togoland**.

8 Montenegro declares war on Austria; the next day it **declares war** on Germany.

11 The Ottoman authorities allow the German cruisers *Goeben* and *Breslau* to pass through **the Dardanelles**, thus revealing the strength of German influence in Turkey.

12 Austro-Hungarian armies **invade Serbia**.

REINFORCEMENTS REQUIRED After the desperate retreat of the British from Mons (below), a British recruiting poster (right) delivers a reproachful message to men who have not yet joined up.

13 France and Great Britain **declare war** on Austria.

14 The **Battle of the Frontiers** begins in Lorraine. Russia promises autonomy to Poland in return for Polish aid.

17 Japan issues an ultimatum to Germany demanding the evacuation of the German treaty port of **Qingdao** (Tsingtao) in China.

17-21 The Serbs repulse the Austrians in the Battles of **Tser** and **Jadar**.

18-19 The Germans defeat the Belgians at **Tirlement**.

19-20 In East Prussia, the Russians defeat the Germans at the Battle of **Gumbinnen**.

20 The Germans enter **Brussels**.

21 The British government orders raising a "**New Army**" of volunteers.

21-24 The French are driven back at **Charleroi**.

23 At the Battle of **Mons**, the British start a two-week retreat. In East Prussia, Hindenburg and Ludendorff take command

will they *never* come?

REPRINTED FROM
"THE WEEKLY DISPATCH"

of the German forces. Japan declares war on Germany.

26 Japan **declares war** on Austria-Hungary. The British stage a rearguard action at **Le Cateau**. German Togoland capitulates.

26-30 In the Battle of **Tannenberg**, the Germans rout the Russians.

28 British cruisers raid German ships in the **Heligoland Bight**.

30 Von Kluck **abandons his advance** on Paris. New Zealanders occupy **Samoa**.

SEPTEMBER

2 The Battle of **Zamosc-Komarov** ends with a victory for the Austrians over the Russians.

3 The **German submarine U-21** sinks the British cruiser *Pathfinder*, the first warship to fall victim to torpedo attack—259 lives are lost. The **French government** starts to move to Bordeaux.

5-10 The Battle of the **Marne** leads to an advance of British and French troops.

6-15 In the Battle of the **Masurian Lakes**, the Germans complete their defeat of the Russians.

7 A British force from Nigeria and a French one from French West Africa invade the German colony of **Cameroon**.

8-12 At the Battle of **Lemberg**, the Russians force the Austrians out of eastern Galicia.

8-17 The Battle of **Drina** ends with the Austrians pushing back the Serbs.

13 On the Western Front, the Germans make a stand north of the **Aisne**.

14 Erich von Falkenhayn succeeds Helmuth von Moltke as German commander in chief.

14-28 In the Battle of the **Aisne**, the British fail to dislodge the Germans.

MARCHING ORDERS French and British troops advance together on the Aisne.

16 The Battle of **Yser** starts: the Belgians flood the district and prevent any further German advances to the Channel ports. The Russians besiege **Przemysl**.

17 The Germans in **New Guinea** capitulate.

18 Hindenburg is made commander in chief of German armies on the Eastern Front. In Britain, the **Irish Home Rule Bill** receives royal assent.

22 The Battle of **Picardy** opens, but the Germans are not dislodged.

22-25 German troops make repeated attacks on **Verdun**. The Germans take **St. Mihiel** on the left bank of the Meuse.

24 The Russians attack the **Carpathian passes** leading to Hungary.

28 The Germans and Austrians **attack Russian troops** south of Warsaw, but are driven back.

OCTOBER

1 Turkey closes its strategically important strait, **the Dardanelles**.

4 The Austrians relieve **Przemysl** and force a Russian withdrawal from the Carpathians.

9 The Belgians are forced to abandon **Antwerp**.

11 In the **Race to the Sea**, the Germans take Ghent, then Lille (12th), Bruges (14th) and Ostend (15th).

12 The First Battle of **Ypres** opens, lasting until November 11. The Germans reach **Warsaw**, but are soon forced back by the Russians.

15 Congress passes the **Clayton Act,** giving unions the right to strike.

18 The Germans attempt a **submarine raid** on Scapa Flow.

NOVEMBER

1 Off **Coronel**, on the Chilean coast, a German cruiser squadron sinks two British ships.

2-5 The Germans in East Africa defeat the British at **Tanga**.

3 German battle cruisers raid **Yarmouth**.

4 Russia and Serbia **declare war** on Turkey.

5 Britain and France **declare war** on Turkey.

9 The Australian cruiser *Sydney* destroys the German *Emden* off the Cocos Islands in the Indian Ocean.

16-25 There is no clear victor after the Battles of **Lodz** and **Lowicz** between the Germans and Russians.

18 The **French government** begins to transfer from Bordeaux back to Paris.

22 A British force from India **occupies Basra**, Mesopotamia.

DECEMBER

1 The first units of **Anzacs** (Australia and New Zealand Army Corps) arrive in Egypt.

2 The Austrians take **Belgrade**.

5-17 The Austrians fail to defeat the Russians at **Limanova**, outside Cracow.

8 In the Battle of the **Falkland Islands**, the British sink four German ships.

9 An Anglo-Indian force takes **Kurna**, in Mesopotamia.

14-24 The Allies attack between **Nieuport** and **Verdun**, to no avail.

15 The Serbs retake **Belgrade**.

16 German battle cruisers raid **Scarborough** and **Hartlepool**.

17 Britain **proclaims a protectorate** over Egypt.

22 The Turkish army starts an unsuccessful attack on Russian forces in the **Caucasus**.

24 The first German **zeppelin** appears over Britain, at Dover.

24-25 Christmas Truce is observed in some sections of the British and German front line.

26 In Germany, the government assumes control of **food supplies** and allocations.

29 The Battle of **Sarikamis** starts, when the Russians blunt the Turkish offensive in the Caucasus.

BESTED IN BATTLE The wrecked German cruiser *Emden* (below) lies off North Cocos Island. Background: British minesweepers, converted from trawlers, go to work clearing the waters of explosives.

1915

JANUARY

2 Russia appeals to Britain for a diversion to relieve Turkish pressure in the Caucasus.

4 The **London Stock Exchange**, which closed at the start of the war, reopens for trading.

13 Britain decides on naval action in **the Dardanelles**.

18 Japan delivers a secret ultimatum to China, demanding mineral and railway rights in the **Shandong peninsula**.

19 In the first German **zeppelin** air raids on Britain, East Anglian ports are bombed.

SKY GIANT For the Germans, Count Zeppelin's invention, the airship, proved its worth in long-range bombing raids.

24 The German battle cruiser **Blücher** is sunk during a naval engagement off Dogger Bank.

FEBRUARY

4 The Germans announce a forthcoming **submarine blockade** of Britain; it becomes effective on February 18.

UNDERWATER RAIDERS German naval strategists quickly spotted the potential of the U-boat for cutting Britain's vital trade links.

8 On the Eastern Front, German and Austro-Hungarian forces attack Russian troops in the Battle of **Masuria**, forcing the Russians to retreat.

16 The French begin a **six-week attack** in eastern Champagne, with insignificant results.

17 After an advance in the northern sector of the Eastern Front, the Germans seize **Memel**.

18 The German **submarine blockade** of Britain starts. The **Olympic Games** scheduled to take place in Berlin in 1916 are cancelled.

19 British and French warships bombard forts guarding the entrance to **the Dardanelles**. The **Norwegian ship** *Belfridge* is torpedoed off Folkestone; it is the first victim of the German submarine blockade.

MARCH

1 Britain orders the **seizure of all goods** at sea bound for Germany.

3 D. W. Griffith's ***Birth of a Nation*** opens in New York.

10-13 A British attack near **Neuve Chapelle** leads to a small advance.

18 British and French warships fail to open **the Dardanelles**.

22 The Russians retake **Przemysl**.

APRIL

5 In Havana, Cuba, white boxer Jess

SCORCHED EARTH Children pick their way through the ruins of a Galician village destroyed by Austrian troops retreating before the Russians.

Willard becomes **world heavy-weight champion** after defeating black boxer Jack Johnson.

8 Start of first wartime deportations and **massacres of Armenians**.

22 The Second Battle of **Ypres** starts. The Germans use **gas** for the first time. No ground is gained by either side in a month-long battle (ends May 25).

23 The English poet **Rupert Brooke** dies from blood poisoning on the Greek island of Skiros.

25 Allied troops land on the **Gallipoli** peninsula—British and French at Cape Helles, Anzacs at "Anzac Cove."

26 In the secret **Treaty of London**, Britain, France, Russia and Italy agree on the terms for Italy's entry into the war. The Germans launch an offensive into the **Baltic states**.

MAY

1 The **American merchant ship** *Gulflight* is sunk without warning by German submarines.

2 The beginning of an Austro-German offensive in **Galicia**. The Russians lose the Battle of **Gorlice-Tarnow**.

7 A German submarine sinks the ***Lusitania*** off the coast of Ireland. More than 1,000 people die, including over 100 Americans.

9 The Second Battle of **Artois** starts. The French assault Vimy Ridge, the British Aubers Ridge. After a massive bombardment, the French break through on a 6 mile front north of Arras. The battle ends on June 18.

13 In London's East End, an angry crowd sets fire to a bakery owned by a German-born baker, having first pulled the baker and his assistant out to safety. Other instances of "**Germanophobia**" multiply.

14 Austro-German armies seize **Jaroslaw** in Galicia.

15 On the Eastern Front, Austro-German forces cross the **San River**

in Galicia. On the Western Front, the British and Canadians mount an unsuccessful assault on **Festubert**.

22 The worst **train disaster** in British history happens when three trains collide near Gretna Green, killing 227 and injuring 246.

23 **Italy mobilizes** and declares war on Austria-Hungary.

26 In Britain, Asquith forms a **coalition government**. Lloyd George heads a new Ministry of Munitions.

JUNE

1 The first attack by zeppelins on **London**.

2 On the Eastern Front, the Russian southern front collapses when the Germans retake **Przemysl**.

7 British air ace **Reginald Warneford** downs a German zeppelin over Belgium and wins the Victoria Cross.

22 The Austrians take **Lemberg**.

23 The Germans advance across the **River Dniester**. In Berlin, the Social Democrats demand a negotiated peace. On the Italian front, the First Battle of the **Isonzo** starts (ends July 7). In all there will be 11 battles for the 60 mile Isonzo front, mostly with no gains.

SOUNDING TROPHY An officer of the Indian army captured this Turkish bugle in Mesopotamia.

25 Mexican general Carranza fails to take Mexico City from rebel leader **Emiliano Zapata;** President Wilson warns U.S. may intervene.

JULY

1 The beginning of the second great **Austro-German offensive** against Russia. It lasts six weeks.

9 In **Southwest Africa**, German forces surrender to South Africans.

18 The Second Battle of the **Isonzo** starts (ends August 3).

AUGUST

6 In the Dardanelles, the British land at **Suvla Bay**. After two days of fighting, the Germans take **Warsaw**.

19 A German submarine sinks the liner *Arabic* in the Irish Sea, with the loss of 44 passengers, including three Americans.

21 Italy declares war on **Turkey**.

25 The Germans take **Brest-Litovsk**.

SEPTEMBER

1 Germany assures America it will not **sink oceanliners** without warning.

5 The **tsar** takes over command of the Russian armed forces from Grand Duke Nicholas.

6 **Bulgaria** concludes an alliance with Germany, Austria-Hungary and Turkey.

18 The Germans capture **Vilna** in Russian Lithuania, ending the summer offensive.

21 **Bulgaria** mobilizes. British Chancellor of the Exchequer Reginald McKenna introduces a 40 percent personal **income surtax** and a 50 percent excess profits tax. He tells the House of Commons: "I know the taxpayer is determined to see the war through."

22 The Second Battle of **Champagne** opens an Allied autumn offensive. The French attack on a front between Rheims and the Argonne. The battle lasts until November 6, with no ground gained.

23 Famed English cricketer **W.G. Grace** dies, aged 67.

25 The Third Battle of **Artois** opens—the British element of the Champagne offensive. The British use **gas** for the first time. In another battle, **Loos** (September 25-October 8), the British fail to hold the ground they win. The offensive ends on October 15.

28 The British defeat the Turks at **Kut**.

OCTOBER

3-5 British and French troops land at **Salonica** (Thessaloniki).

6 The Austro-German campaign in Serbia begins. **Bulgaria enters the war** on the side of the Central Powers.

9 **Belgrade falls** to the Germans and Austrians. The Serbians retreat.

11 The Bulgarians begin a six-week advance into **Serbia**.

12 The British nurse **Edith Cavell** is executed by the Germans in Brussels. The Allies declare that they will assist Serbia.

14 **Bulgaria** and **Serbia** declare war on each other.

15 Britain **declares war** on Bulgaria, as does Montenegro.

16 **France** declares war on Bulgaria.

18 The Third Battle of the **Isonzo** starts (ends November 3).

REST IN PEACE Simple wooden crosses mark the graves of French soldiers killed on the Argonne during the autumn offensive. Background: A German staff officer manages the cumbersome feat of driving while wearing a gas mask.

19 Russia and Italy **declare war** on Bulgaria.

NOVEMBER

2 The Russians begin an advance against the Turks through **Persia**.

6 The actress **Sarah Bernhardt** returns to the Parisian stage; she is 73.

10 The Fourth Battle of the **Isonzo** starts (ends December 10).

12 In the Pacific, Britain annexes the **Gilbert and Ellice Islands** (now Kiribati and Tuvalu).

13 **Churchill resigns** from the British cabinet in the wake of the failure of the Gallipoli campaign.

22-24 In Mesopotamia, the Battle of **Ctesiphon** halts the British advance on Baghdad.

DECEMBER

7 The Turks besiege the British at **Kut** (the siege lasts until April 29, 1916).

19 British forces begin their withdrawal from the Dardanelles (completed January 9, 1916). **Sir Douglas Haig** succeeds Sir John French as British commander-in-chief.

1916

JANUARY

6 After heated debate, the British House of Commons votes for **military conscription**. The Home Secretary, Sir John Simon, resigns in protest.

11 The Russians begin a six-month offensive against the Turks in **Armenia**.

15 The retreating **Serbian army** begins its flight to the island of Corfu.

30 The last zeppelin raid on **Paris**.

FEBRUARY

15 The Fifth Battle of the **Isonzo** begins (ends March 17).

18 The last German garrison in **Cameroon** surrenders.

21 The Battle of **Verdun** opens with a devastating German bombardment along an 8 mile front. The Germans

READY TO FIRE French artillerymen stand by their gun in a lull during the fighting around Verdun.

meet stiff French resistance. The battle lasts for some ten months.

22 A memorandum by Colonel **Edward M. House**, aide to U.S. President Wilson, states Wilson's readiness to propose peace when Britain and France are ready.

25 Fort **Douaumont** (Verdun) is taken by the Germans.

MARCH

1 Germany's extended **submarine campaign** opens.

6 After a brief respite, the Germans renew their assault on **Verdun** (until April 10).

9 Germany declares war on **Portugal**.

14 **Admiral von Tirpitz** resigns in protest against the kaiser's unwillingness to make full use of German sea power.

19 On the Eastern Front, the Battle of **Lake Naroch** is fought, an inconclusive Russian offensive intended to relieve pressure on Verdun.

24 A German submarine sinks the ferry *Sussex* in the English Channel, with the loss of 50 passengers, including three American and the Spanish composer Enrique Granados.

31 General John J. Pershing, future U.S. commander in Europe, defeats the Mexican troops of **General Pancho Villa**. Pershing is retaliating after a raid by Villa into New Mexico, during which 18 Americans were killed.

APRIL

4 **General Alexei Brusilov** is appointed to command the Russian southern front.

21 A German submarine lands **Sir Roger Casement** on the Irish coast to try to postpone a planned Irish uprising.

24 In Dublin, the **Easter Rising** by Irish Republicans takes place.

26 Britain, France and Russia agree on a postwar carve-up of the Ottoman Empire into **spheres of influence**. Britain is to control Mesopotamia, and France Syria. Palestine is to be under

LEADING TO DEFEAT Initial success gave way to surrender for General Townshend (below) in Mesopotamia.

international administration. Russia is to control Armenia.

29 In Mesopotamia, 10,000 British and Indian troops capitulate in **Kut**. Surrender by the Republicans marks the end of the Easter Rising in **Ireland**.

MAY

4 After American protests, Germany agrees to give up unrestricted **submarine warfare**.

9 In the **Sykes-Picot** Agreement, Britain and France refine the Anglo-Russian-French agreement of April 26.

15 An Austrian offensive in the **Trentino** takes the Italians by surprise, leading to the seizure of Asiago and Arserio (May 31). The offensive ends without a breakthrough on June 17.

21 In Britain, clocks go forward an hour. The government believes that **daylight saving time**, due to last until October, will save thousands of tons of coal.

26 A Bulgarian-German force occupies **Fort Rupel** in Macedonia.

31 The Battle of **Jutland** opens. Over two days, the British lose 14 ships and the Germans ten. In tonnage, British losses are double those of the Germans, but the German fleet will remain in port for the rest of the war.

JUNE

4 The **Brusilov offensive**. In a massive southern front advance against the Austrians, the Russians under Alexei Brusilov take Lutsk (June 8) and Czernowitz (June 18). The advance continues with the battles of Strypa (June 11-30), Baranovici (July 2-9) and Kovel (July 28-August 17).

5 **Lord Kitchener**, British Secretary of State for War, dies when the cruiser *Hampshire*, taking him to Russia, strikes a mine off the Orkneys. In **western Persia**, the Turks begin a counteroffensive against the Russians. An Arab attack on the Turkish garrison in Medina signals the beginning of Arab revolt in the **Hejaz**.

7 The Germans take **Fort Vaux** (Verdun). The leader of the Arab revolt, **Hussein**, proclaims independence of the Hejaz from Turkey.

10 The Turkish garrison in **Mecca** surrenders to Hussein.

U.S. Supreme Court Justice **Charles Evans Hughes** resigns to run for president.

17 In the **Trentino**, an Italian counteroffensive against the Austrians recovers land lost in May.

21 France and Britain send the Greek regime an **ultimatum** demanding demobilization and responsible government. Greece complies on the 27th and agrees to new elections.

JULY

1 On the first day of the Battle of the **Somme**,

FLYING THE FLAGS Although officially neutral until 1917, Greeks in Salonica wave an assortment of Allied flags.

British losses are about 60,000. The battle continues for another four months.

11 At **Verdun**, the Germans go on the defensive after six months of attack.

15 In **Armenia**, the Turks begin a counteroffensive against the Russians. The reconstituted **Serbian army**, after being transported from Corfu to Salonica, goes into action with the Allies.

ON GUARD A British sentry keeps watch in a front-line trench during the Battle of the Somme. Background: Successive bombardments reduced Delville Wood on the Somme to little more than splintered trunks and smashed branches.

AUGUST

3 The Irish revolutionary **Sir Roger Casement** is executed for treason.

6-17 During the Sixth Battle of the **Isonzo**, the Italians take Gorizia (August 9).

17-19 On the Salonica front, the Bulgarians and Germans strike back at the Allies at **Florina**.

27 Romania joins the Allies, declaring war on Austria-Hungary. Germany declares war on Romania.

28 Italy **declares war** on Germany. The Romanians begin an invasion of **Transylvania**, taking Kronstadt (Brasov) and Hermannstadt (Sibiu).

29 Hindenburg succeeds Falkenhayn as chief of staff of the German armies, with Ludendorff as his quartermaster general. **Turkey** declares war on Romania.

SEPTEMBER

1 Bulgaria **declares war** on Romania.

2 London is raided by 13 zeppelins at once.

3 British troops enter **Dar es Salaam**, capital of German East Africa.

10 On the Salonica Front, the Allies begin to advance on the Bulgarians in the vicinity of **Doiran**.

14-18 On the Italian front, the Seventh Battle of the **Isonzo** is fought.

15 During the Battle of the Somme, the British use **tanks** for the first time.

18 The **Greek IV Army Corps** surrenders to the Germans and Bulgarians at Kavalla.

26 The Bulgarians and Germans start operations in **Dobrudja**.

27-29 In Transylvania, Austro-German forces counterattack and surround Romanian troops at **Sibiu** (advance ends November 26).

29 Eleutherios **Venizelos** establishes a provisional Greek government in Crete.

OCTOBER

5 In **Macedonia**, Allied forces begin a major offensive.

7-9 Austro-German forces retake **Kronstadt** from the Romanians.

9-12 The Eighth Battle of the **Isonzo**.

10 The Allies **submit an ultimatum** to the Greek government of Spyridon Lambros in Athens, demanding the surrender of the Greek fleet. Lambros complies.

24 The French counterattack at **Verdun** (ends December 18).

29 Hussein is proclaimed king of the Arabs.

31 The Ninth Battle of the **Isonzo** (ends November 4).

OUR MAN An election button promotes President Wilson, who narrowly defeated his Republican rival, Charles E. Hughes, to stay in the White House.

NOVEMBER

2 At **Verdun**, the French retake Fort Vaux.

5 Central Powers proclaim new kingdom of **Poland**, with no king chosen.

7 Woodrow Wilson is narrowly **re-elected U.S. president** on a platform of maintaining peace. The election is decided by the California vote.

10-14 The Germans penetrate the Vulcan Pass (Iron Pass) in the Transylvanian Alps and begin their **invasion of Romania**.

IN MACEDONIA Allied troops shuffle through the streets of Monastir after taking the town on September 19.

18 The Battle of the **Somme** finally ends, with an Allied gain of 125 square miles, and Allied casualties of some 600,000. German losses are estimated at 500,000.

19 In the Macedonian offensive, the Allies take **Monastir** (Bitola).

21 In Vienna, the Emperor **Franz Josef** dies, just days short of the 68th anniversary of his ascending the throne. He is succeeded by his 29-year-old great-nephew Karl.

23 The provisional Greek government **declares war** on Germany and Bulgaria. The Germans cross the Danube into southern Romania.

28 The Germans make their first **airplane raid** on London, using a seaplane. It drops six bombs on Kensington; no one is killed.

DECEMBER

1-5 The Romanians counterattack against the Germans on the Arges river, and are defeated at the Battle of **Argesil**.

6 The Romanian capital, **Bucharest**, falls to Austro-German forces.

7 Lloyd George replaces Asquith as British prime minister.

12 Nivelle succeeds Joffre as commander in chief of the French armies. The German government appeals to the U.S., asking it to inform the Allies that Germany is ready to negotiate peace.

13 In Mesopotamia, British troops begin to advance toward **Kut**.

15 Britain recognizes **Hussein** as king of the Arabs.

18 President Wilson makes **peace proposals** to the belligerents, suggesting that they state their terms and provide guarantees against the renewal of conflict.

19 The British recognize the Greek provisional government of **Venizelos**.

21 By now British forces have built a railway and pipeline across the Arabian desert. In Sinai, Australian and New Zealand troops seize **El Arish**.

30 The Allied governments **reject German peace proposals**. In Moscow, **Rasputin** is assassinated by Prince Felix Yusupov and others.

1917

JANUARY

5 In **Romania**, Austro-German forces continue their advance with the seizure of Braila and later Focsani.

8 In Germany, a top-level meeting at Pless concludes that **unrestricted submarine warfare** is the only method to ensure victory over Britain.

9 In Mesopotamia, the British begin an assault on **Kut**.

16 German Foreign Minister **Arthur Zimmermann** sends a telegram to the German minister in Mexico instructing him to work for an alliance with Mexico against the U.S.

31 Germany warns the U.S. of the imminent resumption of unrestricted **submarine warfare**.

FEBRUARY

3 The U.S. government **severs relations** with Germany. Brazil, Bolivia, Peru and other Latin American states follow suit.

15 In France, all **restaurants** must show their menus to the police. They may serve only two courses, and only one of these is allowed to be meat.

24 The British seize **Kut**.

MARCH

1 The **Zimmermann Telegram** is published in the U.S., and intensifies prowar feeling there.

TELEGRAM DIPLOMACY Zimmermann's clumsy attempt to win over Mexico backfired by hastening America's entry into the war.

2 Continuing their advance through western Persia, the Russians seize **Hamadan**.

8 Strikes and riots break out in **Petrograd** (St. Petersburg). In Germany, the pioneer of dirigible

airships, Count Ferdinand von **Zeppelin**, dies at age 78.

10 In **Moscow**, troops mutiny.

11 In Mesopotamia, the British occupy **Baghdad**.

11-19 In the **Balkans**, the Second Battle of Monastir (Bitola) and the Battle of Lake Presba are fought. Both are inconclusive.

12 In Russia, a **provisional government** is formed under Prince Georgi Lvov. Alexander Kerensky is minister of justice.

15 Tsar **Nicholas II** of Russia abdicates.

24 Emperor **Karl of Austria**, in a secret letter to the Allies, indicates his readiness to negotiate a separate peace.

26-27 The First Battle of **Gaza**. British cavalry surround the town, but are withdrawn.

30 The Russian government recognizes the independence of **Poland**.

APRIL

2 President Wilson delivers a **war message** to the Senate.

5 The British government confirms its policy of supporting an independent and united **Poland**.

6 The **U.S. declares war** on Germany. The Senate voted 90 to 6 in favor of the declaration.

TRANSATLANTIC ALLIES London crowds watch newly arrived American troops march down Piccadilly. Background: A U.S. private bound for Europe bids his family farewell.

9 The Battle of **Arras** opens. The British 3rd Army advances. The Canadians take **Vimy Ridge**. But there is no Allied breakthrough. The battle ends on May 4.

16 The Second Battle of the **Aisne** opens (ends May 9). The French take the **Chemin des Dames** with heavy losses. In Petrograd, **Lenin** and other Bolshevik leaders arrive, after a journey from Switzerland.

17 The first outbreak of **mutiny** in the French army.

17-19 In Arabia, British troops attack **Gaza**, but find that the Turks there have been reinforced by Germans. The British are pushed back.

19 The USS *Mongolia* sinks a U-boat, the **first U.S. shots** of the war.

19-21 By the **Saint-Jean-de-Maurienne Agreement**, Italy recognizes the Sykes-Picot Agreement (May 9, 1916) and receives areas of the Ottoman Empire in Adalia and around Smyrna.

20 German ships **raid Dover**.

23 In Mesopotamia, the British reach **Samarra**, 80 miles north of Baghdad.

MAY

2 Following the success of the German submarine campaign, the first **Atlantic convoy** sets sail. The convoy system proves to be an effective strategy against the submarines.

5-19 In the Balkans, the Battle of **Varda** (or Doiran) confirms the need for support from the Greeks.

12 On the Italian Front, the Tenth Battle of the **Isonzo** (ends June 8).

18 President Wilson signs the **Selective Draft Act** into law.

15 Nivelle is dismissed as French commander-in-chief, and replaced by **Pétain**.

27 On the Western Front, **mutiny** spreads among French troops.

JUNE

7-14 The Battle of **Messines** on the Western Front. The British launch a surprise attack on Messines Ridge and straighten the Ypres salient.

8 In **Persia**, the Russians start to retreat.

11-12 The Allies demand the abdication of the Greek King **Constantine**. Allied troops invade Thessaly and the Isthmus of Corinth.

15 In **Ireland**, an amnesty is granted to the surviving Easter Rising rebels.

26 **Venizelos** becomes Greek premier. The British royal family drops its German titles. It ceases to be the House of Saxe-Coburg-Gotha and becomes the **House of Windsor**.

27 The Greek government **severs relations** with the Central Powers and joins the Allied side.

29 In Arabia, **Allenby** takes command.

JULY

1 On the Eastern Front, **Brusilov** opens another great offensive in Galicia.

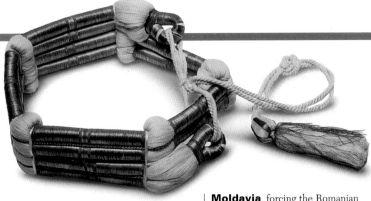

6 After a dramatic desert march, **Colonel T.E. Lawrence** ("of Arabia") leads Arab assault on Aqaba, beginning thrusts against Turkish garrisons and the Hejaz railway.

11 In Ireland, **Eamon De Valera**, the Sinn Fein leader, is released and elected to the British Parliament.

18-28 In **East Galicia**, German and Austrian troops drive the Russians back.

20 In Petrograd, **Kerensky** replaces Prince Lvov as head of the provisional government.

31 Start of the Third Battle of Ypres (**Passchendaele**). The Allies suffer 250,000 casualties to gain 5 miles. The battle continues until November 10.

AUGUST

2 On the Eastern Front, Brusilov is succeeded by General Lavr **Kornilov**.

3 German and Austrian forces seize **Czernowitz** from the Russians.

6 The Germans and Austrians begin an invasion of northern

Moldavia, forcing the Romanian army back at Putna.

14 The **Pope** submits peace proposals to the belligerents, without effect.

17 On the Italian front, the 11th and last Battle of the **Isonzo**. After two years and 11 battles, the Italians have advanced some 10 miles.

20 The Second Battle of **Verdun**, in which the French gain several key positions on the left bank of the Meuse. The battle continues for four months, until December 15.

SEPTEMBER

3-5 The Germans take **Riga**.

9-14 Kornilov marches on Petrograd in an attempt at **counter-revolution**.

12 The Central Powers grant a constitution to **Poland**.

26 The French Impressionist painter **Edgar Degas** dies at age 83.

OCTOBER

11-20 After overrunning much of Latvia, the Germans take the **Baltic islands**.

13 A large crowd gathers at **Fatima** in Portugal, where three shepherd children claim to have seen the Virgin Mary each month since May.

15 In Paris, the Dutch-born dancer **Mata Hari** is executed. A military court had found her guilty of spying for Germany, though she protested her innocence to the end.

23 Battle of **Malmaison**. The French attack along the Chemin des Dames and cut off a German salient northeast of Soissons.

24 The **Caporetto campaign** opens. German and Austrian forces break through the Italian army . The Italians fall back to Piave (battle ends December 26).

25-27 In Dublin, a Sinn Fein convention adopts a **constitution for the Irish Republic** and elects De Valera president.

26 **Brazil** declares war on Germany.

31 In Arabia, the British take **Beersheba** after a month of fighting.

NOVEMBER

2 British Foreign Minister **Arthur Balfour** sends Baron Rothschild a declaration of British support of a Jewish homeland in Palestine.

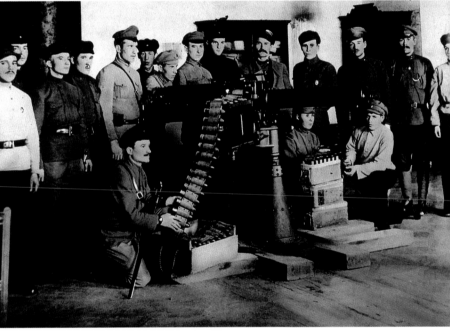

3-4 French and British troops arrive on the **Italian Front** to sustain the Italians after the Caporetto disaster.

6-7 (October 24-25 on Russian Old Style calendar) The **October Revolution** in Russia. In Petrograd, Bolsheviks storm the Winter Palace and seize power in a coup d'état.

7 In Arabia, the Turks abandon **Gaza** to the British, and on the 16th they abandon Jaffa.

17 The French sculptor **Auguste Rodin** dies at age 87.

20 The Battle of **Cambrai** opens. The British launch a surprise attack with tanks, which break through, but leave the infantry too exhausted to consolidate. The **Ukrainians** proclaim a Ukrainian People's Republic.

30 The Germans counterattack at **Cambrai**, forcing the British to give up most of the ground won. The battle ends on December 3.

DECEMBER

3 A Russian delegation arrives at **Brest-Litovsk** to discuss a ceasefire.

6 **Finland** declares its independence from Russia. By the **Truce of Focsani**, hostilities cease between the Central Powers and Romania.

7 The U.S. **declares war** on Austria.

9 Allenby enters **Jerusalem**. In **Russia**, the revolt of the Don Cossacks marks the start of civil war.

12 In **Lisbon**, an army coup ousts the left-wing president, Bernardino Machado. Portugal remains committed to the Allied cause.

22 A week after a ceasefire began, negotiations start at Brest-Litovsk to draw up a **peace treaty** between the Central Powers and the Bolsheviks.

1918

JANUARY

2 Russo-German peace negotiations reach a temporary impasse at **Brest-Litovsk**. They resume again on January 13.

5 Lloyd George formulates **Britain's war aims**: the restoration of the independence of occupied countries, the establishment of an independent Poland, self-determination for Austro-Hungarian and Ottoman minorities.

8 President Wilson outlines the **Fourteen Points** peace program, based on democracy, liberalism, transparency, the restoration of prewar borders in some cases and self-determination in others. In particular, he calls for the establishment of a **League of Nations** to provide international guarantees of peace in the future.

12 **Latvia** declares its independence.

22 By government order, British restaurants and canteens must observe the rule of **two meatless days each week**.

FEBRUARY

1 The Central Powers recognize the independence of the **Ukraine**.

WOMEN'S WORK In an unprecedented contribution to the war effort, women took over many traditionally male roles, including window cleaning.

5 In Britain, the Representation of the People Act receives the royal assent. It gives the **vote to married women** over the age of 30.

9 A peace treaty is signed between the Central Powers and the **Ukraine** at Brest-Litovsk.

18 The Germans resume hostilities against **Soviet Russia**.

21 Australian cavalry takes **Jericho**.

25 The Germans advance into Russia and reach **Narva**, 100 miles from Petrograd.

28 At Lenin's insistence, the Russians resume their negotiations for a peace treaty with the Germans at **Brest-Litovsk**.

29 Under German auspices, General **Paul Skoropadsky** is proclaimed ruler of the Ukraine.

MARCH

1 The Germans and Austrians send an **expeditionary force** into the Ukraine to expel the Bolsheviks.

3 Russo-German **peace treaty** signed at Brest-Litovsk.

9 The Bolshevik government moves the capital of Soviet Russia from Petrograd to **Moscow**.

29 Financier **Bernard Baruch** is appointed by President Wilson to the War Industries Board, responsible for American wartime industry.

LAST CHANCE ADVANCE In April German troops storm through Bailleul during the Battles of the Lys in northern France. Background: A demobilized German soldier shoulders his kit as he sets off for home.

APRIL

1 The Royal Flying Corps and the Royal Naval Air Service are merged to form the **Royal Air Force**.

3 German forces land in **Finland**.

9 The Moldavian Republic (**Bessarabia**) proclaims its union with Romania.

9-29 In the Battles of the **Lys**, the Germans strike south of Ypres, storming Messine Ridge and taking Armentières.

10 In Rome, a Congress of Oppressed Nationalities proclaims the right of **self-determination** for Czechs, South (or Yugo) Slavs, Poles and Romanians.

14 General **Ferdinand Foch** becomes supreme commander coordinating Allied operations on the Western Front.

21 German air ace **Manfred von Richthofen** (the Red Baron) is shot down on the Western Front.

MAY

7 The **Finnish civil war** comes to an end with the German-backed Whites defeating the Reds. By the **Treaty of Bucharest**, Romania is obliged to cede Dobrudja to Bulgaria and place the Carpathian passes under Austro-German control.

27 In the Third Battle of the **Aisne**, the Germans attack across the Chemin des Dames, creating a salient up to 40 miles deep. The battle ends on June 6.

JUNE

3 The Allies declare their support for the **national aspirations** of the Poles, Czechs and South Slavs.

9-14 The Germans attack between **Noyon** and **Montdidier**, pushing toward Compiègne. They are halted after about 6 miles.

15-24 In a last bid for victory against Italy, the Austrians cross the **Piave**, but are forced to withdraw with a loss of 100,000 men.

23 British troops land in **Murmansk** to aid anti-Bolshevik forces.

JULY

10 The **Soviet constitution** is promulgated.

15 The Second Battle of the **Marne**. A German assault east of Rheims is halted after three days by a French and American counterattack. The battle ends on August 7.

16 Tsar Nicholas II and other members of the Russian royal family are murdered at **Ekaterinburg**.

AUGUST

2 British and French troops land in **Archangel** to support anti-Bolshevik forces.

8-11 Battle of **Amiens**. The British advance several miles with 450 tanks.

9 Britain recognizes the **Czechoslovak National Council** as a *de facto* government.

21 On the Somme and near Arras, the French and British launch an offensive that forces the Germans back

ZERO HOUR An American officer took this photo on September 12 at the start of the St. Mihiel offensive.

to the **Hindenburg Line** by September 3.

SEPTEMBER

12-13 The Americans seize the German-held **St. Mihiel** salient.

15 Austria appeals to President Wilson to call an informal peace conference. He refuses.

15-24 On the **Bulgarian front**, the Allies begin a major offensive against the Germans and Bulgarians. The Bulgarians appeal for an armistice.

18 The beginning of the **British offensive** in Palestine. The British breach the Turkish lines at Megiddo, and—with Arabs under Lawrence—push northward.

26 In two great thrusts—the Battles of **Argonne** and **Ypres**—the Americans and British attempt a pincer movement.

29 Ludendorff demands that the German government initiate negotiations for an **armistice**.

30 An armistice between **Bulgaria** and the Allies is concluded at Salonica.

The Bulgarians are demobilized, and their war equipment is made available to the Allies. The **German government** resigns.

OCTOBER

1-2 British and Arab troops take **Damascus**.

4 Prince **Max von Baden** named German chancellor and foreign minister. Austria and Germany appeal for an armistice. Ferdinand of Bulgaria abdicates in favor of his son, Boris.

7 French naval forces take **Beirut**.

14 The new Turkish Sultan Mehmed VI urges President Wilson to arrange an armistice. Allies recognize **Czechoslovak National Council**.

16 Emperor Karl of Austria proclaims the non-Hungarian part of his former empire a **federal state**.

18 The British seize **Douai**.

20 American fighter ace **Eddie Rickenbacker** downs his 22nd German airplane.

24 On the lower Piave, the Italians advance to **Vittorio Veneto.**

27 **Ludendorff** resigns. Austria tells President Wilson that it is willing to make a separate peace.

28 In Prague, the Czechoslovak National Council proclaims an **independent Czech state**.

29 The **Yugoslav National Council** proclaims the independence of South Slavs. Austria offers to surrender to Italy.

30 A **German National Council** is formed in Vienna to administer Austria's German-speaking provinces. An **armistice with Turkey** is concluded at Mudros.

NOVEMBER

1 An independent **Hungarian government** is established under Count Michael Karolyi.

3 The Allies conclude an **armistice with Austria**, by which Austria

LAND FOR ALL Dismembering the huge estates of the nobility was a key policy of the Hungarian nationalist leader, Count Karolyi. Here, he announces the redistribution of his own lands to the peasants.

demobilizes, withdraws from military cooperation with Germany and leaves disputed territory. The German fleet at **Kiel** mutinies. The mutiny spreads rapidly to other naval bases.

3-5 The Italians take **Trieste** and **Fiume** (Rijeka).

7 A **Yugoslav** conference in Geneva opts for the union of Croatia and Slovenia with Serbia and Montenegro.

7-8 **Revolution** breaks out in Munich. A German armistice commission arrives in **Compiègne** to discuss terms with the Allies.

9 Prince Max announces the **abdication** of Kaiser Wilhelm II. Philipp Scheidemann proclaims Germany a republic.

10 The **kaiser** flees to the Netherlands. Allied

forces, having marched across Bulgaria, cross the Danube at Rustchuk and enter Romania. Romania **re-enters the war** on the Allied side.

11 The **Armistice** is signed. At 11 a.m. hostilities cease on the Western Front.

12 A **German-Austrian Republic** is proclaimed.

12-13 An Allied fleet passes through the Dardanelles and lands troops at **Constantinople**.

16 A **Hungarian Republic** is proclaimed.

21 The **German Fleet** surrenders and is interned at Scapa Flow.

DECEMBER

1 **Montenegro** deposes King Nicholas and opts for union with the other South Slavs. The National Assembly of Romanians in Transylvania votes for union with Romania.

4 The United **Kingdom of Serbs, Croats and Slovenes** (later called Yugoslavia) is proclaimed, with King Peter of Serbia as its monarch.

14 In Britain, in the so-called **Khaki Election**, the coalition government wins a huge majority, promising punishment of German war criminals and full reparation for war damage. Women vote for the first time.

18 The French occupy **Odessa**.

A TIME TO BE GLAD Parisians celebrate the Armistice, waving the flags of the different allies.

27 King George V and Queen Mary welcome **President and Mrs. Wilson** to London—the first time a British monarch has welcomed an American president on British soil.

INDEX

ACKNOWLEDGMENTS

Abbreviations:
T = Top; M = Middle; B = Bottom;
R = Right; L = Left

3 Imperial War Museum, L, LM; Image Library New South Wales, RM; Getty Images, R. 6 Ullstein Bilderdienst, MR; Topham Picturepoint, TR; Jean-Loup Charmet, BL. 7 Map by Laurence Bradbury. 8 Getty Images, TR; Topham Picturepoint, MR; Popperfoto, BL. 9 Topham Picturepoint, MR; Mary Evans Picture Library, BL. 10 Corbis-Bettmann, TL; Ullstein Bilderdienst, BR. 11 Punch Library, TR; Roger-Viollet, BM. 12 Collection Viollet/Roger-Viollet, TL. 12-13 Artwork by Christian Hook. 13 Ullstein Bilderdienst. 14 Harlingue-Viollet/Roger-Viollet. 15 Popperfoto background; Imperial War Museum, L; Image Library New South Wales, LM; Culver Pictures Inc, RM; Mary Evans Picture Library, R. 16 Topham Picturepoint, BM. 16-17 Topham Picturepoint. 17 Map by Advanced Illustration; Topham Picturepoint, MR. 18 Mary Evans Picture Library, TL; Imperial War Museum, R. 19 Imperial War Museum, TM; Corbis-Bettmann, BR. 20 ND-Viollet/Roger-Viollet, TM; Jean-Loup Charmet, ML; Corbis-Bettmann, BR. 21 Ullstein Bilderdienst, TR; artwork by Laurence Bradbury. 22 Popperfoto. 23 Topham Picturepoint, TR; Imperial War Museum, B. 24 Mary Evans Picture Library, TR; Ullstein Bilderdienst, L; Getty Images, BR. 25 Map by Advanced Illustration; Mary Evans Picture Library, MR. 26 Jean-Loup Charmet. 26-27 Imperial War Museum. 27 Imperial War Museum, TR; Topham Picturepoint, MR; Ullstein Bilderdienst, BL. 28 Ullstein Bilderdienst, TR; Roger-Viollet, M. 29 Topham Picturepoint, M; Imperial War Museum/CRW Nevinson, BR. 30 Corbis-Bettmann. 30-31 Imperial War Museum. 31 Map by Advanced Illustration; Popperfoto, MR. 32 Map by Advanced Illustration; Imperial War Museum, ML. 33 Ullstein Bilderdienst, TM; Imperial War Museum, MR, B. 34 Jean-Loup Charmet, TM; Imperial War Museum, B. 35 Imperial War Museum/Paul Nash. 36 Getty Images. 36-37 Imperial War Museum. 37 Collection Viollet/Roger-Viollet. 38-39 Artwork by Kevin Gould. 40 Getty Images, TL; Topham Picturepoint, MR; Imperial War Museum/Norman Brand, BL. 41 Imperial War Museum, MR, BL; Ullstein Bilderdienst, BR. 42 Topham Picturepoint, BR; Imperial War Museum/Norman Brand, TM, TR; Imperial War Museum, L. 43 Boyer-Viollet/Roger-Viollet, TR; Imperial War Museum, ML; Ullstein Bilderdienst, BR. 44 David King Collection, ML; Map by Advanced Illustration. 45 Ullstein Bilderdienst, TR, BR. 46 Ullstein Bilderdienst. 46-47 Novosti. 47 Corbis-Bettmann, TR. 48 Corbis-Bettmann, TL; Imperial War Museum, ML. 49 Getty Images, TL; Jean-Loup Charmet, BM; Imperial War Museum, BR. 50 Jean-Loup Charmet, TL; David King, MR; Imperial War Museum, BM. 51 Corbis-Bettmann, T; Imperial War Museum, B. 52 Jean-Loup Charmet, ML; Topham Picturepoint, BM; Getty Images, R. 53 David King Collection, TM; Ullstein Bilderdienst, L; Culver Pictures Inc, R. 54 Corbis-Bettmann, ML; Imperial War Museum, BR. 55 Imperial War Museum/John Singer Sargeant, T; Imperial War Museum/Norman Brand, BR. 56 Corbis-Bettmann, TR; The Tank Museum, BL. 57 Artwork by Graham White, TM; Corbis-Bettmann, BR. 58 Boyer-Viollet/Roger-Viollet, MM;

Ullstein Bilderdienst, BM. 58-59 Ullstein Bilderdienst. 59 Topham Picturepoint, TM; AKG London, MR; Topham Picturepoint, BL; Corbis-Bettmann, BR. 60 Popperfoto, BL; Image Library New South Wales, M. 60-61 Getty Images. 61 Image Library New South Wales, MR; Map by Advanced Illustration. 62 Ullstein Bilderdienst, TR; Imperial War Museum/Norman Brand, ML; Topham Picturepoint, B. 63 Jean-Loup Charmet, TR; Collection Viollet/Roger-Viollet, B. 64 Topham Picturepoint, TR; Map by Advanced Illustration. 65 Topham Picturepoint, TR; Corbis-Bettmann, BL. 66 Harlingue-Viollet/Roger-Viollet, MM; Map by Advanced Illustration. 67 AKG London, TL; Ullstein Bilderdienst, B. 68 Imperial War Museum. 69 Getty Images, TL; Imperial War Museum/Norman Brand, MR; Imperial War Museum, B. 70 Getty Images, TM; Mary Evans Picture Library, BL; Roger-Viollet, BR. 71 Map by Advanced Illustration; Ullstein Bilderdienst, B. 72 Ullstein Bilderdienst, TR; Corbis-Bettmann, BL. 73 Getty Images, TR; AKG London, background; Mary Evans Picture Library, foreground, BL. 74 Topham Picturepoint, ML; AKG London, BM. 75 Map by Roy Williams; Getty Images, MR; Ullstein Bilderdienst, BR. 76 Map by Roy Williams; Topham Picturepoint, BL. 77 Corbis-Bettmann, TL; Getty Images, B. 78 AKG London, MR; Imperial War Museum, BL. 79 Mary Evans Picture Library, MR; Corbis-Bettmann, B. 80 Topham Picturepoint, TL; Roger-Viollet, TM; Ullstein Bilderdienst, MR. 80-81 Ullstein Bilderdienst. 81 Map by Advanced Illustration; Musée des Deux Guerres/Jean-Loup Charmet, MR. 82 Imperial War Museum, MM; Topham Picturepoint, B. 83 Topham Picturepoint, TR; National Archives, Washington, BL. 84 Culver Pictures Inc, TR; Bridgeman Art Library/Imperial War Museum, B. 84-85 Corbis-Bettmann UPI. 85 Boyer-Viollet/Roger-Viollet. 86 Getty Images. 86-87 ND-Viollet/Roger-Viollet. 87 Corbis-Bettmann, TL; Culver Pictures Inc, TR. 88 Getty Images, ML. 88-89 Imperial War Museum. 89 CORBIS, TL; Culver Pictures Inc, MR. 90 Map by Advanced Illustration; Roger-Viollet, MR; Brown Brothers, BL. 90-91 Getty Images. 91 Culver Pictures Inc. 92 Imperial War Museum, TL, BM. 93 Imperial War Museum, TM; Roger-Viollet, B. 94 Culver Pictures Inc, BL. 94-95 Corbis-Bettmann. 95 Ullstein Bilderdienst, TR; Corbis-Bettmann, BM. 96 CORBIS, TL; Collection Viollet/Roger-Viollet, BR. 97 Collection Viollet/Roger-Viollet, TR; Culver Pictures Inc, BL, BM. 98 Culver Pictures Inc, TR; G W Philpot/Bridgeman Art Library, BM. 99 Getty Images, TR; Imperial War Museum/Norman Brand, MR; Paul Nash/Bridgeman Art Library/Imperial War Museum, BL. 100 Imperial War Museum, TL, Imperial War Museum/Norman Brand, MR; G P Leroux/Bridgeman Art Library/Imperial War Museum, BR. 101 Ullstein Bilderdienst, background; Getty Images, L; Brown Brothers, LM; Corbis-Bettmann, RM; Topham Picturepoint, R. 102 Getty Images, L, MR. 103 Brown Brothers, T; Getty Images, BR. 104 AKG London, TL, MR; Image Library New South Wales, B. 105 Topham Picturepoint, MR; Ullstein Bilderdienst, BR. 106 Ullstein Bilderdienst, TR; Jean-Loup Charmet, BM. 107 Roger-Viollet, BM; Brown Brothers, B. 108 Novosti, TR; Ullstein Bilderdienst, BL. 109 Ullstein Bilderdienst, MR, BL. 110 Ullstein Bilderdienst, TL; Topham Picturepoint, MR.

111 Topham Picturepoint, TL; Mary Evans Picture Library, MR; Getty Images, BL. 112 Popperfoto, TL, BR. 113 Imperial War Museum, TR; Branger-Viollet/Roger-Viollet, BL. 114 Getty Images, ML; CORBIS, MR; Brown Brothers, BR. 115 Camera Press, TL; Corbis-Bettmann, BR. 116 Mary Evans Picture Library, MR. 116-17 Novosti. 117 David King Collection, TL; Getty Images, MR. 118 Popperfoto, ML; David King Collection, BR. 118-19 David King Collection. 119 Novosti, BL; Getty Images, BR. 120 C.N. Jones/Bridgeman Art Library/Forbes Magazine Collection, London, TL; Novosti, BR. 121 David King Collection, TR; Jean-Loup Charmet, BR. 122 David King Collection, TL; Jean-Loup Charmet, BR. 123 Corbis-Bettmann, background; Topham Picturepoint, BL; Getty Images, BM; Popperfoto, BR. 124 Topham Picturepoint, TL; Mary Evans Picture Library, MM; Popperfoto, BR. 125 Roger-Viollet, TL; Getty Images, BR. 126 Topham Picturepoint, TL; Getty Images, MR; Corbis-Bettmann, BR. 127 Popperfoto, background; Getty Images, L; AKG London, LM; John Parker, RM; Getty Images, R. 128 Getty Images, MR; Mary Evans Picture Library, BL. 128-9 Getty Images. 129 Getty Images, TR. 130 Getty Images, TR, ML. 131 AKG London, T, MR; Getty Images, BL. 132 AKG London, TL; Ullstein Bilderdienst, BR. 133 Mary Evans Picture Library, ML; Collection Viollet/Roger-Viollet, B. 134 Harlingue-Viollet/Roger-Viollet, MR; Topham Picturepoint, BL. 135 Getty Images, TL; Roger-Viollet, BR. 136 Boyer-Viollet/Roger-Viollet, BM, BR. 137 Getty Images, TR; Jean-Loup Charmet, ML; Corbis-Bettmann UPI, BR. 138 Imperial War Museum, TR; John Parker, BL. 139 Getty Images. 140 Mary Evans Picture Library, TL; Branger-Viollet/Roger-Viollet, BR. 141 Ullstein Bilderdienst, TL; Getty Images, BR. 142 William Orpen /AKG London/Imperial War Museum, TR; Ullstein Bilderdienst, BR. 143 Mary Evans Picture Library, TM; Collection Viollet/Roger-Viollet, MR. 144 Map by Roy Williams; Popperfoto, BL. 145 Corbis-Bettmann. 146 Mary Evans Picture Library, TM; AKG London, ML; Bridgeman Art Library, MR; Imperial War Museum, BR. 147 Imperial War Museum, background, TL, BR. 148 Topham Picturepoint, TR; Ullstein Bilderdienst, ML; Culver Pictures Inc, B. 149 Imperial War Museum, background, TR, BL. 150 Imperial War Museum, ML, BM; Jean-Loup Charmet, MR. 150-1 Imperial War Museum background, TL. 151 Topham Picturepoint, MR, BM. 152 Corbis-Bettmann, background; Imperial War Museum, TM; Culver Pictures Inc, BL. 153 Bath Museum of Costume/Imperial War Museum/Norman Brand, TL; David King Collection, MR; Getty Images, BL. 154 Ullstein Bilderdienst, background; Getty Images, TR, BL. 155 Getty Images, TL; Mary Evans Picture Library, TM; Jean-Loup Charmet, BR.

Front cover: Bridgeman Art Library/Imperial War Museum, T; CORBIS, M; Collection Viollet/Roger-Viollet, B.

Back cover: Imperial War Museum, T; Corbis-Bettman, M; Corbis-Bettman, B.

The editors are grateful to the following individuals and publishers for their kind permission to quote passages from the publications listed below:

BBC Books, from 1914-1918, by Jay Winter & Blaine Baggett, 1996.
Johnathan Cape, from Goodbye to All That, by Robert Graves, 1929.
Constable & Company Ltd., from Peacemaking 1919, by Harold Nicolson, 1933.
Leo Cooper, from Facing Armageddon edited by Hugh Cecil & Peter H. Liddle, 1996; Annette Becker, Jean-Pierre Hirsch, Peter Lowenberg, S. & W. Jacobeit.
Dalton, from Q-Ships, by Carson I.A. Ritchie, 1985.
Deane, from The Defeat of Austria as seen by the 7th Division, by Rev. E. Cross, 1919.
Faber & Faber Ltd., from The Faber Book of Reportage, edited by John Carey.
Victor Gollancz, from The History of the Russian Revolution, by Leon Trotsky, trans. Max Eastman, 1932.
Heinemann, from Lawrence of Arabia, by Jeremy Wilson, 1989.
H.M.S.O. from With a Machine Gun to Cambrai, by George Coppard 1969.
Hutchinson, from The Home Front , by Sylvia Pankhurst, 1938.
Michael Joseph, from 1914-1918; Voices and Images of the Great War, by Lynn McDonald, 1988.
Prentice Hall, from The Russian Revolution of February 1917 trans. by J.L. Richards, 1992.
Schocken Books, from Mmme. Senterre; A French Woman of the People trans. by L.A & K.L. Tilly, 1985.
Secker & Warburg, from The Rise and Fall of the Third Reich, by William Schirer, 1960.
Simpkin, Marshall, Hamilton, Kent & Co., from The Happy Hospital, by W. Muir, 1918.
Weidenfeld & Nicolson Ltd., from First World War, by Martin Gillbert, 1994.